THE ART OF HAPPINESS
in a Troubled World

The ART of HAPPINESS

in a Troubled World

HIS HOLINESS
THE DALAI LAMA

and

HOWARD C. CUTLER, M.D.

First published in Great Britain in 2009 by Hodder & Stoughton
An Hachette UK company

This paperback edition published in 2020 by Yellow Kite
An imprint of Hodder & Stoughton

11

A CIP catalogue record for this title is available from the British Library

Paperback ISBN 978 0 340 79440 1
eBook ISBN 978 1 848 94666 8

Typeset in Weiss

Printed and bound in Great Britain by Clays Ltd, Elcograf S.p.A.

Hodder & Stoughton policy is to use papers that are natural, renewable and
recyclable products and made from wood grown in sustainable forests. The logging
and manufacturing processes are expected to conform to the environmental
regulations of the country of origin.

Yellow Kite
Hodder & Stoughton Ltd
Carmelite House
50 Victoria Embankment
London EC4Y 0DZ

www.yellowkitebooks.co.uk

CONTENTS

AUTHOR'S NOTE

In this book, extensive conversations with the Dalai Lama have been recounted. The Dalai Lama generously allowed me to select whatever format for the book I felt would most effectively convey his ideas. I felt that the narrative format found in these pages would be most readable and at the same time impart a sense of how the Dalai Lama incorporates his ideas in his own daily life. With his approval, I organized this book according to subject matter, and in doing this I have chosen to combine and integrate material that may have been taken from several different conversations. The Dalai Lama's interpreter, Dr. Thupten Jinpa, kindly reviewed the final manuscript to assure me that there were no inadvertent distortions of the Dalai Lama's ideas as a result of the editorial process.

A number of case histories and personal anecdotes have been presented to illustrate the ideas under discussion. In order to maintain confidentiality and protect personal privacy, in every instance (unless otherwise indicated) I have changed names and altered details and other distinguishing characteristics to prevent identification of particular individuals.

INTRODUCTION

A while back, I was invited to Australia to deliver the opening keynote address at an international conference on human happiness. This was an unusually large event, which brought together fifty leading experts from around the world to speak about happiness, thousands of attendees, and even the Dalai Lama, who appeared on the second day as the featured speaker.

With so many professional colleagues gathered in one spot, there was plenty of lively discussion on a wide range of topics. During a lunch break, I overheard several colleagues arguing about the merits of some recent articles in the Australian newspapers, touching on a debate going on in positive psychology circles. Positive psychology is a new branch of psychology often referred to as "the science of human happiness." The question being debated was: If the goal is to increase human happiness, which is the better approach—to focus on inner development or social welfare? In other words, should efforts be devoted primarily to developing techniques that individuals can practice to increase personal happiness, or should we focus on improving social conditions, creating conditions that allow the members of a society to thrive and result in greater happiness for the population as a whole?

It seemed that the debate could be quite contentious at times. Some championing the social approach were characterizing positive psychology, which largely focused on finding effective methods of increasing personal happiness, as little more than another self-indulgent pop-psychology fad, concerned only with a self-centered pursuit of personal gratification. Of course the positive psychology camp had some powerful arguments in rebuttal. While not denying that having one's survival needs met was a prerequisite for happiness, they went on to point out that since happiness is a subjective state, involving an individual's attitudes, perceptions, emotions, and so on, ultimately it was necessary to focus on a person's inner state, on an individual level, to increase happiness. In addition, addressing the claims that working on increasing personal happiness is a self-absorbed, selfish pursuit, they pointed to studies showing that increasing personal happiness makes an individual more charitable, more giving, more willing to reach out and help others, and it is *unhappy* people who are more self-focused and selfish.

Until that moment I had been unaware of the extent of this debate, which in a way could be boiled down to a fundamental question of one's basic orientation: *"Me" or "We"?* So when I first heard people debating this issue, I was riveted. As it turned out, the Dalai Lama and I had spoken about that very same issue during the course of some recent discussions we were having about the relationship between the individual, the greater society, and human happiness, seeking to answer questions such as: What is the effect of society on an individual's happiness? If societal problems undermine our happiness, what can we do about it? What is an individual's responsibility to try to bring about social change? And how much can a single individual do, anyway?

Those discussions, which include some of the conversations chronicled in this book, were part of an ongoing dialogue about human happiness that we originally began in 1993. In order to put these conversations in the proper context, I think it will be helpful to step back and briefly review the history of the *Art of Happiness* book series, and the radical changes that have taken place within both the scientific community and the general public with regard to our perception and understanding of happiness.

History of *The Art of Happiness*

It was the beginning of the 1990s when I first began to think about collaborating with the Dalai Lama on a book about happiness. The Dalai Lama had already written three dozen books by that time, but since they appealed primarily to students or practitioners of Buddhism, his books had failed to find a wide readership among a general Western audience. I had known the Dalai Lama for about a decade by then, enough time to realize that he had much wisdom to offer non-Buddhists as well as Buddhists. So, I began to envision a book written for a general Western audience, distilling the essential principles that had enabled him to achieve happiness. By focusing on the practical application of his ideas in daily life and by framing his views within the context of Western science and psychology, I hoped to ultimately come up with an effective approach to finding happiness that combined the best of East and West. The Dalai Lama readily agreed to my proposal, and we eventually began work on the project in 1993, during his first visit to my home state of Arizona.

Inspired and excited by the project, I decided to temporarily give up practicing psychiatry in order to devote my full attention to writing the book. I estimated that it would take six months to complete the book, and with the Dalai Lama as a coauthor, I was certain I'd have my choice of the top publishing companies.

I miscalculated. Five years later I was still working on the book and still adding to the thick, demoralizing, ever-growing stack of rejection letters on my desk—letters from literary agents and publishers who were uniformly convinced that there was no mainstream audience for books by the Dalai Lama, no market for a collaboration between him and a Western psychiatrist, and no public interest in the subject of happiness. With my financial resources depleted, it seemed I had few options left, and I was just on the verge of self-publishing a few copies of the book and returning to the practice of psychiatry when I had a stroke of luck at last. It was right at that point that an offhand remark made by the mother of a close friend to a stranger on a New York subway—a stranger who turned out to be in the publishing industry—initiated an unlikely series of connections that finally led to securing an agent and mainstream publisher. And so it was in 1998, with a small first printing and modest expectations, *The Art of Happiness: A Handbook for Living* was at last released.

Life is unpredictable. To our immense surprise, the book enjoyed an overwhelmingly positive response. It seemed to strike a chord in readers, resonating deep in the hearts of so many people yearning for something better in life. The book soon began to appear on bestseller lists around the world, including ninety-seven weeks on the *New York Times* bestsellers list. It was eventually translated into fifty languages and became a perennial classic with a readership in the millions.

As a result of the book's popularity, we received many wonderful and moving letters, some of which expressed the request for a sequel, pointing out topics that had been omitted from the first book. For example, in focusing primarily on inner development as the path to happiness, I included discussion of inner obstacles to happiness but largely avoided any mention of wider societal problems even though the Dalai Lama regularly raised these issues in our private discussions and in his public talks.

But it was now time to face the fact that human beings do not live in a vacuum—we live within a society, and that society has many problems that can affect our happiness. So, wishing to explore these societal and global issues in greater depth with the Dalai Lama— and respond to readers' requests at the same time—I approached him with the idea of collaborating on a sequel, seeking to answer the fundamental question: *How can we find happiness in such a troubled world?* He agreed.

Although I originally intended to address this vast question in a single sequel to *The Art of Happiness: A Handbook for Living*, we quickly realized that the subject was too broad and included far too many topics to fit into just one book, so we divided the topics into a series of volumes. The second book in the series, *The Art of Happiness at Work*, published in 2003, applied the Art of Happiness principles to the setting where most of us spend the bulk of our waking hours during adulthood—the workplace. Like the first book, *The Art of Happiness at Work* was very well received and was a *New York Times* bestseller—but also like the first book, it focused primarily on the level of the individual.

In this volume we finally turn to the broader societal issues that undermine human happiness. The Dalai Lama begins by identifying the lack of a sense of community as well as the erosion of trust in many societies today and, as our conversations continue, we go on to discuss issues such as prejudice, racism, terrorism, violence, and fear. The Art of Happiness series continues to be a work in progress, with three more volumes tentatively planned to complete the series. One volume will address violence in greater depth, including its causes, remedies, and the Dalai Lama's vision of the twenty-first century as the "Century of Dialogue." Another will include topics related to personal lifestyle, wealth, poverty, consumerism, economic issues, education, and the Dalai Lama's call for us to develop a sense of "Universal Responsibility." And finally, there will be a practical workbook, offering an effective science-based program for training in happiness, combining Buddhist principles and practices with Western science and psychology.

A Happiness Revolution

The Dalai Lama's perception of happiness as an achievable goal, something we can deliberately cultivate through practice and effort much like any other skill, is fundamental to the Buddhist view of happiness. In fact, the idea of training the mind has been the cornerstone of Buddhist practice for millennia. Coincidentally, shortly after the publication of *The Art of Happiness*, this same idea began to take root in society from another direction—as a "new" scientific discovery—leading to a fundamental shift in many people's perception of happiness. More and more people seemed to be rejecting the idea of happiness as something that is merely a by-product of our external circumstances, in favor of seeing happiness as something that can be systematically developed. This change was part of a worldwide Happiness Revolution, characterized by a sudden explosion of interest in the subject of human happiness among both the scientific community and general public.

Although there are always multiple factors fueling the rapid growth of a new movement like the Happiness Revolution, in this case the watershed event appeared to be the formal establishment of a new field of psychology focusing on positive emotions, human strengths, and flourishing. Dr. Martin Seligman, the influential psychologist who is widely considered to be the founder of this new field, dedicated his term as president of the American Psychological Association to promoting this new area of study, which he called "positive psychology." Seligman teamed up with another brilliant researcher, Dr. Mihaly Csikszentmihalyi, to lay the groundwork for this new field, and the two were soon joined by a core group of top researchers from various universities in America and Europe who shared a greater interest in human strengths and virtues than in human weakness and pathology.

When *The Art of Happiness: A Handbook for Living* was being written, there were relatively few studies available on human happiness and positive emotions, and other than a handful of mavericks, few researchers were interested in investigating these largely unpopular subjects. With the inception of positive psychology, however, that changed dramatically—*For the first time in human history, happiness had finally become a legitimate field of scientific inquiry*. As result, we have seen the exponential growth of new research on happiness over the past decade. And throughout this period it has been particularly gratifying for me to see that the rapidly growing body of scientific evidence has consistently supported and validated the Dalai Lama's views. As the evidence continues to mount, we are seeing Buddhist principles and Western science beginning to converge in many ways.

The Benefits of Happiness

One of the primary factors fueling the Happiness Revolution has been the startling research that reveals the many benefits of happiness—benefits extending far beyond merely "feeling good." In fact, cultivating greater happiness can be seen as "one-stop shopping" for those seeking greater success in every major life domain: Happiness leads to increased success at finding a mate, better marriages, stronger relationships, better physical and mental health, and a longer life (up to ten years longer!). It increases creativity, cognitive abilities, and resilience. Happy people are also far more successful at work and earn substantially higher incomes. In fact, organizations with happy employees are also more successful and consistently demonstrate greater profitability.

Despite the substantial personal rewards of cultivating greater happiness, it is critical to point out that *cultivating greater happiness not only benefits oneself, but also one's family, community, and society at large.* In fact, this is one of the key principles underlying the Art of Happiness series. While this principle was introduced in the first volume of the series, it takes on a profound new meaning in the context of this book and the recent scientific research on positive emotions.

Earlier, I mentioned the debate about which of the approaches to happiness is more "valid," the path of inner development or the path of social change—that is, should we work toward personal happiness or societal happiness? Nobody bothered to solicit the Dalai Lama's opinion on the debate that week in Australia, but it is a question that he answered during the course of our conversations—and his answer was one that I had not heard widely expressed so far by those on either side of the question. His answer to the debate? *There is no debate!* The best approach? *Both!* This was not an either/or situation, where we need to choose one or the other. *He feels that we can and should work toward our own personal happiness and societal happiness at the same time.*

In regard to cultivating greater personal happiness, the Dalai Lama offers several methods. In Part III of this book, for example, he begins by revealing a practical approach to coping with the problems of today's world while cultivating a sense of hope, optimism, trust, and other positive states of mind. Since positive emotions and states of mind have direct effects in increasing our overall levels of happiness, ultimately this shows us how to find happiness in our troubled world.

When it comes to increasing "societal happiness," of course, there are an infinite variety of activities that a person can undertake to help build a better world—the specific actions that a person chooses is generally determined by his or her personal interests, resources, abilities, circumstances, and so on. Specific activities to help reduce social problems such as poverty or the environment will be discussed in the next volume of the Art of Happiness series, along with a discussion of subjects such as altruism and prosocial or helping behavior.

The Intersection of Personal and Societal Happiness

In this volume, however, we begin by proposing a different approach, a powerful and rather radical approach to simultaneously working toward inner happiness and overcoming societal problems: In the closing chapters of this book we present *our key argument that positive emotions in general—and the supreme "positive emotions" of compassion and empathy in particular—lie at the intersecting point between inner and outer happiness, with the capacity to simultaneously bring about personal happiness and provide a potential solution to many of the problems plaguing society today (at least as the first step in overcoming these societal problems).*

For example, we provide direct scientific evidence demonstrating how the cultivation of compassion can be an effective technique to increase personal happiness. In addition, we show how *empathy and compassion cause specific changes in brain function that alter the way we perceive and interact with others*—for example, causing us to perceive others as being more similar to ourselves. These changes result in relating to others based more on our similarities than our differences, removing the barriers between "us" and "them." This also produces characteristic ways of thinking and acting that seem to be "custom-designed" as antidotes to some of the societal problems we will explore in later chapters—even the instinctual, "automatic and unconscious" bias that human beings experience toward those whom we perceive as different, which until recently was considered to be impossible to prevent. Finally, we will explain how this approach to overcoming societal problems could even have several unique advantages over more conventional approaches, due to factors such as the contagious nature of positive emotions and happiness.

In the closing chapter of this book, we explain how there are specific exercises or techniques that anyone can practice to deliberately cultivate a greater capacity for empathy and compassion—one does not necessarily need to be a naturally empathetic or "warm hearted" person in order to experience higher levels of empathy or compassion. Thus, anyone can use these techniques to increase their customary level of day-to-day happiness. However, to use this method to overcome widespread societal problems, a significant portion of the population would likely need to practice these techniques. This could be accomplished, for example, by providing education and training in these techniques as a routine part of our children's education in the public school systems, along with actively promoting greater awareness of the benefits of the techniques through the media and so on.

Before this could take place, it is likely that many more people would need to become aligned with the Dalai Lama's view of compassion: perceiving compassion as a source of personal happiness, something that genuinely benefits you and not just "the other guy." It would require seeing compassion as something of great practical value and importance, with real concrete benefits, not merely as a "warm and fuzzy" abstract philosophical concept or a "soft" topic that is religious, spiritual, or moral in nature. In fact, it should even be seen as a necessity, something critical to our survival and not a luxury or something we only practice in church on Sundays or after we retire to Florida with our millions.

Needless to say, adopting broad educational initiatives that would include nationwide training in these methods could be a slow process. Meanwhile, the problems of our world today are varied and complex, and there are no secret formulas or magic bullets that are going to suddenly eradicate all of our human problems, both personal and global, overnight. But, at least we have a place to start. As the Dalai Lama reveals in the following pages, there are practical steps we can take to cope with our troubled world, strategies that we can use to maintain genuine day-to-day happiness while we are seeking solutions to broader problems. Ultimately, we will find that the Dalai Lama's message is one of hope, based on an absolute belief in the fundamental goodness of human nature, and the inner sense of peace that comes from knowing that there is a clearly defined path to happiness—in fact, many paths.

The Art of Happiness in a Troubled World

I, Us, and Them

Chapter 1

ME VERSUS WE

I think this is the first time I am meeting most of you. But whether it is an old friend or a new friend, there's not much difference anyway, because I always believe we are the same: We are all just human beings. —H.H. THE DALAI LAMA, SPEAKING TO A CROWD OF MANY THOUSANDS

TIME PASSES. The world changes. But there is one constant I have grown used to over the years, while intermittently traveling on speaking tours with the Dalai Lama: When speaking to a general audience, he invariably opens his address, "We are all the same . . ."

Once establishing a bond with each member of the audience in that way, he then proceeds to that evening's particular topic. But over the years I've witnessed a remarkable phenomenon: Whether he is speaking to a small formal meeting of leaders on Capitol Hill, addressing a gathering of a hundred thousand in Central Park, an interfaith dialogue in Australia, or a scientific conference in Switzerland, or teaching twenty thousand monks in India, one can sense an almost palpable effect. He seems to create a feeling among his audience not only of connection to him, but of connection to one another, a fundamental human bond.

It was early on a Monday morning and I was back in Dharamsala, scheduled to meet shortly with the Dalai Lama for our first meeting in a fresh series of discussions. Home to a thriving Tibetan community, Dharamsala is a tranquil village built into a ridge of the Dauladar mountain range, the foothills of the Himalayas in northern India. I had arrived a few days earlier, around the same time as the Dalai Lama himself, who had just returned home from a three-week speaking tour in the United States.

I finished breakfast early, and as the Dalai Lama's residence was only a five-minute walk along a mountain path from the guesthouse where I was staying, I retired to the common room to finish my coffee and review my notes in preparation for our meeting. Though the room was deserted, someone had left on the TV tuned to the world news. Absorbed in my notes, I wasn't paying much attention to the news and for several minutes the suffering of the world was nothing but background noise.

It wasn't long, however, before I happened to look up and a story caught my attention. A Palestinian suicide bomber had detonated an explosive at a Tel Aviv disco, deliberately targeting Israeli boys and girls. Almost two dozen teenagers were killed. But killing alone apparently was not satisfying enough for the terrorist. He had filled his bomb with rusty nails and screws for good measure, in order to maim and disfigure those whom he couldn't kill.

Before the immense cruelty of such an act could fully sink in, other news reports quickly followed—a bleak mix of natural disasters and intentional acts of violence . . . the Crown Prince of Nepal slaughters his entire family . . . survivors of the Gujarat earthquake still struggle to recover.

Fresh from accompanying the Dalai Lama on his recent tour, I found that his words "We are all the same" rang in my head as I watched these horrifying stories of sudden suffering and misery. I then realized I had been listening to these reports as if the victims were vague, faceless abstract entities, not a group of individuals "the same as me." It seemed that the greater the sense of distance between me and the victim, the less real they seemed to be, the less like living, breathing human beings. But now, for a moment, I tried to imagine what it would be like to be one of the earthquake victims, going about my usual daily chores one moment and seventy-five seconds later having no family, home, or possessions, suddenly becoming penniless and alone.

"We are all the same." It was a powerful principle, and one that I was convinced could change the world.

"Your Holiness," I began, "I'd like to talk with you this morning about this idea that we are all the same. You know, in today's world there is such a pervasive feeling of isolation and alienation among people, a feeling of separateness, even suspicion. It seems to me that if we could somehow cultivate this sense of connection to others, a real sense of connection on a deep level, a common bond, I think it could completely transform society. It could eliminate so many of the problems facing the world today. So this morning I'd like to talk about this principle that we are all the same, and—"

"We are all the same?" the Dalai Lama repeated.

"Yes, and—"

"Where did you get this idea?" he asked.

"Huh?"

"Who gave you this idea?"

"You . . . *you* did," I stammered, a bit confused.

"Howard," he said bluntly, "we are *not* all the same. We're different! Everybody is different."

"Yes, of course," I quickly amended myself, "we all have these superficial differences, but what I mean is—"

"Our differences are not necessarily superficial," he persisted. "For example, there is one senior Lama I know who is from Ladakh. Now, I am very close to this Lama, but at the same time, I know that he is a Ladakhee. No matter how close I may feel toward this person, it's never going to make him Tibetan. The fact remains that he is a Ladakhee."

I had heard the Dalai Lama open his public addresses with "We are all the same" so often over the years that this turn of conversation was starting to stagger me.

"Well, on your tours over the years, whenever you speak to big audiences, and even on this most recent, you always say, 'We are all the same.' That seems like a really strong theme in your public talks. For example, you say how people tend to focus on our differences, but we are all the same in terms of our desire to be happy and avoid suffering, and—"

"Oh yes. Yes," he acknowledged. "And also we have the same human potential. Yes, I generally begin my talk with these things. This is because many different people come to see me. Now I am a Buddhist monk. I am Tibetan. Maybe others' backgrounds are different. So if we had no common basis, if we had no characteristics that we share, then there is no point in my talk, no point in sharing my views. But the fact is that we are all human beings. That is the very basis upon which I'm sharing my personal experience with them."

"That is the kind of idea I was getting at—this idea that we are all human beings," I explained, relieved that we were finally on the same page. "I think if people really had a genuine feeling inside, that all human beings were the same and they were the same as other people, it would completely transform society . . . I mean in a genuine way. So, I'm hoping we can explore this issue a little bit."

The Dalai Lama responded, "Then to really try to understand this, we need to investigate how we come to think of ourselves as independent, isolated or separate, and how we view others as different or separate, and see if we can come to a deeper understanding. But we cannot start from the standpoint of saying simply we are all the same and denying that there are differences."

"Well, that is kind of my point. I think we can agree that if people related to each other as fellow human beings, if everyone related to other people like you do, on that basic human level, like brothers and sisters, as I've heard you refer to people, the world would be a far better place. We wouldn't have all these problems that I want to talk to you about later, and you and I could talk about football games or movies instead!

"So, I don't know," I continued, "but it seems that your approach to building the sense of connection between people is to remind them of the characteristics they share as human beings. The way you do whenever you have the opportunity to speak to a large audience."

"Yes." He nodded.

"I don't know . . ." I repeated again. "It is such an important topic, so simple an idea yet so difficult in reality, that I'm just wondering if there are any other methods of facilitating that process, like speeding it up, or motivating people to view things from that perspective, given the many problems in the world today."

"Other methods . . ." he said slowly, taking a moment to carefully consider the question while I eagerly anticipated his insights and wisdom. Suddenly he started to laugh. As if he had a sudden epiphany, he exclaimed, "Yes! Now if we could get beings from Mars to come down to the earth, and pose some kind of threat, then I think you would see all the people on Earth unite very quickly! They would join together, and say, '*We,* the people of the earth!'" He continued laughing.

Unable to resist his merry laugh, I also began to laugh. "Yes, I guess that would about do it," I agreed. "And I'll see what I can do to speak to the Interplanetary Council about it. But in the meantime, while we're all waiting for the Mothership to arrive, any other suggestions?"

Thus we began a series of conversations that would continue intermittently for several years. The discussion began that morning with my casually tossing around the phrase "We are all the same" as if I was coming up with a slogan for a soft drink ad that was going to unite the world. The Dalai Lama responded with his characteristic refusal to reduce important questions to simplistic formulas. These were critical human questions: How can we establish a deep feeling of connection to others, a genuine human bond, including those who may be very different? Is it possible to even view your enemy as a person essentially like yourself? Is it possible to really see all human beings as one's brothers and sisters, or is this a utopian dream?

Our discussions soon broadened to address other fundamental issues dealing with the relationship between the individual and society. Serious questions were at stake: Is it possible to be truly happy when social problems invariably impact our personal happiness? In seeking happiness do we choose the path of inner development or social change?

As our discussions progressed, the Dalai Lama addressed these questions not as abstract concepts or philosophical speculation but as realities within the context of our everyday lives, quickly revealing how these questions are directly related to very real problems and concerns.

In these first discussions in Dharamsala, we dealt with the challenge of how to shift one's orientation from Me to We. Less than a year later, I returned to Dharamsala for our second series of conversations— September 11 had occurred in the interim, initiating the worldwide War on Terror. It was clear that cultivating a We orientation was not enough. Acutely reminded that where there is a "we" there is also a "they," we now had to face the potential problems raised by an "us against them" mind-set: prejudice, suspicion, indifference, racism, conflict, violence, cruelty, and a wide spectrum of ugly and terrible attitudes with which human beings can treat one another.

When we met in Tucson, Arizona, several years later, the Dalai Lama began to weave together the ideas from our many conversations on these topics, presenting a coherent approach to coping with our troubled world, explaining how to maintain a feeling of hope and even happiness despite the many problems of today's world.

But that Monday morning we began on the most fundamental level, exploring our customary notions about who we are and how we relate to the world around us, beginning with how we relate to those in our own communities and the role that plays in our personal and societal happiness.

"No Sense of Community, No Anchor"

On a recent Friday afternoon, an unemployed twenty-year-old posted a message on YouTube, simply offering to "be there" for anyone who needed to talk. "I never met you, but I do care," he said.

By the end of the weekend, he had received more than five thousand calls and text messages from strangers taking him up on his offer.

Continuing our discussion, I reviewed. "You know, Your Holiness, our discussions over the years have revolved around the theme of human happiness. In the past we discussed happiness from the individual standpoint, from the standpoint of inner development. But now we are talking about human happiness at the level of society, exploring some of the societal factors that may affect human happiness. I know of course that you have had the opportunity to travel around the world many times, visiting many different countries, so many different cultures, as well as meeting with many different kinds of people and experts in so many fields."

"Yes."

"So, I was just wondering—in the course of your travels, is there any particular aspect of modern society that you have noticed that you feel acts as a major obstruction to the full expression of human happiness? Of course, there are many specific problems in today's world, like violence, racism, terrorism, the gap between rich and poor, the environment, and so on. But here I'm wondering if there is more of a general feature of society that stands out in your mind as particularly significant?"

Seated upon a wide upholstered chair, the Dalai Lama bent down to unlace his plain brown shoes while he silently reflected on the question. Then, tucking his feet under him in a cross-legged position, settling in for a deeper discussion, he replied, "Yes. I was just thinking there is one thing I have noticed, something that is very important. I think it could be best characterized as *a lack of sense of community*. Tibetans are always shocked to hear of situations where people are living in close proximity, have neighbors, and they may have been your neighbors for months or even years, but you have hardly any contact with them! So you might simply greet them when you meet, but otherwise you don't know them. There is no real connection. There is no sense of community. These situations we always find very surprising, because in the traditional Tibetan society, the sense of community is very strong."

The Dalai Lama's comment hit home with me—literally and figuratively. I thought, not without some embarrassment, that I myself didn't know the names of my neighbors. Nor had I known my neighbors' names for many years.

Of course, I was not about to admit that *now*. "Yes," I said, "you will certainly see those kinds of situations."

The Dalai Lama went on to explain, "In today's world you will sometimes find these communities or societies where there is no spirit of cooperation, no feeling of connection. Then you'll see widespread loneliness set in. I feel that a sense of community is so important. I mean even if you are very rich, if you don't have human companions or friends to share your love with, sometimes you end up simply sharing it with a pet, an animal, which is better than nothing. However, even if you are in a poor community, the poor will have each other. So there is a real sense that you have a kind of an anchor, an emotional anchor. Whereas, if this sense of community is lacking, then when you feel lonely, and when you have pain, there is no one to really share it with. I think this kind of loneliness is probably a major problem in today's world, and can certainly affect an individual's day-to-day happiness.

"Now when we speak of loneliness," he added, "I think we should be careful of what we mean. Here I don't necessarily mean loneliness only as the feeling of missing someone, or wanting a friend to talk to, or something like that. Because you can have a family who has a close bond, so they may not have a high level of individual loneliness, but they may feel alienated from the wider society. So here I was speaking of loneliness more as a wider kind of isolation or sense of separation between people or groups."

The decline of our sense of community has increasingly become the subject of popular discourse during the last decade, due in part to books such as *Bowling Alone,* by Robert D. Putnam, a political scientist at Harvard University. Putnam argues that our sense of community and civic engagement has dramatically deteriorated over the last thirty years—noting with dismay the marked decline of neighborhood friendships, dinner parties, group discussions, club memberships, church committees, political participation, and essentially all the involvements that make a democracy work.

According to sociologists Miller McPherson and Matthew E. Brashears from the University of Arizona and Lynn Smith-Lovin from Duke University, in the past two decades the number of people who report they have *no one* with whom they can talk about important matters has nearly tripled. Based on extensive data collected in the University of Chicago's General Social Survey, the percentage of individuals with no close friends or confidants is a staggering 25 percent of the American population. This number is so surprising that it left the researchers themselves wondering if this could really be an accurate estimate. The same organization conducted a similar nationwide survey back in 1985, shocking Americans then by revealing that, on average, people in our society had only three close friends. By 2005, this figure had dropped by a third—most people had only two close friends or confidants.

The investigators not only found that people had fewer social connections over the past two decades but also discovered that the pattern of our social connections was also changing. More and more people were relying on family members as their primary source of social connection. The researchers, noting that people were relying less on friendships in the wider community, concluded, "The types of bridging ties that connect us to community and neighborhood have withered."

While the study did not identify the reasons for this decline in social connectedness and community, other investigators have identified a number of factors contributing to this alarming trend. Historically, advances in modern transportation created an increasingly mobile society, as more and more families pulled up roots and moved to new cities in search of better jobs or living conditions. As society became more prosperous, it also became a common practice among larger segments of the population for children to leave home to attend universities in other cities or states. Easier travel and communication have allowed young people to move farther from the parental home than ever before, in search of better career opportunities.

More recent studies show that working hours and commutes are both longer, resulting in less time for people to interact with their community. These changes in work hours and the geographical scattering of families may foster a broader, shallower network of ties, rather than the close bonds necessary for fulfillment of our human need for connection.

Solitary TV viewing and computer use, ever on the rise, also contribute to social isolation. The growth of the Internet as a communication tool may play a role as well. While the Internet can keep us connected to friends, family, and neighbors, it also may diminish the need for us to actually see each other to make those closer connections. Researchers point out that while communication through tools such as the Internet or text messaging does create bonds between people, these types of connections create weaker social ties than communication in person. Words are sometimes poor vehicles for expressing and communicating emotions; a great deal of human communication is conveyed through subtle visual cues that can be better perceived in face-to-face encounters.

Whatever the cause, it is clear that the decline in our sense of community and the increasing social isolation have far-reaching implications on every level—personal, communal, societal, and global. With his characteristic wisdom and insight, the Dalai Lama is quick to point out the importance of this issue, and its impact on human happiness both on the individual level as well as on a wider societal level. Here the views of both the Dalai Lama and Western science converge. In fact, echoing the Dalai Lama's view, and summarizing the latest scientific research from many disciplines, Robin Dunbar, professor of psychology at the University of Liverpool in the UK, asserts, "*The lack of social contact, the lack of sense of community, may be the most pressing social problem of the new millennium."*

Building the Spirit of Community: The First Steps

"Well, the medication is finally working!" said David, a well-groomed, nicely dressed young man sitting in my Phoenix office. "My depression has completely lifted, and I'm back to my normal state of unhappiness." He was half joking—but only half. A bright, successful, single thirty-two-year-old structural engineer, David had presented to treatment about a month earlier with a familiar spectrum of symptoms: sudden loss of interest in his usual activities, fatigue, insomnia, weight loss, difficulty concentrating—in short, a pretty ordinary, garden-variety depression. It didn't take long to discover that he had recently moved to Phoenix to accept a new job and the stresses related to the change had triggered his depression.

This was years ago, when I was in practice as a psychiatrist. I began him on a standard course of antidepressant medication, and his acute symptoms of severe depression resolved within a few weeks. Soon after resuming his normal routine, however, he reported a more long-standing problem, a many-year history of "a kind of mild chronic unhappiness," an inexplicable pervasive sense of "dissatisfaction with life," and general lack of enthusiasm or "zest" for life. Hoping to discover the source and rid himself of this ongoing state, he asked to continue with psychotherapy. I was happy to oblige. So, after diagnosing him with the mood disorder dysthymia, we set about in earnest, exploring the usual "family of origin" issues—his childhood, his overly controlling mother, his emotionally distant father—along with past relationship patterns and present interpersonal dynamics. Pretty standard stuff.

Week after week, David showed up regularly, until terminating therapy a few months later, due to another job-related move. Over the months his major depression had never returned, but we had made little to no headway with his chronic state of dissatisfaction.

Remembering this patient now, who was by no means unique, I recall one aspect of his personal history that seemed rather unremarkable at the time. His daily routine consisted of going to work five or six days a week, at least eight-hour days, then returning home. That about summed it up. At home, evenings and weekends, he would generally watch TV, play video games, maybe read a bit. Sometimes he would go to a bar or to a movie with a friend, generally someone from work. There was the occasional date, but mostly he remained at home. This daily routine had remained essentially unchanged for many years.

Looking back on my treatment of David, I can only wonder one thing: *What in the world was I thinking?!* For months I had been treating him for his complaints of a sense of dissatisfaction ("I dunno, there's just something *missing* from my life. . . ."), exploring his childhood history, looking for patterns in past relationships, yet right in front of us his life had at least one significant gap, a gap that we failed to recognize. Not a small, obscure, or subtle gap, but rather a huge gaping cavern—he was a man with no community, no wider sense of connection.

During my years of psychiatric practice, I rarely looked beyond the level of the individual in treating patients. It *never even occurred to me* to look beyond the level of family and friends to a patient's relationship to the wider community. This reminds me of British prime minister Margaret Thatcher at a time when she was at the pinnacle of her power and influence announcing, "Who is 'society'? There is no such thing! There are individual men and women and there are families." Looking back on it now, it almost seems as if I was practicing a brand of Margaret Thatcher School of Psychotherapy.

From my current perspective, I would have done my former patient David a greater service had I handed him a prescription reading: "Treatment: *One act of community involvement per week. Increase dosage as tolerated. Get plenty of rest, drink plenty of fluids, and follow up in one month.*"

In seeking an effective treatment to cure the ills of our society, as the Dalai Lama will reveal, forging a deeper sense of connection to others, and building a greater sense of community, can be a good place to start.

Having identified this erosion of community bonds as a significant problem, we now turned to the question of what to do about it.

"Your Holiness, you have mentioned that this lack of sense of community is a big problem in modern society. Do you have any thoughts about how to increase the sense of community, strengthen those human bonds?"

"Yes," the Dalai Lama answered. "I think the approach must begin with cultivating awareness. . . ."

"Awareness specifically of what?" I asked.

"Of course, in the first place, you need to have awareness of the seriousness of the problem itself, how destructive it can be. Then, you need greater awareness of the ways that we are connected with others, reflecting on the characteristics we share with others. And finally, you need to translate that awareness into action. I think that's the main thing. This means making a deliberate effort to increase personal contact among the various members of the community. So, *that* is how to increase your feeling of connection, increase your bonds within the community!"

"So, if it is okay, I'm wondering if you could very briefly touch upon each of these steps or strategies in a bit more detail, just to delineate them clearly."

"Yes, okay," he said agreeably, as he began to outline his approach. "Now, regarding cultivating greater awareness. No matter what kind of problem you are dealing with, one needs to make an effort to change things—the problem will not fix itself. A person needs to have a strong determination to change the problem. This determination comes from your conviction that the problem is serious, and it has serious consequences. And the way to generate this conviction is by learning about the problem, investigating, and using your common sense and reasoning. This is what I mean by awareness here. I think we have discussed this kind of general approach in the past. But here, we are not only talking about becoming more aware of the destructive consequences of this lack of community and this widespread loneliness, but we are also talking about the positive benefits of having a strong sense of community."

"Benefits such as . . . ?"

"Like I mentioned—having an emotional anchor, having others with whom you can share your problems and so on."

"Oh, I was thinking more in terms of things like less crime, or maybe health benefits of connecting to a wider community . . . ."

"Howard, those things I don't know. Here you should consult an expert, see what kind of evidence there is, scientific evidence. I am not an expert in these things. But even without looking at the research, I think anyone can do their own investigation, keeping their eyes open and reflecting on these things.

"For example, even in the same city or community, you might find two different kinds of neighborhoods. Let's say that in one neighborhood people don't really get along with each other, neighbors don't really communicate with each other, and nobody cares much about the general community. Then compare that with another neighborhood where people talk to each other, where there is a sense of friendship and community, so when some things happen, either good or bad, people get together and share it. Comparing the two, you'll definitely find that the people living in the more community-oriented neighborhood will be much more happy and will have a greater sense of security, safety. That's just common sense."

Pausing momentarily, the Dalai Lama continued. "You know, Howard, I think that it's during the hard times, like when a family suffers a tragedy, especially the death of a loved one, it is then that a community becomes so important. It's during such times of grief that you can really see the value of community. . . . This reminds me. I heard, for example, that in some of the Tibetan settlements in South India, when there is a death in one family, all the other families of the camp pull together to support and comfort them, even bringing firewood to the cemetery for the cremation of the body."

"What do you mean by a 'camp' here?" I asked.

"Oh, many of these settlements were originally organized into camps of around one hundred and sixty people, when they were first established," he replied.

"In these camps," the Dalai Lama continued, "neighbors also look out for one another, especially after those elderly ones whose children or grandchildren may not be living in the vicinity. If they are sick or unable to care for themselves or by their own family, the community will also make sure that they are properly cared for. This is wonderful. Isn't it?"

"So, Your Holiness, having recognized that there are clear-cut benefits from connecting with a community, can you explain the next strategy you mentioned, your suggestion to increase awareness of the ways that we are connected with others?"

The Dalai Lama considered the question for a moment. "Yes. Now, one thing. When we talk about sense of community, basically we are talking about a feeling of connection to others, a feeling of affinity to a wider group beyond oneself, where you feel a sense of belonging. So, Howard, if we are seeking to build a sense of community, strengthen community bonds, we need to find a way to connect with others, establish a feeling of connectedness. The point here is that you should become aware of, on what basis you relate to others, and investigate the various ways you can connect, or relate to them. Look carefully. Analyze. Ask yourself, what are the different characteristics that you share with others? What are the common bonds?"

"So here," I clarified, "you're talking about things like, for instance, how members of the Tibetan community relate on the basis of a shared culture and spirituality, and how that creates strong community bonds?"

"That's right. But remember, a shared cultural or spiritual background or tradition is not the only basis for these strong community bonds, this sense of community. This is on one level. But one can also relate to others on other levels, such as belonging to the same family, or based on living in the same neighborhood, or local region, or you can find others who share your same personal interests or hobbies. Each of these can be considered a different kind of 'community.' It is a matter of the underlying feeling of belonging to a wider group. That is what is important."

"So, this brings us to the final step," I said, "or maybe it's actually the first step: taking action—making an effort to establish personal contact with others of your community, however you define or conceive of your 'community.'"

"That's right."

"You know, Your Holiness, I was just thinking that there can be so many different causes of the deterioration of our sense of community, and a lot of these no doubt have to do with the basic characteristics of modern society. For example, one of the factors in Western societies which might affect this is mobility. People will often move from one city or state to another in order to improve themselves in some way, for a better job, to make more money, to try to improve their living conditions. This idea of uprooting oneself in search of better opportunities is actually promoted in our society."

"Yes," the Dalai Lama agreed, "this mobility may play some role. For example, there would be a real affinity for others and a greater sense of community if you are living among individuals who you have grown up with, gone to school with and so on. And in modern society, with people moving so often, we don't always have such situations."

"So, that's one cause of the problem," I concluded. "But I mean, how can we build a sense of community when people are always being encouraged to pick up and move, based on . . . 'Oh, that job over there is better,' and so on?"

"Howard, I don't think that moving automatically has to make one lose a sense of community," he replied confidently, "*because even if one is new to a community, one can make an effort to get to know the people in the neighborhood.* Even if you move to a new area, you can still create a community there. This sense of community is based on individuals and families making an effort to meet and get to know one another. You can always make an effort to get to know the people you're living with locally, *join local organizations, participate in community activities,* and so on.

"So, it is often simply a matter of *willingness*. And how can we help increase this willingness? Again, through awareness, through the recognition of the real importance of a sense of community, of how that may have a direct impact on your own happiness, and the happiness of your family.

"The fact is that wherever you go, you can't run away from community. Isn't it?* There it is. Unless you choose to isolate yourself. Choose to become indifferent. Choose to have no commitment. It is really up to you."

By now the Dalai Lama's attendants were hovering just outside the screen door on the veranda, signaling our time was up. "So, I think we will end for today," he said cheerfully. "We will meet again tomorrow." With that, he slipped on his shoes and quickly left the room.

So, we begin our investigation of human society and happiness with several basic premises. First, there is no doubt that societal factors can influence an individual's happiness. Second, in looking for specific factors that can influence human happiness, there is no doubt that a sense of connection to others and a wider sense of community play a key role in human happiness. Third, in looking at the trends of modern society, as the Dalai Lama points out, there is no doubt that there has been a deterioration of our sense of community, growing social isolation, and a lack of a deep feeling of connection among people.

While I had never given much thought to this trend before, once the Dalai Lama highlighted the growing lack of community in modern society, I became profoundly aware of the pervasiveness and seriousness of this problem. The more I reflected on this critical issue, it seemed that the entire course of modern civilization was behind this problem, creating it, fueling it, pushing it onward—and leading us to greater and greater problems and potentially even disaster. Underlying

---

* When speaking English, the Dalai Lama often uses the expression "Isn't it?" to mean "Don't you agree?"

this erosion of community bonds were complex social forces, forces of such tremendous power and pervasiveness as modern technology and even the fundamental values of our society. In a society that was moving faster and faster, these social forces seemed to be creating a current that was sweeping us along involuntarily. How can we slow down the current of this mighty river that seemed to be carrying us toward greater misery and possibly even destruction?

Fortunately, the Dalai Lama offers us a well-defined approach to reestablishing community bonds, and as always, his approach is immensely practical. With his natural, spontaneous wisdom, he explained how to create the spirit of community in three basic steps. . . .

STEP ONE: AWARENESS OF THE BENEFITS

If a mysterious stranger sidled up to you and whispered, "I can offer you a secret method to cut in half your chances of dying within the next year—without giving up your cigarettes, Big Macs, or beer, without a single push-up, or a minute of exercise!" what would the information be worth? Well, for those suffering from the pervasive social isolation and alienation of modern society, such a method does exist. "Connectedness really matters," Robert Putnam explained at one White House conference. "Wonderful studies, controlling for your blood chemistry and how old you are and your gender and whether you jog and whether you smoke and so on, show that your chances of dying over the next year are cut in half by joining one group. Cut in a quarter by joining two groups," reported Putnam.

In outlining his approach to building a stronger sense of community, the Dalai Lama advises us to begin by investigating the benefits of connecting to a wider group. Based on many studies, there is no question that the physical, mental, and emotional health benefits of intimate relationships and social ties are legion: Lower death rates, faster recovery from illness, better mental health, and better immune function are just a few. The scientific evidence comes from many sources, ranging from massive surveys of thousands, to small-scale laboratory experiments— such as the slightly unsettling study conducted at Carnegie Mellon in which samples of cold virus were directly squirted into the nostrils of a few brave subjects, finding that those with rich social networks were four times less likely to get sick!

In addition to the personal health benefits of close relationships, evidence has been accumulating that a sense of belonging to a wider community, extending beyond one's intimate circle of friends or family, has equally compelling benefits that can manifest in many other ways. As Robert Putnam points out, "Communities that have tighter social networks have lower crime and lower mortality and less corruption and more effective government and less tax evasion."

The ultimate purpose of my discussions with the Dalai Lama was to discover an approach to finding happiness within the wider context of living in modern society. Thus, in assessing the benefits of having a sense of community, it is important to look at the role (if any) this plays in human happiness. In his wonderful book *Happiness: Lessons from a New Science,* leading economist Lord Richard Layard outlines six key factors that can largely explain the differences in average levels of happiness between one country and another. One of them is the percentage of the population that belongs to a social organization.

STEP TWO: AWARENESS OF THE WAYS WE ARE CONNECTED

According to the Dalai Lama, the way to build a stronger sense of community is to develop a deep awareness of the ways we are connected to others. Such awareness can be developed by deliberately reflecting on the characteristics we share with others, our common interests, background, and shared experience. The Dalai Lama points out, for example, how the Tibetan people are bound tightly by a common cultural and spiritual heritage, whether living in exile in India or other countries throughout the world. These common bonds have deep roots: with the spiritual heritage dating back to the seventh century, when Buddhism began to spread in Tibet, and the cultural heritage extending back even further. It seems reasonable to suppose that the deeper the roots of the shared heritage, the stronger one's sense of identity or spirit of community will be. But the Dalai Lama also reminds us that there are many other qualities through which we forge a sense of connection. If we investigate carefully, we can always find some characteristic or experience that we share with others, some common bond.

In thinking about this approach to cultivating a deeper sense of community, I couldn't help but wonder what characteristics the residents of my own hometown, Phoenix, might have in common—beyond living in the same city, which seemed unlikely to foster a deep connection all by itself. What might be the shared heritage or common bond for engendering a sense of unity among the diverse inhabitants of this city?

Like the mythical phoenix bird for which it was named, rising from its own ashes, this city grew out of the barren Sonoran desert on the ruins of an ancient unknown community. A city with more than two million inhabitants today, it didn't even exist a mere 150 years ago. The city has sprung up essentially overnight, with most of the inhabitants moving here only in the past few decades. In stark contrast to the strong community ties based on the deep roots of the Tibetans' rich heritage, it seems that only weak bonds could be formed by such shallow historical roots in this case. What else could provide the people of Phoenix common ground that would not be swept away at the first sign of community unrest?

Seeking an answer to this question, I conducted my own little survey polling long-time residents. What was the common cultural heritage I discovered? For thirty-five years, almost every schoolchild in Phoenix was sharing the exact same experience at the exact same time, five days a week—watching a local children's cartoon show on TV called *Wallace and Ladmo,* which featured a fat guy wearing a polka-dot shirt and a straw hat (later traded for a bowler hat and bow tie) and a tall skinny guy wearing a top hat and a giant necktie. As Phoenix-raised filmmaker Steven Spielberg explained, "When my mom saw me and my three sisters parked in front of the TV set watching *The Wallace and Ladmo Show,* she knew, except for bathroom breaks, we wouldn't be anywhere else." A similar statement could be uttered by a generation of Phoenix residents, cutting across ethnic, racial, gender, religious, or socioeconomic barriers—a generation that shared the exact same words and same visual images being imprinted and stored in their brains at the exact same moment for hours every week.

Well, okay, maybe this isn't the strongest basis on which to forge common ground, but at least it shows that if you dig deep enough, you're bound to uncover some kind of shared experience, a basis for camaraderie. As my conversations with the Dalai Lama continued, he would reveal a way to form a common bond on a much more fundamental level, encompassing a much wider slice of humanity than a city of kids, who at the very same instant were all absorbing the wisdom of Popeye: "I am what I am and that's all that I am!"

STEP THREE: TAKE ACTION; INCREASE PERSONAL CONTACT

The final step: Take action. Clearly the first two steps of the Dalai Lama's method of building a sense of community, which involve developing greater awareness, mean nothing unless that awareness is translated into action. Years later as I reviewed the transcript of that conversation, I came to his comments about not knowing one's neighbors. While acutely aware that his words applied to me at the time, I had promptly forgotten about it. Now here it was, years later, in fact, and I realized I *still* had not bothered to find out my neighbors' names. Of course, I hadn't been ignoring them over the years, but whenever I saw a neighbor, the interaction had always been limited to a nod of the head, perhaps a smile, sometimes a friendly "How's it goin'?" or rarely a brief chat about the weather. Yet there was never an attempt to connect in any meaningful way.

As I read the Dalai Lama's words in the transcript "*it's simply a matter of willingness*" and recalled our conversation, I suddenly stood up from my computer. "Better late than never," I thought, and walked outside, determined to meet at least one of my neighbors. By chance I noticed one who was having car trouble. I walked over to offer help. We introduced ourselves and as it turns out, we had quite an interesting conversation. I walked back indoors, returned to my computer, and went back to work.

My professional colleagues might disparagingly label this a mere "anecdotal report" and dismiss my observations as biased and of no value as proof of anything. Well, no matter. But I swear that just taking that one small step, that simple act of connecting with my neighbor, gave me a sudden and dramatic boost in mood, energy level, and even mental clarity, as I was able to return to my work with a renewed freshness and enthusiasm, as if returning from a weekend vacation instead of a brief conversation with a neighbor.

When contemplating the deterioration of our sense of community, the growing alienation in our society, and the destructive social forces causing them, these had initially seemed to be virtually unsolvable problems. But now, they seemed possible to resolve. In presenting these complex and seemingly overwhelming social problems to the Dalai Lama, he seemed to slice through them like Alexander the Great cutting the Gordian knot. His answers were so basic, they were disarming. What if you move to a new place? *Simply join a group.* What if you feel unmotivated? *Understand the benefits more.* What if you feel isolated, alienated, unconnected to any community? *Take stock of your own interests, and get involved with others with similar interests.*

Showing us the way to begin to build a renewed sense of community, a feeling of belonging, he pointed out the truth with utter clarity: It is up to us. He places the responsibility squarely in our own hands, rather than in the hands of the overwhelming forces of society. We don't need to turn back the clock to earlier days; we don't need to revert to agrarian societies. We don't need to change the course of modern society in order to create a greater sense of community. We only need to act, one person at a time, reaching out to connect with others with similar interests.

But while the principles the Dalai Lama expressed were simple, they are not simplistic, nor are they necessarily easy to achieve. As I was to discover, the ideas he presented were much more profound and nuanced, and his approach was not as straightforward as it seemed upon first glance. This was only the first step in exploring the relationship between the individual, society, and the pursuit of human happiness.

Chapter 2

ME *AND* WE

Relating on a Basic Human Level

THE NEXT morning we continued our discussion of community.

"Your Holiness, yesterday we were speaking about this problem of people feeling isolated and the benefits of this sense of community," I began, "so, essentially, what we are talking about here is identifying with a wider group, kind of moving from the focus on 'me' to the focus on 'we.'"

"That's right."

"Now the benefits for that shift of orientation are very clear. There are personal benefits such as better health, as well as benefits for the welfare of the community and the society in which we live. Also, there's no doubt that our interpersonal relationships, our social networks and so on, provide our greatest potential source of human happiness. In our discussions over the years, even before identifying the importance of a sense of community, you've often mentioned how you feel that our connection to others, relating to others with human affection, a sense of caring and compassion and so on, is integral to personal happiness. . . ."

"That's right," he reaffirmed.

"Well," I continued, "I think there could be a potential problem here. Certainly it is natural that people may strongly identify with their particular group or community. But this can highlight our differences from other groups, which can often lead to a feeling of superiority. Strong group identification not only produces pride for one's own group but also creates the very real potential of developing bias and prejudice against other groups. And then all sorts of problems can arise as a result. So, the question is, How can one encourage the transition from 'I' to 'Us', moving from a feeling of isolation to a feeling of identification with a group, yet prevent that from progressing to 'Us' *against* 'Them'? It seems that human beings have a long history of that kind of thing occurring, and from there it is a very short step to conflict and even violence."

"This is true," the Dalai Lama agreed; "that is why it is important to recognize, as I mentioned yesterday, that there can be different levels to the concept of 'community'—and I think *it is important that one's cultural or national identity, or whatever, does not override one's basic identity as a human being,* as also being a member of the human community. This is critical."

"Well, I guess here we are talking about connecting on a deeper level, on the basic human level, connecting with others based on that fundamental human bond. And I think the problem is that many people still lack that underlying deep sense of connection to others. The absence of that fundamental human bond can result in a sense of indifference, a lack of concern for others' welfare that can in turn lead to problems ranging from poverty to the destruction of the environment. Also, without that deep connection there is a sense of separateness, a sense that others are fundamentally different, which can open the door to prejudice and possibly even to the kinds of dehumanization that can lead to unimaginable atrocities. Human history is filled with examples of this. So, since this seems to be at the core of so many human problems, how do you suggest cultivating a greater sense of connection with others, even to all human beings?"

"Of course, there can be many causes, many components to these problems you mention," he reminded me. "But now in answering your question about cultivating a deeper feeling of connection, I think the key is how we relate to one another. *It comes down to our basic outlook, on what basis we relate to those around us.*"

"Just to clarify, when you say, 'on what basis,' you mean . . . ?"

"The question is whether we relate to others based on what differentiates us or on the characteristics we share. This can determine whether we have an underlying sense of separation from others, or a feeling of affinity and a bond to a wider community."

"I suppose that is true," I agreed, "but I think that people naturally tend to view others based more on their differences. In fact, I think we *like* to see ourselves as unique, as different from others. I don't think it is easy to change the way we relate like that."

"That's true," he said. "To have a real sense of brotherhood, sisterhood, based on identifying oneself first and foremost as a human being is not easy. It does not happen overnight. But I feel that part of the problem is that in day-to-day life, the majority of the people don't give serious thought to their common connection to all other human beings. They do not spend time reflecting on it. I think in general in society there is much greater emphasis on our individual differences. So, for many people, their connection to others is normally not so apparent. Yet that human bond is always there."

The Dalai Lama picked up the simple ceramic mug he kept on a table beside him and removed the lid. Taking a sip of hot water, his customary beverage, he continued. "I was just thinking—maybe you could imagine a situation where someone was stranded on an uninhabited barren island for a long time, and if you happen to come across another human being, even if that person was very different from you and a complete stranger, you would immediately feel a sense of affinity to that person. Then our common bond as human beings would become very apparent."

"Well," I said, "I guess you pointed out one of the main problems—we don't often think about these things. After all, we don't often get stranded on deserted islands! So, in our everyday lives we get caught up in our individual problems and we tend to forget our basic connection and bonds as human beings. If we really want to change our perspective, and develop that genuine sense of connectedness to others, to *all* human beings, where do we start?"

"Once again, it comes down to awareness—cultivating an even wider awareness of the ways that we are connected, the characteristics that we share as human beings, and the deliberate promotion of these ideas in our society."

"You know, Your Holiness, I'm not sure if 'awareness' alone would make such a huge difference in overcoming our sense of separateness. I mean there is enough evidence available of the ways in which we are so similar as human beings, such as when the Human Genome Project was completed. There were stories in the media everywhere about how we share 99.9 percent of our genetic code with every person on the planet."

"Yes, but I think that learning about something is only the first step," he reminded me. "We need to really investigate it, analyze it, think about it over and over, until we develop a deep conviction, until it becomes part of our basic outlook, our natural way of responding to the world around us. And then, once we have this deep conviction, we need to work on changing our behavior—again, this takes effort.

"But all this begins with simple learning, simply to become aware of some facts, through reading or through hearing about something—then we can take the next step, make the effort to deepen our understanding and reinforce what we have learned."

We do indeed tend to focus on our differences more than our commonalities. Yet the Dalai Lama identifies "awareness" of our commonalities, the characteristics, qualities, and traits we share, as the first step in cultivating a deep feeling of "affinity and connectedness" to others—and not just to one's own ethnic, cultural, religious, or political group, but to all human beings. It is no surprise that he also points out that this will not be easy, that it will take time since it involves a fundamental shift in the ways we perceive and respond to others. It is unlikely that just by thinking about this issue once or twice, suddenly we will start to feel the same sense of closeness and affinity for every human being that we might feel for our team members in our Sunday-afternoon softball league.

The Dalai Lama recognizes that we will need to reflect on our common characteristics as human beings, over and over again, until we are conditioned to think of others in a new way—after all, every human being is not issued a matching T-shirt at birth, printed with "Team Humanity." But with the profound impact such an outlook could have in reducing prejudice, hatred, and violence in the world, there is no question that it is worth the effort to adopt a new outlook—or at least consider the possibility that we can learn to relate to others in a new way.

Still, we will inevitably meet with some internal resistance as we struggle to adopt this new outlook. In study after study, people are found to exaggerate their differences from others, as well as minimize the similarities among human beings in general. We overestimate everyone's uniqueness, not just our own. In his book *Stumbling on Happiness,* Harvard social psychologist Daniel Gilbert concludes, "If you are like most people, then like most people, you don't know you're like most people."

In seeking reasons for this very human trait, he points out that our day-to-day social life involves constantly making choices—selecting particular individuals "to be our sexual partners, business partners, bowling partners, and more." This requires "that we focus on the things that distinguish one person from another and not on the things that all people share." The implication is clear: A lifetime spent on focusing on the differences among human beings results in a fundamental distortion, in exaggerating the degree to which people are unique and different. After all, in the normal course of day-to-day life, there is not much call to investigate or reflect on the characteristics that we share—little need to think about how all human beings breathe oxygen, or all share characteristic emotional responses and patterns of behavior, or all want happiness and to avoid suffering—unless, that is, you are a biologist, a psychologist, or a Buddhist monk. The fact is that under normal conditions, people like to think of themselves as unique and different from others. As Gilbert reports, "Research shows that when people are made to feel too similar to others, their moods quickly sour and they try to distance and distinguish themselves in a variety of ways."

We cherish our differences, our specialness. It is this feature of human psychology that Gilbert laments in the closing passages of his book, as our greatest untapped and unused strategy to lead us to greater happiness. Throughout our lives we continuously make choices and decisions, based on what we believe will make us happy. The problem is that, for a variety of solid reasons, our underlying assumptions and beliefs about what will make us happy are often simply incorrect. However, because human beings are so similar in many ways, we have at our disposal a very reliable and effective method to help us accurately predict what course of action will or will not make us happy in the future: observing others who have made the same decisions we are contemplating, those who have previously charted that course, and keenly observing how happy those individuals are under those exact circumstances. Yet, sadly, because of our belief that we are unique, that our minds are so different from one another, and that all people are so different from each other, we often reject the lessons we could learn from others about what will bring us true happiness.

There is no doubt that if we developed a deep awareness of our similarities as human beings we could set a direct course toward greater happiness by observing the relationship between other people's behavior and their experience of happiness or misery. This sense of similarity could also provide the basis for cultivating a profound empathy for all other human beings that could act as an antidote to prejudice, hatred, and violent conflict.

Yet if we strictly adhere to the Dalai Lama's suggestion to view others on the basis of the most fundamental human qualities we share, how would we distinguish one human being from another? How would we make decisions about which mate to choose or which employee to hire?

What would it be like if we were relating to others *only* on the basis of the traits we all share, seeing each other merely as "human beings"? It is true that if we did that, there would be no basis for bias, either for or against any particular person, no basis for prejudice, discrimination, or hatred to arise. But would it be the same as relating to a wide variety of tasty dishes merely as "food"? As an example, let's say that one went to a restaurant and was presented with a menu with many delicious dishes, each one well balanced and having the same percentage of proteins, fats, and carbohydrates. If one was to look at those dishes purely on the basis of the traits they share—such as they all are composed of proteins, fats, and carbohydrates, or even that they are all composed of carbon, hydrogen, and oxygen atoms—then on what basis could you select your meal? From that perspective, they would all be the same.

Fortunately, we do not have to make a choice between viewing other human beings solely in terms of our differences, from the perspective of what differentiates us, or viewing others solely from the perspective of the fundamental human characteristics we share. As our discussions progressed, the Dalai Lama would go on to explain how we can do both, adopting a radical new perspective in which we hold both views and transform our outlook and attitudes about others—but it was not without a bit of struggle first, as we attempted to reconcile our differing perspectives.

Extreme Individualism

Every night, millions of Americans spend their free hours watching television rather than engaging in any form of social interaction. What are they watching? In recent years we have seen reality television become the most popular form of television programming. To discover the nature of our current "reality," we might consider examples such as *Survivor,* the series that helped spawn the reality TV revolution. Every week tens of millions of viewers watched as a group of ordinary people stranded in some isolated place struggled to meet various challenges and endure harsh conditions. Ah, one might think, here we will see people working cooperatively, like our ancient ancestors, working cooperatively in order to "win"! But the "reality" was very different. The conditions of the game were arranged so that, yes, they had to work cooperatively, but the alliances by nature were only temporary and conditional, as the contestants plotted and schemed against one another to win the game and walk off with the Grand Prize: a million dollars! The objective was to banish contestants one by one from the deserted island through a group vote, eliminating every other contestant until only a lone individual remained—the "sole survivor." The end game was the ultimate American fantasy in our Age of Individualism: to be left completely alone, sitting on a mountain of cash!

While *Survivor* was an overt example of our individualistic orientation, it certainly was not unique in its glorification of rugged individualists on American television. Even commercial breaks provide equally compelling examples, with advertisers such as Burger King, proclaiming, *HAVE IT YOUR WAY!* The message? America, the land where not only *every man* and *every woman* is an individual but also *where every hamburger is an individual!*

Human beings do not live in a vacuum; we live in a society. Thus it is important to look at the values promoted and celebrated in a given society and measure what effect this conditioning has on our sense of independence or of interdependence.

It is easy to see how Western societies promote the value of Individualism. However, there are many societies in the world, primarily in Asia, that promote a different kind of outlook, what researchers generally refer to as Collectivism, essentially the opposite of Individualism. Collectivism in this context does not refer to some kind of political philosophy, such as Communism, but instead refers to a basic orientation focusing on one's interdependence and interrelatedness with others.

One can often identify the fundamental values that a particular culture promotes by looking at the traditional proverbs in that culture—in this case, for example, we see that proverbs such as "The squeaky wheel gets the grease" have taken root in the West, extolling the virtue of an individual standing out from the crowd and speaking one's mind, while in Asian cultures such as Japan you'll find proverbs such as "The nail that stands out gets pounded down," hinting at the reception one can expect for, arrogantly, stepping out from the group.

The fundamental question was, which cultural value—Individualism or Collectivism—is more likely to promote happiness among the members of a society, a question I hoped the Dalai Lama could answer as we continued our discussion.

Still examining the question of Me versus We, but shifting the level of our discussion from the level of an individual's outlook and attitudes to the level of societal attitudes and values, we continued our conversation.

"You know, Your Holiness, we have been discussing an individual's capacity to form social bonds and connect to others. In forming these bonds, you not only mentioned the need for a wider awareness of the ways that we are connected and the importance of the deliberate promotion of these ideas in our society. You also mentioned earlier how people can be affected by the values promoted by their society or culture.

"I'm wondering to what degree one's sense of community might be affected by the values of the society in which one lives. Specifically, I'm wondering about the effects of Individualism. People living in individualistic societies tend to have a sense of 'self' that is more independent, compared with some Asian countries that tend to venerate the ideal of Collectivism, associated with more traditional values and a greater awareness of our interdependence and interrelatedness with others.

"From one perspective, one could say that individualistic cultures have a general Me orientation while the collectivist cultures have a We orientation. But the basic question is which society will be happier. For example, it seems that the promotion of Individualism, with its focus on 'Me,' may contribute to the sense of separation and lack of community you spoke about. On the other hand, there seem to be some benefits to Individualism: a sense of independence, self-reliance, and so on. In fact, I think that the promotion of independent thinking, self-sufficiency, and autonomy can lead to greater creativity, personal initiative, achievement, discovery, and then—"

"Now, one thing," the Dalai Lama interrupted, "when you say 'Individualism,' I think it is important to recognize that there can be different levels. On one level it can be a positive thing, and it can bring creativity, or a sense of self-confidence, these kinds of very positive things. But it can also become more extreme, where you will feel so independent and self-sufficient that you feel, 'Oh, I don't need others.' It can also become a sense of self-centeredness, or selfishness, where you completely disregard the welfare of others. So, it is the more *extreme* forms of Individualism that can cause problems."

Growing up in America, being so indoctrinated with the ideal of individualism, it never occurred to me to analyze if there were healthy or extreme forms or to look for examples of any destructive effects of this on the individual. But as the Dalai Lama made these distinctions, it was easy to come up with illustrations of the dangers of extreme individualism. I thought of Ted Kaczynski, for example, the infamous Unabomber, for years America's most dangerous domestic terrorist— perhaps the poster child for extreme Individualism. Despite having a brilliant mind for mathematics, Kaczynski ended up living a miserable life in a remote, squalid shack in Montana, conducting a one-man war against technology, industry, society, and all forms of Collectivism. He spent his days in solitude, making letter bombs to kill and dismember people he didn't like.

Of course, aside from the dangers of extreme individualism, there was still a question about the negative effects of the less extreme varieties, leading me to ask, "Your Holiness, you mention how extreme Individualism can cause things like selfishness, but to clarify, do you also think that the promotion of less extreme forms of Individualism can cause or contribute to the widespread loneliness and alienation you mentioned earlier?"

He paused thoughtfully before replying. "I feel that it is not so much the consequence of promoting this Individualism that is the factor for making people feel alienated from others. I feel that it is more that the countervailing outlook is not presented. That is the element that is missing.

"Also, Howard, I think it is important to remember that there can be different degrees of Individualism between different nations. Even in the West there can be communities that enjoy a greater appreciation of our interconnectedness, and spirit of cooperation. Although it may not be the case in the States, in European countries such as Sweden and other Scandinavian countries, and also in the kibbutz movement in Israel, there is a very strong social ideal. Similarly, it is well known that in the Swiss model of democracy, there is a greater autonomy at the district level, and when people have more of a say in creating policies that directly affect their lives, I think that they may feel a greater sense of community. And I believe that individuals living in these kinds of models of society will probably be a lot happier."

He was right. According to the first "Map of World Happiness," created well after the Dalai Lama's prediction of higher happiness levels in these countries, the Scandinavian country of Denmark was rated #1 in happiness, Switzerland #2, and Sweden came in at #7.

"So," the Dalai Lama continued, "I think it comes down to this: *If a society promotes narrow-minded Individualism or narrow-minded Socialism, in either case it is shortsighted, and does not ultimately promote the greatest happiness of the members of that society.* For example, if a society is too extreme in its socialist approach to the point that it is at the expense of the individual, then it will be like a huge tree that has only trunk but no branches. Apart from the strong government, there is nothing else. There is no individual freedom, there is no creativity. There is nothing. On the other hand, if a society places too much emphasis on the individual, to the point where he or she feels too independent, has a sense of not needing others, and feels totally self-sufficient, then it is sort of like a person who sits on the limb of a tree while he is sawing it off. It's foolish!"

As with extreme Individualism, it was easy to see the dangers of extreme Collectivism. In fact, the world has seen far too often the destructive effects of the state trampling upon the rights of the individual in the name of the collective: the gulags, the repressive regimes, the horrors that occur when human beings are stripped of their individual human rights. There is something about even the more benign forms of extreme Collectivism that seems to squelch human creativity, personal initiative, and growth. I recalled my first visit to China, in 1981, a time when all one needed to do was step onto any street in Beijing to witness how Collectivism was glorified in that society. There was something unsettling about strolling down a street in a town of millions of inhabitants, where everyone you see, *everyone,* was dressed in the same dark blue Mao suit—well, except for the rare renegade daring to show their nonconformist attitude by sporting a dark gray Mao suit instead of a dark blue one.

As I remembered that visit, I thought of our Chinese tour guide, a pleasant young guy fresh out of college. He wasn't a professional guide, but had been assigned to our tour group because of his skill in both English and French, since our party included several French Canadians. Fully expecting that our group would automatically and uniformly adhere to the government's carefully scripted agenda, he hadn't been prepared to deal with a group that included individuals with their own personal preferences about the things they wanted to see or do. Not long after our arrival, our group was scheduled to spend several hours exploring some local gardens. After agreeing to meet back at our bus at a designated time, our group broke up into smaller units, and several couples and single individuals started to head off to explore the various features of the gardens on their own. Our guide immediately called out, "Please stay together! Please stay TOGETHER!" He ran back and forth, trying to round us up, but as members of the group drifted in different directions, he became visibly more agitated. As it dawned on him that he was not going to be able to herd us together and march us through the gardens in formation, he completely cracked. Sputtering and seething with rage and total exasperation, he screamed, "YOU PEOPLE *HAVE NOT THE TRUE SPIRIT OF COLLECTIVITY!!!"*—as if it was the ugliest, most shameful insult he could hurl at us.

Summarizing his view, the Dalai Lama concluded, "I think it is possible for a society to encourage the development of the individual and recognize individual rights, while at the same time paying attention to the welfare and well-being of the overall community or society. After all, both of these levels—the individual as well as the society—need to be addressed in order to maximize human happiness. Now, on the individual level, since happiness is always a subjective state of mind, in order to create a happier society, we need to begin at the level of the individual mind. After all, a happy society is composed of happy individuals. So, all of this argues strongly in favor of paying attention to the welfare of individuals.

"However, we also need to look at the level of society as a whole and pay attention to the interests of the group, to create the conditions where individuals and groups can thrive, where there is an overall sense of security, attention to the social welfare, and so on. So we need a wider, more holistic outlook that includes both approaches. And it all comes down to balance."

There can be a multitude of factors that affect the average level of happiness in a nation, but what type of society is happier? *The answer to this question leaves us squarely aligned with the Dalai Lama's view!* In looking at the traits of the *happiest* nations on earth, one discovers a pattern that appears to follow the Dalai Lama's key principle: balance. Here we find a balanced approach that avoids extremes of independence and interdependence, Individualism and Collectivism, but rather *incorporates both* perspectives. In Scandinavian countries, for instance, one finds a Western industrialized culture, which is traditionally more individualistic, with the typically Western tradition of respect for individual rights and independent thinking. At the same time, you also find collectivist values, such as the cultural value that you shouldn't stand out, the "nail gets pounded down" ethic. A similar pattern exists in other countries with the very highest levels of happiness, like Switzerland, demonstrating a balance between a sense of independence and a sense of interdependence, respect for individual freedom and initiative yet with a stronger sense of social welfare and a more active involvement in the affairs of the local community than is found in less-happy Western countries.

When it comes to identifying the kind of society that we should seek to create for a happier world, all of the available evidence seems to support the Dalai Lama's view: We must work toward building societies that maintain respect for an individual's human rights and dignity, one that encourages cultivation of personal strengths, personal integrity, and self-confidence yet at the same time promotes a deep sense of connection to others and concern for the welfare of others. Balance is the key.

"Not Me or We, But Me and We"

An attendant, a tall monk wearing the traditional maroon and saffron robes and a perpetual smile, glided in silently, and unobtrusively set down a tea service on the low, red lacquer coffee table in front of us. After pouring me some tea and refilling the Dalai Lama's mug with hot water, he seemed to vanish. The short tea break allowed the Dalai Lama's private secretary to enter the room and confer with him for a few moments, but we quickly resumed our conversation.

"Your Holiness, we were discussing your view that the happiest society is one in which there is a balance—where both welfare of the individual and the community are respected and promoted, and where that is reflected in the social policies and the values that are promoted in that society. But now I want to switch back to the level of the individual. Earlier we were talking about the importance of establishing a deep sense of connectedness with others, how that can bring greater personal happiness as well as help overcome societal problems like prejudice, conflicts, and so on. So, essentially we were speaking of the many benefits that can result from a fundamental shift in our inner orientation from Me to We. This involves focusing less on our differences and more on our similarities, on our common characteristics."

"Yes."

"Yet now we have also acknowledged the benefits of a healthy sense of individualism. So the question is, How do we reconcile this conflict between cultivating this healthy sense of independence, a sense of Me, with a sense of connection with the group, a sense of We?"

"I see no conflict here," the Dalai Lama stated flatly.

"Well, it's the question of how to find the right balance between these two differing perspectives. On one hand you have a sense of uniqueness, a self-identity, and on the other hand a feeling of belonging, a group identity. So, the basic issue is essentially the question of Me Versus We, and how can we—"

"Howard," the Dalai Lama cut in, "I think in discussing this topic we should first make something more clear. Now, I have noticed that sometimes people in the West have this tendency to see things in black or white terms, all or none. So here you are speaking of this Me *Versus* We, as if one needs to make a choice, as if to achieve a sense of unity, our goal must be to forget our differences, and look *only* at the areas we have in common with others.

"But that is not the goal here," he said firmly. "The approach we are advocating in bringing about positive changes is to develop a more realistic view, a view that is more consistent with reality. So, we are not saying to forget about oneself, one's own concerns. That is not realistic. We are saying that you can think about *both* one's own welfare and the welfare of others at the same time."

Nonetheless I persisted with my original question. "It still seems to me that on some level, if we want to have a strong feeling of connection with others and a kind of identification with one's group, whether it is a small group or the local community or the society in which one lives, that one still needs to somehow reconcile one's individual identity on the one hand, one's individuality and feeling of independence, separateness, and isolation, with the opposite feeling of connection, on the other."

We continued along the same lines for several more moments, as I pressed him for a way to deal with the "opposing" sensibilities of a Me or a We orientation. The Dalai Lama absently rubbed his palm over the crown of his shaved head as I spoke, a gesture of frustration that was also reflected in his rapidly shifting facial expression. As his expression settled on a priceless mixture of three parts bewilderment, one part amusement, and a dash of disgust, he shook his head and laughed. "I'm just not clear as to where the contradiction lies! From my perspective there is no *inherent opposition* here."

It *was* clear there was a basic difference of perspective that was acting as a barrier. Of course, this was nothing new. We'd begun this series of meetings with a brief struggle when I casually tossed around the phrase "We are all the same" and the only response he could come up with to such a simplistic concept was to jokingly suggest a Martian invasion as the solution to our global problems.

This struggle to reconcile our divergent points of view—his as a Buddhist monk, mine as a Western psychiatrist—is something that we had first encountered in our original series of discussions many years earlier, chronicled in the first volume of *The Art of Happiness.* It continued periodically over the years, although it has become somewhat less frequent as we have become more familiar with each other's perspectives.

Evidence of our divergent points of view would still surface occasionally, however, when in my zeal for clear-cut, definitive solutions to broad human problems, I asked questions that he felt were so all encompassing that they were impossible to answer. Generally, he attributed these kinds of questions to my characteristic Western "absolutist" thinking, the tendency to see things in terms of black and white—a contrast to his customary view that human problems are often more complex, nuanced, composed mostly of gray areas. (Yet the roles were sometimes reversed when I would occasionally explain an individual's maladaptive behavior in terms of complex psychological dynamics, while he might attribute the behavior to simple conditioning: "Oh, they just got into the habit of that behavior," or the influence of previous lifetimes.)

Although overly simplistic or generalizing questions would frustrate the Dalai Lama at times, we developed a way of dealing with these kinds of questions: They would usually be dismissed with a joke. We had a running joke that was woven throughout our discussions. We put such questions into either one of two categories: Impossible or

Silly. If I was going to ask a question that I knew he would react to in that manner, but I wanted to ask anyway, I'd preface my question by, "Now, Your Holiness, this is in the Impossible category, and the question is . . ." So, in that manner we got through our differing viewpoints quite easily, helped by his natural good humor and easygoing manner.

That morning when the Dalai Lama had trouble understanding how I couldn't grasp such a simple concept—that one could be connected to others while simultaneously maintaining one's individuality—he merely chalked it up to that ol' wacky Western absolutist thinking, and broke into his good-natured laugh. Nonetheless, I confess I didn't fully abdicate my position that one had to give up *part* of one's individuality if one was going to "merge" with a group identity, didn't fully buy his view, until much later, when I began to find scientific evidence supporting his view.

Scratching his head, and still laughing, the Dalai Lama continued. "I was just thinking . . . I was thinking that the difference between the Tibetan language and English might possibly suggest a basic difference of perspectives. In Tibetan, the word we use for 'I' and 'me' is '*nga*' and the word we use for 'us' and 'we' is '*ngatso*.' So on the basic level of the words themselves there is, in the Tibetan language, an intimate connection between 'I' as an individual and 'we' as the collective. '*Ngatso*,' the word for 'we,' literally means something like 'a collection of "I"s' or 'many "I"s.' So it's like multiple selves, this kind of idea. So when you are identifying with a wider group, becoming part of that group, it's like *extending* the individual sense of self, rather than *losing* it. Whereas the English terms 'we' and 'I' seem to be completely unrelated, the roots of the words are different, they are not related. . . . What is the word?"

"Etymology, etymologically?"

"Yes, etymologically. So, in your questions about Me Versus We, maybe this indicates in the West there is a sort of feeling on some level of Me in opposition to We. So, maybe when you are identifying with a group, or becoming part of a wider group, it is almost as if you are giving up or losing your individual identity. I don't know." The Dalai Lama pondered.

"Well," I said, "of course I can see the benefits of developing a greater sense of a group identity, feeling a part of a wider group. But it still seems on some level at least, that the more you move in that direction, there may be the risk of sort of weakening your own self-identity, which has to do with a sense of how you are unique, how you are different from others."

"No, that is not necessarily the case," he responded. "And, in fact, this process of expanding your identity as being part of a group can actually be a very natural process that occurs without losing your individual identity. For example, in a single family, there are various individuals, and they are all different. But when people think in terms of 'our family,' then there is an inclusiveness, because we relate to one another on the basis of being related. So, here you expand your identity to include the family, and you have this collective family identity. It's really a question of expanding your horizons or scope, because if people are not willing to expand this, they can even have a division within their own family. There could be a family where they make a distinction within the family based on all sorts of things—different political views or financial arrangements or anything.

"Then you could have a family who has a collective family identity, but your sense of 'community' or affinity is very confined to that nuclear family. So you have your spouse, your children, but if you're not able to reach out and extend that perimeter of your circle, then again, it will be quite narrow. This family would differentiate themselves from their neighbors, and keep themselves totally cut off, and then live independently. But you could also have families which will not only identify themselves as a family but also identify themselves as being part of a neighborhood. And if your family is able to reach out, broaden that circle beyond your immediate neighborhood, you could develop a feeling of connection and a bond with others based on 'we as the community.' And that will make a huge difference.

"If individual families living in a community can really relate to each other as members of the same community, of course sometimes there might be a conflict and arguments and so on, but at least there will be a sense of belonging. If you feel sometimes you need to talk to someone, you can just knock on someone's door, or share your problems, share your joys, invite people around."

He paused, then concluded. "So, in this same way you could expand your identity to include 'we as the region' or 'we as the country,' and so on. And ultimately, in the case of society, the human community, we can extend this unity to include everybody, so we can say, 'we, the people of the earth.' So at the level of humanity, there are differences among the individual members but at the same time we can see a 'sameness,' we can relate to each other on a deeper, more fundamental basis. . . . You know," he added, as he prepared to end the session, "these days I've noticed that there's a lot of usage of the word 'humanity.' I think that's a wonderful development—because this is very inclusive."

Setting down his mug of hot water and reaching for his shoes, the Dalai Lama wrapped up: "So, the important thing here is that a person can still have a concern for one's own welfare, to have a sense of Me, but one can expand the scope of one's identity, and of one's concern, to include others—*it is not so much forgetting our differences, but rather remembering our similarities*, giving it equal attention and importance. Basically, it is not a matter of Me *or* We, but rather Me *and* We."

We began our discussion of human happiness within a societal context by investigating the fundamental issue of Me Versus We—separateness versus connection. The Dalai Lama argues that human beings are designed to connect to others, explaining how our capacity for human affection, warmth, friendship, and love are rich and reliable sources of human happiness—like some alchemical process of transmuting lead into gold, the transformation of I into Us, cultivating a sense of belonging, brings rich rewards of human satisfaction, along with better physical, mental, and emotional health. At the same time, connecting with others helps to strengthen the wider community and help build a better society. In fact, whether looking through the lens of the

Buddhist ideal of compassion or citing recent scientific evidence, one could reasonably argue that human connection and community bonds, based on a sense of caring, can be the single greatest source of human happiness and satisfaction.

But, as we have witnessed throughout human history, sometimes things can go wrong. Terribly wrong. While the feeling of belonging, the sense of Us, may bring great rewards, what happens when Us *and* Them becomes Us *Against* Them? How does the mere perception of Us and Them escalate into prejudice, hatred, conflict, and violence? These were critical questions that we had to face as our discussions continued.

Chapter 3

PREJUDICE (US VERSUS THEM)

IN 1992 a Croatian farmer named Adem told a horrific story. In an interview with American journalist and author Peter Maas, Adem sat hunched over, mumbling a narrative of events so devastating that they seemed to have drained the strength and spirit from his body. Even his voice couldn't seem to register much more than a whisper. Over the previous year, he said, relations between local Serbs and Croats had deteriorated. In just a year they saw individual identities dissolve, absorbed into a greater undifferentiated mind-set: Us Against Them. And then one night, the hostilities suddenly became a nightmare from which Adem could not awaken. That night Serbs from a neighboring village rounded up thirty-five men from Adem's village and slit their throats. . . .

The previous autumn, the killers had helped their victims harvest their fields. These Serbs had been their friends, those with whom they had shared their lives—and now, had incomprehensibly brought their deaths.

Two years later, on another continent, it was a pleasant spring afternoon, and life had been good for many in the African village of Nyarubuye. Friends and neighbors worked together in the fields, cultivating their crop of sorghum, and, on their day of rest, attended church together. Though people were distinctly divided by tribe, being either Tutsi or Hutu, Gitera, a local farmer, said, "Life was normal. For us, as long as there was a harvest good enough to save us from buying food from the market, I would say that we were happy."

The village was in Rwanda, a country of long-standing tension and conflict between the two main "ethnic groups," the Hutu and the Tutsi. On April 6, 1994, the Hutu president, Juvénal Habyarimana, was assassinated, shattering the shaky cease-fire that had been in place since the signing of peace accords between the two parties the previous fall. The assassination ignited the resentments and hatred that had been simmering for so long just underneath the surface, precipitating the genocide of the minority Tutsis at the hands of the ruling Hutus.

Only nine days later Gitera found himself wielding a bloody machete, hacking his next-door neighbors to death, the mother, the children, everyone—inside the village church. The local Tutsis had fled there, certain a safe refuge could be found in the place where they had learned together with their Hutu neighbors that murder was a sin. Instead, seven thousand Hutu men had surrounded the church and were massacring almost everyone inside, slashing and bludgeoning their neighbors to death with clubs and machetes. Gitera described a scene of unimaginable horror, seeing "people whose hands had been amputated . . . people rolling around and screaming in agony, with no arms, no legs . . ." He added finally, "These people were my neighbors."

Such events had been occurring nationwide, with countless incidents—a ten-year-old boy buried alive, a Hutu housewife strolling over to next-door neighbors and slaughtering the children who had been her children's closest playmates, untold tortures—as what started out with well-organized militias sent out to the villages to massacre Tutsis turned into a frenzied bloodbath, a killing spree by civilians, who were encouraged by the government and whipped up by the Rwandan state radio blaring out a continuous stream of dehumanizing propaganda, referring to Tutsis not as people but as "cockroaches" that must be exterminated. Much of the civilian population participated in the mass extermination.

The figures of the genocide are staggering—an estimated eight hundred thousand to one million of their fellow Tutsi countrymen (as well as Hutu moderates) were massacred in one hundred days! Not with bombs, machine guns, or gas chambers—but mostly one on one, up close, personal. One witness reported he saw "husbands killing wives, wives killing husbands, neighbors killing neighbors, brothers killing sisters, sisters killing brothers, and children killing parents." For a hundred days, it seemed that all social categories or designations, such as husband, wife, sister, neighbor, friend, old, young, farmer, doctor, or clergyman had all disappeared—only two remained: "us" and "them."

"Your Holiness," I began, "in our last discussion we were focusing on the importance of connection with others, of a feeling of belonging, a basic human bond. You mentioned how we can identify with a group without losing our sense of self and there are many kinds of groups one can identify with, whether it is with one's family, or community, or nation, and so on. And in fact there is a lot of research on how social connectedness is not only associated with greater happiness, but also with better physical and mental health and many other rewards, even a longer life.

"At the same time, we have identified the problem that once you have an 'us,' you'll also have a 'them,' which sets up the potential for prejudice, hatred, and in the most extreme cases the kinds of dehumanization where you will perceive the differences between your group and the other group to be so vast that you don't even recognize them as human. And from there it is only a short step to atrocities and even genocide."

"Seeing another group as 'subhuman' is an extreme example of what is otherwise a natural tendency to separate ourselves into Us and the other as Them," said the Dalai Lama. "So in order to tackle the roots of these problems you mention, I feel that we need to seriously look at the very natural tendency to separate into groups and look at the world in terms of Us and Them."

"Then let's make this the first topic we explore today—this natural human tendency to divide ourselves into groups: the 'in-group' and the 'out-group.'"

The Dalai Lama seemed fresh, ready to explore. "Yes. Very good!" Catching him in the morning was always a good thing.

I said, "Well, in starting on the most basic level, first I think there is a biological basis, from an evolutionary standpoint, why people tend to divide themselves this way. But of course, as you like to remind me, these things can be complex. So, there may be other causes of these 'us and them' divisions, such as psychological causes. For example, right now the World Cup is going on. So if you like a particular team, you're a fan, and if someone asks you the outcome of a particular game, you don't say, 'Oh, they won.' You say, '*We* won!' You know, you identify with the successful group. Of course, people like to feel good about themselves. And one way of doing that is by identifying with a group that is successful.

"But there can also be a great danger," I went on. "Last year, for example, there was an incident in which over a hundred people were killed in a riot at a soccer match in Africa. You know, this reminds me, a friend was recently telling me about the growing tide of football hooliganism around the world, with violent assaults, stabbings, shootings, fans trampled in human stampedes—thousands of cases around the world. He called it the English Disease. And if this kind of violence can erupt just over as seemingly benign a dispute as a soccer match, then what hope is there?" I sighed.

For a moment, both of us were silent, then I continued. "But I guess the first question is, why is this Us Versus Them mentality such a powerful characteristic of human beings?"

The Dalai Lama was silent for a moment longer while he considered the issue, then began. "Now, the sense of self and the attachment to one's existence is of course a very natural trait. And I think that this sense of Us is simply an extension of this sense of self—it becomes extended so others get included in it, especially your immediate kin. You expand your horizon of identification, of personal identity, to include others, those to whom you look for support. So, as this expands, first it extends to your family, then your cultural group, then your nation, wherever it takes.

"In the ancient past, humans needed to band together in these close groups to help ensure survival. If there was competition for scarce resources, then there was an advantage to closely identifying with one's particular group; in order to survive oneself, one needed supporters. And of course, in the past, in those days the world was such that it was possible for groups or communities to remain relatively isolated, and to develop and thrive independently from other groups."

The Dalai Lama continued. "However, even though the feeling of Us Versus Them may have been a positive thing in the past, helpful for survival, the fact is that the world has changed. Today's reality is so different. Today's world is more interdependent, where a spirit of cooperation is critical for our survival. So, what was once productive is actually now counterproductive, and potentially very destructive.

"Therefore just because we can say that this sense of Us Versus Them is a natural trait, that does not mean that we should not do anything about it. Even though this sense of selfhood and the extension that gives rise to the feeling of Us Versus Them may be natural, if it leads to negative consequences, then we need to actively try to counter this tendency."

Friends and Foes

The Dalai Lama's suggestion to trace the development of these group divisions was not simply a matter of intellectual curiosity. Understanding the basics of this process can not only help us better understand why we behave the way we do but also provide the possibility of changing our behavior, of creating a better world, a better future for our children.

In tracing the process of how human beings separate into groups that can sometimes seek to destroy and harm one another, we begin by classifying people into two categories, the in-group and the out-group (what I've been referring to as Us and Them)—those groups that I identify myself as a member of, and those groups that I perceive to be different from me, those groups to which I do not belong. The process of dividing people into two groups, Us and Them, is one example of *categorization*. The brain really likes to categorize everything it can into groups—categorizing objects, concepts, and people. Why? We live in a very complex world, and the brain's ability to process information is limited. Categorization is one of the brain's favorite strategies to help simplify the torrential flood of sensory information that we're inundated with every moment.

Knowing what category something belongs to tells us something about its general properties and how to respond to it without having to analyze all the specific properties of the object from scratch, as if we were seeing an unknown object for the very first time. This helps us respond to the world around us as quickly and efficiently as possible, enhancing our odds for survival. Forming categories based on general characteristics requires less complex analysis, and this helps us to conserve our brain resources and expend less mental energy.

The most important type of categorization in our daily life is the way that we categorize people: *social categorization*. This involves identifying that person as belonging to a particular racial, ethnic, gender, or other type of group, and then classifying the individual as belonging to Us or Them.

Our social environments in the modern world can be very complex, and since the brain likes to conserve its resources, it looks for ways to simplify our world and make it easier to navigate the course of our social interactions. *Stereotypes* are one way of doing this. Stereotypes are beliefs we have about the traits or attributes that are typical of particular groups. Once the brain assigns a person to a particular social category, *stereotypes* about that category are evoked. So, instead of trying to assess the unique characteristics and attributes of every individual we meet, we quickly determine to which category this person belongs, then rely on stereotypes to tell us something about him or her. Stereotypes are an example of *heuristics*, mental shortcuts that can quickly give us information about how to behave.

The Dalai Lama pointed out how the formation of Us and Them divisions, along with our natural responses to Us and Them, are there for a reason. Therefore, these responses were once adaptive, helping our remote ancestors survive. In order to understand why we react the way that we do, it is important to briefly examine the evolution of the human brain.

The basic anatomy and structure of the human brain gradually evolved over millions of years. As the brain evolved, the human being's natural and innate responses, shaped by evolutionary forces, were hardwired into neural circuits. For most of the period of human evolution, our hominid ancestors, with our remote cousins dating back more than 5 million years, lived as hunter-gatherers or scavenger-gatherers, roaming over vast territories in small bands, picking up whatever food they could find or animals they could kill with their crude stone weapons. Their job description was to survive and pass down their genes to the next generation. Throughout the period of human brain evolution, beginning when our own *Homo* genus appeared on the scene roughly 2 million years ago, humans struggled along in the Pleistocene epoch, which lasted until the end of the last Ice Age around 10,000 years ago. It was during this time that the human brain rapidly evolved, more than tripling in size.

Our early ancestors did not have an easy go of it. This was an age of extreme fluctuations of climate, drought, famine, both human and nonhuman predators to contend with, and a precarious life full of uncertainty—except for one thing: There were bound to be plenty of catastrophes and adversity. The brain was custom-built to help our remote ancestors survive, to efficiently respond to the types of everyday problems that those living in the Pleistocene epoch were most likely to encounter over and over again, generation after generation. This has left us with a legacy of a brain that is good for overcoming danger and life-threatening situations, what some researchers call the catastrophic brain—a brain that was on the constant lookout for things that might go wrong, things that might be a threat to our survival, a brain that might tend to ignore the good things in life, in favor of the bad, good at sensing the tiny pebble in our shoe but not as good for appreciating the beautiful sunset or scenery we encounter as we stroll.

Thus, from an evolutionary perspective, it is easy to understand why our brains are hardwired to have in-group favoritism. Resources were not always plentiful, and it was surely to one's advantage to belong to a group, all working cooperatively to help maximize the odds of survival: working together to hunt large animals, gather scarce resources, defend against attacks and predators. In addition, an instinctual in-group favoritism would tend to draw us to a group resembling us, whose social rules and norms we are familiar with, and thus assure smoother and more effective social functioning—increasing our odds of successfully finding a mate, reproducing, and passing down our genes.

The benefits of feeling a special feeling of affinity to a group isn't limited to the evolutionary advantage of having your own team to bring home a fat haunch of bison or take down a cranky saber-toothed tiger, a matter of survival. Even today, it is easier to work cooperatively with a group that you are familiar with, a group in which one knows what the social norms are, the proper codes of behavior, and so on. We feel more comfortable and trusting with those who are like us, and as we have mentioned, humans thrive and flourish when they are connected with a group.

Now, ordinarily there is really nothing wrong with merely recognizing differences between groups, merely identifying Us and Them. Similarly, there is also nothing wrong with favoring one's own group. But the problem is that the evolutionary forces and pressures that acted to shape the architecture of the human brain did not stop there—we do not only form an automatic positive bias toward our own group, but we also have an *instinctual negative bias* toward other groups. As soon as we categorize an individual as belonging to Us or Them, the brain continues to process that information by classifying them as Friend or Foe—immediately stamping that image with an emotional tone, instinctively imbuing these categories with positive feelings toward "friends" and negative feelings toward "foes." And as we will discuss, that is where things can begin to go wrong—very wrong.

Prejudice

"Your Holiness, you mention the potential for negative consequences to arise from the underlying feeling of Us Against Them. I was just thinking how our goal is happiness, and of course that's the overall theme of our discussions. When it comes to human happiness, studies have shown that people are actually happier living in homogeneous communities or societies, where there simply isn't many of Them around. Which I guess isn't surprising, but it is a bit discouraging for those of us living in multicultural societies like America.

"You know, I'm curious about some of your own personal experiences in this regard. Of course, traditionally Tibet was a very homogenous culture. It's not like America where you have all sorts of different cultures and races coming together. Tibet was historically very isolated, in fact one of the most isolated countries in history, and was almost all ethnically Tibetan people. In fact, when I visited Tibet for the first time, you could probably count the number of Westerners who had visited Tibet in the hundreds. . . ."

As soon as I said this, I recalled the tragic situation in Tibet in which the Chinese were virtually assuring the final destruction of traditional Tibetan culture through the policy of population transfer of ethnic Han Chinese into Tibet. I felt very awkward, wondering if my words were causing the Dalai Lama to feel sadness or pain by reminding him of the current crisis. But he gave no indication of this, his demeanor unchanged—alert, attentive, listening.

Trying to mask my embarrassment, I quickly moved on. "You know, we've been talking about how humans naturally divide groups into Us and Them. But beyond merely dividing people into these two categories, it seems it is equally natural to have an automatic bias or negative reaction to Them, an instinctual fear or suspiciousness of those who we perceive as different. And of course this can sometimes escalate into discrimination, prejudice, and so on. . . . So, out of curiosity, since you were raised in a very homogeneous culture, do you remember the very first time you saw or met a Western person, a Caucasian, or a member of a different race? Do you remember how you reacted to other races? Was there a sense of bias against them?"

The Dalai Lama thought for a while. "No, I don't remember the very first time. But of course—" Suddenly the Dalai Lama stopped and he started to laugh uproariously.

"I just remembered," he said, still laughing, "the first time my younger brother met a foreigner. He was a small child. There was this striking-looking Muslim gentleman, with a big red beard. He was a Uighur of the East Turkistan race. I was not there at the time, but I found out later that my brother, who was very young at the time, was completely overwhelmed when he saw this man! He was so scared that he almost fainted!" The Dalai Lama continued laughing, barely catching his breath. "And he couldn't even speak for three or four days after that, and they apparently had to perform a healing ritual to bring him back to normal!"

As his laughter died down, he continued. "In my own case, though, I don't recall any particular incident, or reaction of surprise. Of course growing up I had seen some white people who were living at the British Mission in Lhasa. And in the early days we had some Uighur Muslims in Tibet, and of course ethnic Chinese. When I met these people it was obvious that they were different, that recognition was definitely there. But on my part I don't remember there being any sense of distance or feeling of bias on those grounds."

A legacy from our remote past as a species has left us with a natural bias in favor of those whom we perceive as in-groups and against those whom we consider out-groups. This immediate, instinctual emotional response in the brain to out-groups, a reaction of fear and even hostility, can range from subtle to overt, from an unconscious response below the threshold of the person's conscious awareness to an overwhelming sense of fear or hostility. The automatic reaction of the Dalai Lama's brother as a small child serves as a vivid illustration of how powerful these fundamental responses can be.

Again, like our positive bias, or favoritism, toward our in-group, this negative bias toward out-groups makes sense from an evolutionary perspective—because during the period when the human brain evolved, competition with neighboring bands of humans for scarce resources was a tough business. The business of the day was *survival*, and in the Pleistocene age business competitors were more likely to beat the competition with a stone ax instead of a clever ad, or even put you out of business for good—but by cutting your throat instead of by cutting prices.

So, if we remember that our brains were actually custom built to deal quickly and efficiently with the most common dangers and problems of the Pleistocene age—a time when homicide was the very latest, most modern conflict-resolution technique and when strangers could be an unknown quantity—then we can see that hardwiring the brain to react to members of another group with a good old-fashioned danger alert, to keep us on our toes, was no doubt the smart thing to do.

This negative bias toward out-groups became the basis for the creation of prejudice. A common way of conceptualizing prejudice is as a general attitude toward others consisting of two components: the instinctual, automatic bias, which is a negative emotional response, such as fear or hostility, combined with a set of stereotyped beliefs about the other group. These stereotypes are generally false beliefs, such as the belief in inherent superiority of the in-group and inferiority of the out-group.

NEUROLOGICAL ORIGINS OF PREJUDICE

What happens inside the brain to produce the distorted ways of thinking and the negative emotions associated with prejudice?

To trace the pathway of information in the brain, we can begin with the pure sensory information that we perceive in our environment, the sights, sounds, smells, and tactile information. The visual information about *every object* you observe is picked up by the retina, a group of cells inside the eye, and that information is transmitted to your brain via the optic nerve, carried along in bundles of nerve fibers, traveling to the occipital region, an area in the back of the brain that processes vision. The eye itself does not know what it is seeing; it simply records everything in our environment as nothing more than patterns of shapes, colors, and shading, light and dark. It is the brain that assigns a meaning to those objects, telling you what you are seeing, labeling it. It also simplifies what you are seeing, by filtering out a lot of what the eye is seeing, forming some initial impressions about the objects you are seeing, and separating them into general categories, making a decision about what is important for you to be aware of.

To understand how the brain edits our world, filtering out a lot of information to create a simplified representation of the world, a simple experiment can be very effective: First, close your eyes, turn in the opposite direction, then open them for around ten seconds, carefully looking at and noting everything you see in the room in front of you. Then turn back around and write down everything that was in the room in your direct field of vision. Then turn around again and compare your list to all the objects actually in the room—by carefully examining each and every object in the room in detail. You may be surprised by the many objects that you had directly looked at but which you did not "see." Despite clearly looking at them with both eyes wide open, the brain made these objects invisible to you.

Having identified an object we encounter as belonging to the category of "human being," we further categorize that human as belonging to Us or Them. Some of this information goes to what is known as the limbic system, a collection of structures deep inside the brain that play an important role in the regulation of emotion, motivation, and memory. From an evolutionary point of view, the limbic system is very old, part of the more primitive parts of the brain that can also be found in lower animals. Structures in the limbic system are responsible for our immediate instinctual response to the things or people we encounter, our "gut" reaction—do we have a positive or a negative feeling about the object, a general feeling of attraction or aversion, is it good or bad?

Now, within the limbic system is a small almond-shaped structure buried deep in the brain called the amygdala. *The amygdala is part of our danger-alert system, responsible for evoking emotions such as fear and anger, strong emotional responses that are helpful in dangerous, life-threatening situations.* The emotions produced by the amygdala prepare us for the famous fight-or-flight response, to fight or escape the dangerous situation, predator, or enemy. The amygdala is critically important in our social interactions.

There has been a growing body of scientific evidence identifying the amygdala as the primary biological culprit responsible for prejudice and hatred, which ultimately lead to so many of the conflicts going on in the world today. Amygdala activity represents perception of a potential threat and is involved in the biased or prejudiced response in the context of social evaluation, reacting as if one is prepared for fear in particular, or hostility against what it perceives to be out-groups. This may have been appropriate or helpful for our prehistoric ancestors, but it is slow to unlearn, and today the amygdala can produce false alarms.

Information about our environment is sent to many parts of the brain. At the same time that information is transmitted to the limbic system, other neural pathways carry information to the cerebral cortex, the crowning glory of human evolution, the hallmark of human beings. Located on the outer surface and toward the front of the brain, and representing the most recent development in brain evolution, this is the part of the brain associated with the higher functions of reasoning, analysis, and logic—the seat of rational thought. It is here that a more thorough analysis of the object or person can take place, and a more nuanced and accurate understanding can emerge. This is the "thinking" part of the brain that forms our conscious thoughts and beliefs about others. It is here where our stereotypes arise. And when negative stereotypes or false beliefs about an out-group are combined with the negative emotional response produced by the amygdala, prejudice

arises. As we continue, we will examine how these false beliefs are created and how to overcome them.

One final point is significant here: The areas of rational thought in
the brain's neocortex and the areas of emotion in the limbic system
can communicate with each other, with neural pathways connecting
them, resulting in the ability to intentionally modify our customary
reactions to some degree through new learning, new experiences, and
conditioning. As we will later see, it is the neocortex that may be our
salvation, that part of the brain with the capacity to free us from the
primitive reflexive responses of fear, hostility, hatred, and prejudice
inherited from our remote ancestors.

STEREOTYPES AND FALSE BELIEFS

Following the destruction of New Orleans by Hurricane Katrina, the
media was filled with stories and visual images of the aftermath, often
focusing on the plight of the survivors. In many of these stories, white
survivors forced to flee their homes due to hurricane winds were described by the accurate word "evacuees," while black survivors were
often described by the incorrect term "refugees," a word that carries
a connotation of someone forced by circumstances to seek refuge in a
foreign land—i.e., a foreigner, one of Them. In one notorious pair of
photographs, a black man carrying a large bag through the waist-deep
waters carried a caption with a description of "looting," a word that
evokes images of theft, violence, and danger. A photograph of a white
couple performing the exact same activity described the action as "for-
aging," a word that evokes a very different image—perhaps of cute
white bunnies searching for carrots or harmless little squirrels hunting
for acorns.

"Your Holiness," I continued, "in thinking about the various kinds of
negative consequences of this Us Against Them attitude, as an American living in a multicultural society, racism comes to mind immediately.
This has been a significant problem in American society, the source
of a lot of suffering over the centuries, although less now than in the
past. . . . Since right now we are focusing on the causes of the destruc-

tive consequences of an Us Against Them outlook, do you have any thoughts as to any additional specific causes of prejudice and racism?"

"So, Howard, here you are asking about racism. But I feel that prejudice is not really a matter of racism based on color alone—prejudice against color of the skin—it has a lot to do with mental projection, this false premise that one group is inherently inferior to another.

"For example, if you look at even a single society that is racially uniform, you will find discriminations based on a variety of false premises. For example, my first visit to Africa was in Gabon, where I went to participate in a function at the Albert Schweitzer Center there. On the way to the center there were some villages. They were so poor, so underdeveloped. And I saw children, completely naked, running around with blood all over them from one of these tall water birds they had just killed, a crane or maybe a flamingo. The blood was dripping everywhere. It made me feel so sad. But then very near these villages was the center I was going to, where the ruling elite of the country, including the president, were clearly living a luxurious lifestyle. I could really feel the huge gap between the ruling elite and the general public, the masses. It was very disheartening. So here within the same group of people I also sensed certain prejudice based on this false belief in inferiority versus superiority.

"Of course, in dealing with issues like prejudice or racism, there are always many factors at play, many contributing factors. For example, we are conditioned to hold these false views, and this conditioning can come from different levels—they can be views that have been promoted by one's family in some cases, or one's particular group, or ideas one picks up from the society that one grows up in. Then there may also even be historical factors that are involved on some level—for example, a history of colonialism may also play a role in giving rise to some of these prejudices.

"So, there may be many things . . . and of course there are many things that people can base discrimination on. . . ."

"By 'things,' you mean . . . ?"

"For example, factors such as how much money a person has or how much power, education, or social status are all commonly used as a basis for feeling this sense of intrinsic superiority over others. The British use titles like 'Sir' and 'Lord,' for instance; that sets up these class distinctions that imply these kinds of differences, a kind of inborn superiority, creating a sense of separation. Of course there are other criteria too, such as the idea that one's own religion is superior to another's or more true than another's.

"So, there can be many forms of discrimination and prejudice, but the principles are the same. And no matter what criteria one might choose for one's sense of superiority, inevitably it would be detrimental to both sides, and it can cause problems."

Pressing the point further, he said, "*No matter what kind of prejudice and discrimination it is, at the root you will find a distortion of reality, false views or beliefs in the inherent superiority of one group over another.*"

The Dalai Lama looked at his watch, and I realized our time was coming to a close. So wrapping it up, I said, "So, just to summarize . . ."

He said, "No matter what is the basis for one's prejudice, on whatever characteristic one is basing their sense of superiority, it leads to problems in the long run, so we need to find ways of reducing this."

As our session was about to end, a final question occurred to me: "Your Holiness, we are talking about prejudice and how the grounds upon which people base the idea of superiority are just mental projections, false beliefs. But in some cases there are differences among people, and people *are* superior in some ways; for example, some groups are actually better educated. Well, if people are basing their feeling of superiority on the fact that they are better educated than someone else, and if they *are* better educated, then this is not a false belief; it has a valid basis in reality."

The Dalai Lama replied, "Howard, as I mentioned, when we are dealing with human behavior and attitudes, there are many factors at play. This is actually a very complicated issue." He added, with a slight tone of exasperation, "And after all, our discussions and this book that we're working on isn't going to be judged by the United Nations—we don't have to come up with a solution to all the problems in the world.

So here, not only are false beliefs involved in these kinds of attitudes, but from the Buddhist point of view, the root of the problem really is the mental afflictions. You have attitudes like arrogance and conceit, which are rooted in ignorance.

"So, yes, some people may be more capable because of better education, some less educated; some more affluent, some less affluent; some better looking, some not as good looking. But one big factor remains: that despite these kinds of differences, we still need to always be able to maintain respect for all. They are all human beings, worthy of human dignity and respect on that fundamental level. That's an unchangeable truth."

The Dalai Lama put his shoes back on to end the session. Our discussion of the way to overcome prejudice would have to wait until our next meeting.

The Rwandan War between the Tutsis and Hutus, mentioned earlier, is perhaps the most extreme illustration of this principle from the latter half of the last century. Following the Rwandan genocide, an International Criminal Tribunal for Rwanda was established by the UN to try the perpetrators of the crime of genocide—the deliberate attempt by the Hutu leaders to exterminate the Tutsi ethnic group. When the very first case came to trial, the term "ethnic group" came under scrutiny. "Ethnic group" was generally defined as a distinct group whose members share a common language or culture. Since both the Tutsi and Hutus shared a common language, religion, and culture, the judges quickly realized that the Tutsi could not be considered a separate ethnic group. The concept of genocide of course applied to race as well, but the Tutsi did not meet the definition of a separate race either. The judges discovered that they could not legally conduct these trials for "genocide" unless the Tutsi were a distinct ethnic group or race.

For more than a year, a shifting roster of judges and legal scholars on board the Rwanda Tribunal issued a flurry of confused opinions and decisions—completely changing their position and reversing themselves four times in an attempt to find a way to perceive the Hutus and Tutsis as two distinct racial or ethnic groups, but without success. The judges finally ruled that the definition of a victim in these cases would have to be done on a case-by-case basis—with the result that every genocide trial would begin by reviewing the same confusing and inconclusive evidence on Hutu and Tutsi identity all over again. Of course, the hatred that had fueled the war and genocide was based on the absolute conviction on both sides that there were fundamental ethnic and even racial differences between them. Yet it was apparent that these racial and ethnic "differences," the basis for unimaginable horror and human slaughter, were purely imaginary, with no basis in reality.

How did such illusions and false beliefs arise? In this case, the long and complicated history of Rwanda—with shifting ruling parties, political agendas, and power structures—gradually created the belief among both Tutsi and Hutu that they were ethnically distinct races, but in fact the terms *"Tutsi" and "Hutu" originated as social and economic, not ethnic or racial, identities, and the terms were actually flexible and fluid, meaning different things to different people in different places at different times.* Generally, "Tutsi" originally referred to either those of noble status, or those who held a certain level of power and wealth, while "Hutu" generally referred to those of "common" status. The terms were so fluid, however, that Hutu lineages that acquired enough wealth, power, and influence could actually become Tutsi, and gradually their Hutu roots would be forgotten.

The "ethnicization" of the terms "Hutu" and "Tutsi" came about as a more recent political construct, which some scholars believe was started by the ruling Tutsi court in the eighteenth and nineteenth centuries, in order to claim Tutsi superiority over Hutu. Later German and Belgian colonizers *solidified any remaining fluidity of definitions,* formally institutionalizing a system of ethnic classification, complete with their views of racial and ethnic superiority and inferiority. This was politically expedient in setting up the Tutsi to help them govern—at the same time assuring the increasing divisiveness and polarization between the two groups. The formalized definitions of the separate "races" and ethnic groups was so arbitrary, however, that *in 1933, the*

Belgians classified an individual with fewer than ten cows as Hutu and an individual with more than ten cows as Tutsi!

The quandary that the Rwanda Tribunal faced underscores the tragic aspect of racial hatred and prejudice in all its forms. As the Dalai Lama mentioned, it is generally based on distorted and false beliefs, whether it is the illusion of fundamental racial differences between two groups or the false beliefs in the innate inferiority or superiority of one or another of the two groups.

The Dalai Lama points out how at the root of prejudice you will find false beliefs and a distortion of reality. By examining the underlying brain mechanisms in the formation of prejudice, it is easier to understand how such distortions of reality can occur. Earlier we saw how the brain, inundated with a massive amount of incoming data, likes to sort out the objects and people it encounters into general categories. Further, once a person is categorized as belonging to a particular social category or group, stereotypes about that group are immediately evoked. Stereotypes are a form of heuristics, a kind of mental shorthand the brain uses to help us deal more easily with a complex world. While this has certain advantages—such as helping us react quickly to the things going on around us or helping to conserve brain resources—there is a big price we pay for this. It can result in distorting reality, forming false beliefs or stereotypes about other groups, and potentially lead to prejudice, hatred, and eventually violence.

How does this occur? Social categories are based on simplifying information, generalizing, and forming quick judgments. Distortion of reality begins right there. It is virtually impossible to form a full understanding and an accurate picture of a complex human being, their entire character, attributes, talents, skills, values, and so on, based on a few generalities about a group that you think they belong in. At the same time, it is easy to overgeneralize; there have been many studies showing that human beings tend to significantly magnify *differences between* groups and to overestimate *similarities within* groups, overlooking the distinctive features of individuals within the group—the "they all look alike" phenomenon.

Our stereotypes about a particular social category or group may be positive or negative and they can vary in their degree of accuracy. However, even an "accurate" stereotype, which may reflect a real difference in averages between groups, is based on distortion—and the more we boil a complex human being down to a couple of primary attributes, perceiving that person simply as a member of a group, the more unreliable our judgment about that person is bound to be. After all, stereotyping involves making a judgment about a person even before you get to know them. On top of that, when you judge someone based on being a member of a particular social group, you tend to forget that the person may also be a member of many other social groups, and you ignore all the rest.

The problem with prejudice is not simply that we tend to have distorted and false beliefs about other groups—but that these false beliefs and prejudice tend to mutually reinforce each other. Prejudice begins with a negative emotional response to another group, and we have a natural tendency to form beliefs about the group that are consistent with our emotional, "gut-reacton" bias. In the same way, we tend to attribute positive characteristics to our own group—thus tending to perceive our group always to be superior and the out-groups inferior. A study of thirty tribes in Africa, for instance, found that each one thought that they were superior to all of the others.

Of course, these beliefs develop regardless of whether they are true or not. Sadly, once we develop these erroneous beliefs or stereotypes, they tend to be particularly fixed and rigid. Studies have shown that the brain tends to pick up information from the environment that is consistent with our beliefs, such as the belief in the innate inferiority of other groups, and filters out contradictory data. When an observed behavior or trait is ambiguous, we will distort and filter the way we perceive things to fit our biases.

Although, as the Dalai Lama points out, our false beliefs about other groups are the direct cause of much of the cruelty in the world, tragically we are generally not even aware of how the brain selectively filters, minimizes, or exaggerates information to make it fit with our beliefs.

THEN AND NOW

A few years ago, some researchers conducted an experiment on in-group favoritism. In that study subjects were assigned membership in one of two groups playing a game over the computer, and they had the ability to award real money to other players of either team. However, subjects were told that they would not receive any money themselves from anyone in this experiment. In-group favoritism was measured by how much money the subject awarded to his own team. As one might expect, the subjects favored and rewarded their own group. But here's the significant part: First, there was no material advantage to the subject for favoring his group, no advantage of any kind. Second, the subject had been told absolutely nothing about the members of either team—the "game" was conducted anonymously over the computer. The subject had been assigned to his group based on a coin toss. Thus, the subject's tendency to show group favoritism, or to feel that his group was superior or better in some way, was completely *arbitrary*, based only on the fact that he was in the group.

This experiment underscores an important point made earlier by the Dalai Lama. In our distant past as a species, it was adaptive to practice in-group favoritism and out-group bias or prejudice. At a time when out-groups could often threaten our own existence, reacting to out-groups with an automatic, instinctive danger alert could save our lives. Favoring our own group also offered very real rewards, helping us survive and reproduce. Of course, occasionally even today these responses can be helpful under some circumstances. For example, a feeling of favoritism toward one's own group can contribute to a feeling of affinity and connection, a sense of belonging. Even the negative biases that are part of the brain's danger-alert system can be helpful, and even save our lives if we are in a life-threatening situation, under attack from members of another group.

But the problem is that now we are walking around with a brain which was developed to deal with the common problems our ancestors faced in the Pleistocene epoch a million years ago, brains that have not changed anatomically for over a hundred thousand years. The world is very different, and yet our brains are still automatically, instinctually, blindly reacting in the same ways as hundreds of thousands of years ago, even when there is now no adaptive value for reacting that way, no benefit at all, such as in the computer game experiment just mentioned.

Of course, as the Dalai Lama points out, the problem here is not simply that we act in ways that offer no benefit or advantage to us, but that acting on some of these more primitive instinctual responses can potentially be disastrous. In fact, the strategies the brain developed to deal with the problems of the Pleistocene world, to promote human welfare and survival of our ancestors, are the same strategies that can potentially be our downfall today.

Our brains are good at detecting dangers, threats, and reacting quickly, but when we form stereotypes based on imaginary differences, form prejudices based on those stereotypes, and blindly act based on programs designed for our remote ancestors, and encoded into our brain circuitry, the results can be disastrous. In today's interdependent world, for example, with *our survival dependent on cooperation* with other groups, it is to our great disadvantage to automatically react to these groups as if they are enemies. The violence and atrocities that we have witnessed up to the present are largely the result of basing our behavior on some of these more primitive brain mechanisms.

Chapter 4

OVERCOMING PREJUDICE

I N NOVEMBER 2008 the American public elected America's first African American president, a milestone event that would have been considered impossible only a generation ago. Only two generations have passed since segregation was a commonplace practice in the American South, when individuals from all strata of American society openly expressed bigotry and racism. From a global perspective, it has not been three generations since the world witnessed the horrors of the Holocaust, the very worst expression of human prejudice and hatred imaginable, a low point in human history. When we look back to the blatant discrimination and overt bigotry seen in our grandparents' day, it seems that great strides have been made in reducing discrimination, prejudice, and racism.

Lest we become too complacent, however, recent research suggests that the problems of prejudice are far from over. Bias is much more widespread than people are aware of. Rather than disappear, the manifestations of prejudice have just become more subtle. According to some estimates, 80 percent of Western democratic populations will report that they have no prejudiced views and do not display significant discriminatory behavior, while only a small minority, maybe 10 percent, of individuals will say they are openly racist, or prejudiced. However, research reveals that even those who consider themselves to be totally unbiased are often shocked to find that they still hold subtle biases when they undergo psychological testing. Although less visible, the effects of such unconscious biases can also be destructive, affecting our judgment and behavior in more subtle but very real ways.

Having taken a look at how prejudice arises and acknowledged its destructive effects, it was now time to explore ways to overcome prejudice, seeking an approach to breaking down the barriers that may exist among diverse individuals and groups—and hopefully discovering a way to forge a basic human bond even with those who we would normally perceive as being different from us.

I began, "Your Holiness, this is our last meeting for the time being. This week we have discussed the benefits of shifting one's outlook from Me to We, and establishing a feeling of belonging to a wider community, as well as the potential dangers when the healthy feeling of Us transforms into an Us Against Them outlook—which can lead to prejudice, discrimination, and racism."

"That's right."

"Yesterday you spoke about the need to overcome our prejudices, racism, and false beliefs about other groups. So, this brings us to the final topic for the week, which is how to overcome prejudice."

"Very good."

"So, the question is, how do you suggest that we go about doing this?" I asked.

"I would say that *there is no single approach*," he replied. "We need many approaches."

"Well, let's say that a particular society is troubled by a significant degree of racism and prejudice—there are a lot of individuals who feel that their particular group is superior and have a strong prejudice and hostility against another group. So, where would you start? How would you begin to go about getting them to abandon their prejudice and racist views?"

"Of course," responded the Dalai Lama, "we will always have some level of preference towards members of our own group, but here we are talking about reducing our prejudices and biases against other groups. And as I mentioned, there may be several methods.

"But the first step is to *motivate people*. Of course, here there must be a willingness to look at their prejudiced attitudes. That is critical. Then, there must be some level of openness to revising their customary outlook."

"So, how do you begin to motivate people to revise their prejudiced attitudes?" I asked.

"By increasing awareness of the disadvantages of their attitudes, having them reflect on the ways in which belittling other fellow human beings is detrimental to oneself in the long run."

"Then the next step?"

"The next step is challenging the beliefs that the prejudice is founded on, these false beliefs about the other group, such as the belief in inherent superiority and so on. Generally, these prejudices, on whatever basis, are a result of conditioning . . . that is picked up from their culture, or their family, and so on. So, we need to overcome this conditioning. This is done by actively disputing the distorted ideas and false beliefs, presenting a case for revising these beliefs, by pointing out where there are false premises upon which they base their belief, false projections, and so on. It is a matter of discovering the reality."

Paradoxically, part of the reason why up to 80 percent of Western societies may continue to harbor subtle prejudices could be the climate of "political correctness" that has been so prevalent in our culture. The desire for social acceptance and genuine embarrassment over their views may lead people to suppress or deny prejudiced thoughts or feelings. There have been research studies showing that merely trying to suppress such thoughts, to quickly try to "sweep them under the rug," *does not get rid of prejudice—and in fact it can increase it.*

This happens, at least according to some investigators, due to the "don't think of an elephant" phenomenon; the harder you try not to think of an elephant, the more likely you are to think of an elephant. This may explain why most people do not espouse racist views in American society today—far fewer in fact than in our grandparents' era—while at the same time our society is still filled with racial tension due to the subtle biases people may not even be fully aware of. Research shows that when there are widespread subtle biases lurking just under the surface of a seemingly peaceful and tolerant society, a period of social unrest, economic decline, or stress can sometimes spark an eruption of overt racial prejudice and even conflict, as people regress to more primitive ways of interacting.

The Dalai Lama offers a sound approach to dispelling both subtle bias and overt prejudice. He begins by pointing out the importance of recognizing and openly acknowledging one's biases and stereotyped beliefs, rather than hiding, suppressing, or denying them. This is followed by actively challenging and disputing any beliefs found to be inconsistent with the truth. Research has confirmed that instead of repressing one's prejudices, if one openly acknowledges one's biases, and directly challenges and refutes them, one can overcome them. And there is no question that some of our false beliefs are so deeply conditioned, that it requires a strong motivation to overcome them, motivation that can come from a deep understanding of the harm our prejudice does to ourselves in the long run.

This approach alone has been shown to reduce our prejudices—but as our conversations continued, the Dalai Lama went on to identify several additional strategies to overcome our biases and prejudice. . . .

Continuing our discussion of how to overcome prejudice, his suggestion that one could rise above conditioning by actively refuting false beliefs seemed to be sound. Yet this might not be so easy for the average person. After all, most people did not have decades of training in logic and debate and lifelong practice of training their minds like he did. So I went on to observe, "But it just seems that sometimes this kind of conditioning is so strong, that it is difficult to get people to change their deeply ingrained beliefs. . . . Actually, out of curiosity, have you ever personally witnessed anyone revise their thinking about these kinds of false beliefs?"

"Oh, yes," he said with obvious enthusiasm. "For example, I remember one experience in South Africa. In fact, this was a very powerful and moving experience for me."

"Can you tell me about that?"

"Yes, this was in Soweto Township, in an inner city slum in Johannesburg, South Africa. Arrangements were made so I could visit the home of an ordinary family. I spent about two hours there and they offered me tea, and we had time to chat. A friend of the family, who was introduced to me as a schoolteacher, joined us. This was very soon after the end of apartheid. So, I happened to mention to them, 'Now this country has had a change of government and achieved democracy, you have achieved political equality, so I think now all opportunities are open to you. But it takes time to change people's minds and attitudes, so it may take a little time for some people to embrace this equality psychologically.' So the schoolteacher told me, 'Even if we have equal opportunities, we cannot compete with the whites because by nature we are less intelligent.' He really believed that the black people living there were genetically inferior, their brains not as good as the white brains. I was so sad that he actually believed this. So, I argued with him. I told him it was not true, this was a false idea, but he did not believe me. His conditioning was so strong that he truly believed in this idea of racial inferiority.

"So, I spent a long time in his home, talking to him, using various arguments, trying to convince him that he was not inferior. Finally, by the end of our time together I finally convinced him. He then sighed deeply and said, 'Yes, I think you are right. Now I'm convinced that we are equal.' That was a day that I still remember very clearly. I felt so happy and a sense of relief. He changed his outlook. I felt that, oh, at least here was one person where I made a difference."

In recounting this story, there was a certain kind of intensity and excitement in the Dalai Lama's voice, a certain look of earnestness in his eyes that created an unmistakable impression of deep gratification and pleasure and conveyed a genuine sense of accomplishment, as if he were describing one of the truly great achievements in his life. His was a life marked by great achievements—countless honors and awards, even the Nobel Prize—and yet in all the years I had known the Dalai Lama, I had rarely heard him speak about anything with the same unbridled enthusiasm and obvious sense of pride and satisfaction as he did in describing his visit to this African schoolteacher.

I asked, "What arguments did you use to try to convince him?"

"I used several arguments. First, I tried to share my own experience with him, my experience with the Chinese. I explained to him how Chinese consider the Tibetans backward, inferior; there is the perception that the Tibetans are not equal. Then I explained how that was not the case, it was a false belief, and told him of our experiences as refugees. I told him stories of how, through our own hardship, our hard work, we can become equal, and once educational opportunities were open to us, we were as good as the Chinese. I demonstrated how it is just a matter of opportunity, access, and the self-confidence to embrace these that make the difference. Then I spent some time explaining that from a scientific viewpoint, as far as the brain is concerned, at the fundamental level, the biological level, there are no differences. *All people have the same potential.* So, these are the kinds of arguments I used."

"You know, Your Holiness, the situation with this schoolteacher is a somewhat different case than we have been discussing. So far we have been talking about how people favor their in-groups and feel bias against out-groups, such as racial minorities. As a result, humanity has an ugly history of oppression of minorities and stigmatized groups.

"But here is a tragic case where a member of the oppressed group may also adopt the false beliefs in their inferiority. Of course, as we have discussed, all else being equal, people tend to believe in the superiority of their own group. But in this case other dynamics complicate the picture. And your story reminded me about some of the theories about the underlying psychological mechanisms in cases like this. . . ."

"What is the theory?" he asked.

"One factor," I replied, "is that the group may need to rationalize the inequity, and it may be easier for some to believe that they, or their group, have done something wrong or have some inherent weakness, than to believe that they are the helpless victims of a discriminatory society. I guess that on a deep psychological level it causes less anxiety to believe in your group's inherent inferiority than to believe in an unfair, arbitrary, and indiscriminate universe, where bad things happen for no reason. Thus, it seems that the stereotypes we possess are often in the service of rationalization, or trying to make sense of a senseless world. So, it can work both ways—negative stereotypes about a group can lead to inequities, and these inequities can perpetuate stereotypes.

"Of course," I added, "this kind of rationalization can perpetuate prejudice among oppressors as well as the oppressed. There have been research studies indicating that people don't like to believe in an unjust world, and the idea of a world in which bad things happen randomly is unsettling to most people on a deep level—'If someone receives bad treatment without reason, without deserving it, the same thing could happen to me!' Because of this, if something bad happens to someone, at least a part of us likes to believe they somehow deserved it. So, when we see groups discriminated against in our society, who are low in status, or who are even actively oppressed, we tend to believe they must possess some trait that is responsible."

The Dalai Lama nodded thoughtfully as I continued. "Anyway, this case you mentioned also reminded me about one of the most damaging and tragic effects of racial prejudice, the concept of *stereotype threat*."

"What is that?" he asked.

"It's a situation in which members of a stereotyped social group will underperform an activity in a way that is consistent with the negative stereotype. The underlying mechanism is thought to be that the individual subconsciously fears that his behavior or performance will confirm an existing stereotype about the group. This creates a kind of anxiety that then affects multiple mental functions, such as memory and critical thinking, and that leads to an impairment of performance—which then confirms the negative stereotypical image the person may have.

"There have been lots of studies documenting this effect, showing that sometimes it only takes a simple reminder that one is in a stereotyped group to trigger this effect—for example, just having a group of black male students fill out a form in which they had to check a box identifying their race prior to taking a standardized test was enough to depress their performance, subconsciously activating the stereotype that black students are less intelligent and do worse on these kinds of tests. One interesting study indirectly reminded a group of female Asian students that they were Asian, which improved their scores on a math test, activating the stereotype that Asian students are better at math. Then in a later test—with the same group—a reminder of the student's gender depressed their scores, activating the stereotype that girls are worse at math. These kinds of studies have led some researchers to conclude that stereotype threat may play some role in the long-standing gap in academic performance in the U.S. between white students and racial minorities, like black and Latino students."

Sensing that the Dalai Lama might be becoming bored from my monopolizing the conversation, and wishing to hear his views, I said, "Anyway, Your Holiness, I'd like to return to the discussion of ways to reduce prejudice against others. You just mentioned some of the arguments against racism that you used to convince a member of a minority that they were not inferior. But I'm wondering what reasoning you would use for somebody on the opposite side, somebody who feels that other people are inferior in some way, you know, a racist or religious bigot. Would you use the same arguments against racism? How would you argue with them to help them overcome this prejudice?"

The Dalai Lama paused for a moment. "The arguments would be equally valid, no matter who you are presenting the argument to. It is still a matter of trying to overcome false beliefs that may be part of his cultural conditioning—explaining that the idea that one's race is superior to another race is, in short, sheer ignorance; it is just stupidity," he said with conviction. "The reality is that there is no scientific basis, no moral basis, and no ethical basis for these kinds of discrimination. One can forcefully point out that their sense of racial superiority is really a form of delusion. For example, some may point to gaps in wealth and claim natural inferiority of others—but you can point out that given some opportunity over time, that gap disappears. Because you can argue with them logically, that if the opposite race has been given the opportunity and the chance to prove themselves they also have all the natural potentials."

I argued, "But still, I think it would be more difficult to convince the person who feels they are superior. Are there any additional arguments you might use?"

The Dalai Lama considered that question. "In that case, as I mentioned earlier, I might appeal to their own self-interest, pointing out the detrimental effects or disadvantages of those beliefs. For example, let's say that one is engaged in business. The success of one's business often depends on one's reputation, and a reputation for being prejudiced would be detrimental to the person's financial success. He will also lose the respect of those who are working with him or for him, and there will be less cooperation. So, eventually, he himself will suffer. So one can see how one's racism can have negative effects in one's personal life, at least in the long term.

"Another thing. I would ask that person to really reflect on the insecurity and tensions they experience within a racist society. There is a big psychological toll that one must pay for living in a community with such racial tension. And a potential physical toll too, as such communities or societies can more easily erupt in violence."

The Dalai Lama took a sip of hot water, then added, "You know, this reminds me. Earlier, you were wondering how this natural feeling of Us and Them can progress into destructive things, to violence. One important factor is lack of contact with others, those on the other side. And if you analyze this, investigate, you can trace step by step how this can lead to violence: This lack of contact with others, or isolation from others, is an important factor here, because lack of contact or isolation results in ignorance about the other groups. This ignorance can then lead to this 'stereotyping' you mention. This can also lead to more suspicion of the other side. And this suspicion can easily become a kind of fear. And when people act out of fear, aggression is one potential response. In fact, it is one of the most common responses. So you see, out of fear, out of mistrust, then their behavior sometimes becomes more aggressive, of a more violent type.

"So, whenever you have these strong divisions between people, there is a potential for violence. I remember, for example, several years ago that there was rioting in one community in Los Angeles, in an area that was predominantly Korean, that was a result of interracial tension. So it's in everyone's best interest to live in a more stable society, a more stable environment. That is common sense. I would ask that individual to reflect on the feeling of suspicion, fear, and unease he may experience if he finds himself walking in a neighborhood that was composed predominantly of that minority, and ask if he sees any benefit in living in an environment where he could walk anywhere without feeling insecure."

"Well," I pointed out, "I don't know if that would be a powerful enough argument for some of these racists, though. They would say then, 'Well I would just avoid walking in those areas.'"

The Dalai Lama laughed. "Then the other option would always be to have some members of the different race knock on his door, and present their arguments with bats and clubs!" He laughed again and continued. "But seriously, there will always be those who you cannot change. There are so many differences among human beings. But, on your part, you can always try to make some difference, making a plea by asking them to try to imagine living in a society with less tension, less fear, less hostility and how wonderful that would be; ask him if he would rather have his children live in a society filled with hatred and fear. After all, everyone wants to live in a safer environment for themselves and for their family."

"You know, Your Holiness, I was just thinking about a conversation in which I asked about your reaction the first time you met a member of a different race. You said that you didn't remember any bias or negative response to them. But it occurs to me that of course there can be many differences between groups besides racial differences. So, I'm just wondering, even if you did not have racial discrimination when you were growing up in Tibet, surely there must have been other forms of discrimination in that society. Didn't you ever feel a sense of bias against other groups in *some* way?"

The Dalai Lama considered the question. "Yes, maybe I felt some prejudice on religious grounds."

"In what way?"

"In the past I had some feeling of distance, even bias, against other traditions. For example, in Tibet there were some who practiced Islam, and also our native pre-Buddhist Bon religion. So I do recall having a certain feeling of distance like this, but later over time I overcame these prejudices."

"And how did you overcome those prejudices?"

"As a result of learning more about the other's viewpoint, developing a greater understanding of them.

"Just to be clear, in identifying learning as one strategy to help overcome prejudice, do you mean learning through more formal kinds of academic education, like reading about the others' groups and so on?" I asked.

"Yes, this can be helpful," replied the Dalai Lama. "But here, I was referring to an understanding that came about especially through personal contact with people of these other traditions. *That* was the most important factor.

"Now in the case of Tibetans, for example, there may be a lot of talk about the Chinese, and sometimes initially, when they think of Chinese people, on the surface there may be a feeling that, yes, this is a Chinese person, and they might feel a sense of distance and opposition. But when they actually *meet* a Chinese individual in person, then there is the possibility of lessening such feeling if the Tibetans can relate to the other as another human being. Then it becomes clear to them to really be aware of the difference between those who are responsible for perpetrating the atrocities against the Tibetans, as opposed to Chinese people in general. So in my case, for instance, these days, actually I enjoy meeting Chinese people.

"So, in general, it's important to relate to members of other races, especially those with whose group or nation you are having a conflict, not simply seeing them as a *representative* of their entire group. But rather seeing them as an *individual* human being."

※

None of us are born bias-free. Including the Dalai Lama. Admitting to his own brand of bias and prejudice when he was younger—prejudice against other religious traditions—he went on to identify the factors that had enabled him to eliminate that bias. His comments about how he overcame his own prejudices, uttered with such simplicity and so casually, would be easy to dismiss as little more than a few brief generalities, even commonplace or trite. But in these concise comments, taking up just a brief moment in the course of our lengthy conversation, the Dalai Lama offered profound truths, identifying three separate and distinct powerful strategies to overcome prejudice, strategies with the potential to transform society: personal contact, education, and seeing others as individuals. Each of these approaches has a body of scientific evidence confirming its effectiveness, including some surprising recent cutting-edge research that has broadened our understanding of prejudice and the possibility of eliminating it. It is worthwhile, therefore, to take a closer look at each one of these.

Personal Contact

The idea that personal contact among different groups can reduce bias and prejudice has been in scientific literature since as early as the 1930s, and by the 1940s there was a growing interest in conducting studies on contact and racial prejudice, stimulated in part by soldiers returning from World War II. Despite the general racial policy of segregation in the armed forces during World War II, a few limited experiments in integration very late in the war, such as integrating Officer Candidate

Schools, did not go unnoticed by social scientists, who discovered that in many cases, integrated training schools and combat experiences reduced prejudice.

In 1954, one of the founders of the field of social psychology, Muzafer Sherif, conducted a highly influential study along with his wife, Carolyn Wood Sherif, called the Robbers Cave Experiment. It is a classic study not only on how easily prejudice and hostility form between groups, but on the potential benefits of contact between groups in overcoming prejudice and conflict. This is one of the principles the Dalai Lama had found to be beneficial in his own life.

The research was conducted at a boys' camp near the Robbers Cave State Park in Oklahoma, with Muzafer Sherif posing as the camp janitor. The study was comprised of three planned phases. In the first phase, twenty-two eleven-year-old boys with similar backgrounds were selected and divided into two groups. Each group was picked up by a separate bus and taken to the camp, where they were assigned living quarters far enough apart so that each group remained completely ignorant of the other's presence for the first few days. This phase was designed to facilitate bonding within each group and to quickly develop a strong in-group identity. The boys chose the names the Rattlers and the Eagles for their groups, and as expected they bonded rapidly, developing internal social hierarchies within just two or three days.

The second phase was designed to induce "friction" between the two groups. After arranging for the two groups to become aware of each other, the experimenters organized a highly competitive sports tournament between them, throwing in a dash of built-in frustration in the way the games were set up and run. The experimenters had more success than they bargained; the hostility started almost immediately, even before the first meeting, merely by anticipating the competition. The hostility escalated very rapidly, from name-calling, to "raids" on the other's cabins with destruction of property, to the point where the two groups didn't even want to eat in the same cafeteria. In fact, the experimenters had to end Phase 2 prematurely, fearing for the boys' safety after physical fights broke out between members of the two groups.

The key to this experiment was the third and final phase, in which researchers developed a method to cease hostilities and promote reconciliation through intergroup *contact*. Their method was simple yet tremendously effective: They introduced sudden "problems" and tasks that required cooperation between the groups—tasks that required their attention and resolution, but that neither group could do alone. These were problems that *transcended the intergroup conflict*. Challenges set up by the researchers included a water-shortage problem; a "broken down" camp truck that needed enough "man power" to be pulled back to camp, requiring all of them to pull together, and finding a movie to show. These and other necessary collaborations *caused hostile behavior to subside almost miraculously*. The groups overcame their bias toward each other and bonded to the point that, by the end of the experiment, the boys unanimously insisted they all ride back home on the same bus.

Despite these experiments, it is Gordon Allport who is commonly credited with doing the original work investigating this method of reducing prejudice and intergroup conflict, introducing the Contact Hypothesis in his book *The Nature of Prejudice*. In studying this idea of contact reducing prejudice, it was very apparent that face-to-face, personal contact *alone* will not necessarily lead to a decrease in prejudice. Slave owners in the Old South came into contact with slaves every day of their lives, were even raised by black nannies, but that didn't eliminate prejudice. Allport identified several factors that he felt must be present in order for contact to be successful at reducing intergroup conflict and achieving intergroup harmony: First, he argued that efforts should be made to create a *sense of equality* in social status. Next, the two groups should work together on a *common goal*, problem, or task. Intergroup *cooperation* is another critical ingredient, in which the groups are mutually dependant on each other. Ideally, contact should occur in ordinary purposeful pursuits, avoiding a sense of artificiality. Finally, if possible, the group contact and working together should be *supported by the community* in which they occur—sanctioned by authorities, the law, or local customs.

Learning and Education

Another key strategy recommended by the Dalai Lama is *education*. The Dalai Lama's hypothesis that learning about the other group will weaken and eliminate prejudice over time is supported by both common sense and substantial scientific evidence.

This can occur in three main ways: First, the more information one has about others, the more likely one will be able to see others in individuated and personalized ways, as unique human beings instead of one-dimensional representatives of a group. Second, greater knowledge of others may reduce uncertainty about how to interact with them, which can reduce the likelihood of avoiding members of other groups and reduce discomfort in interactions that do occur. Third, enhanced intercultural understanding, in terms of better historical background or increased cultural sensitivity, might reduce bias by increasing recognition of injustice. Learning about the suffering and discrimination of a group while empathizing with the victims may lead people to come to believe that the victims do not deserve the mistreatment. If the victims do not deserve this unjust treatment, it may no longer be tenable to hold negative attitudes about them.

To understand how education can genuinely overcome prejudice, it is helpful to take another look at the neurological correlates of prejudice and what happens in the brain as we learn more about an oppressed group. Earlier, we mentioned how prejudice is a result of neural pathways that are hardwired into the human brain—in a sense we come into the world equipped with a built-in predisposition for prejudice. As we've discussed, this is a very old feature of normal brain function, calling upon the older, more primitive parts of the brain—such as the limbic system, and that rascal the amygdala, the culprit in producing our negative emotional response to out-groups.

This might seem to be a depressing fact of human existence, but fortunately, that is only half the story. *Our brains also come prewired with the capacity to overcome prejudice.* This is possible because there are neural pathways running between the newer, more advanced areas of the brain, the prefrontal cortex—the seat of higher thinking—and the ancient, more primitive areas such as the amygdala. These neural circuits allow the areas of rational thought and the areas of emotion in the brain to communicate with each other. So, using our capacity for reason, logic, and critical analysis to combat our false beliefs, distorted views, and prejudices can result in messages being sent out from the prefrontal cortex that travel along neural pathways to the amygdala, inhibiting its activation. This is the mechanism that allows learning and education to modify our instinctive negative response to out-groups and thus overcome prejudice.

The greater the contact we have with out-group members, the more information we will gain about them. The more information we have, the more likely we will be able to see others in individuated and personalized ways, as a unique human being instead of a one-dimensional representative of a group. This leads to the Dalai Lama's next approach to overcoming prejudice: *viewing members of the stereotyped out-group as individuals.*

Perceiving Individuals: The Vegetable Method

Until recently scientists thought that our negative biases were automatically evoked when encountering a member of an out-group, but that this response could be reduced through learning, education, and methods such as challenging our false beliefs about the group. But it was believed that there was nothing that could be done to *prevent* the negative response from arising in the first place—it happened too fast. In other words once our negative bias or stereotyped beliefs were activated, there were methods to deactivate it and to prevent acts of overt prejudice or discrimination. But nothing could be done to prevent it from being spontaneously activated.

Why? The more primitive areas of the brain evoking emotion, such as the amygdala, were built by nature to help us respond to threats or danger quickly and efficiently. So, when we encounter another person, the analysis of the individual that takes place in those areas of the brain is very crude, looking at only one trait—friend or foe, in-group or out-group. This happens very fast, in a fraction of a second. If categorized as "foe," the danger alert is given, evoking negative emotions such as fear or hostility. In contrast, the "thinking" area of the brain, the neocortex, the area that produces our conscious thoughts, beliefs, ideas, reasoning, and so on, analyzes the person in more depth, assessing multiple traits and attributes of the individual, not just one. So, logically, this more complex analysis takes more time. Thus, by the time we are consciously aware of the person, and our stereotypes and beliefs about the person surface in our conscious mind, our emotional reaction has already occurred.

Until recently we seemed to be faced with an insurmountable challenge: Not only are these biased reactions automatic and spontaneous, but they can also be totally unconscious. We may harbor innate biases against another group yet at the same time believe that we are completely bias-free and unprejudiced. We like to think of ourselves as fair and unbiased, and yet we have been conditioned by the society around us, sometimes without even being aware of it. The conditioning we are indoctrinated with does not necessarily come from explicit bigoted or biased propaganda or messages promoted in our culture, such as in past generations. The biased response can even be learned through subtle social signals communicated by others—for example, simply by perceiving other people's fearful facial expressions when encountering a member of an out-group. Of course, the problem is that unconscious instinctual biases can still have subtle adverse effects on our judgments, interactions, and relationships with members of the other race or group.

If we are not even aware of our biases, how can we combat them? Was it the case that some level of negative bias against other groups will always be inevitable?

As it turns out, our prejudices are much less intractable than was previously believed and the effectiveness of a simple technique (one mentioned by the Dalai Lama to see members of a stereotyped group as individuals) has completely overturned the previous scientific understanding.

Some of the seminal experiments in this field have been conducted by psychologist Susan Fiske and her colleagues at Princeton University using fMRI brain imaging and cognitive testing. Functional magnetic resonance imaging (fMRI) is a kind of live X-ray of the brain that shows what areas of the brain are most active at any given moment. Lying flat on a table, the subject is slid into this brain-scanning machine, which surrounds the head like a giant doughnut. The fMRI machine shows a series of highly refined cross-section images of the interior of the brain, which can be viewed on a monitor or screen. Beyond simply taking still-life photos of brain anatomy, the machine can also show live images of brain function, as different regions of the brain "light up" in different colors according to which areas of the brain are activated at that moment.

In a series of significant experiments, Fiske and colleagues began by showing a group of white subjects a series of photos of unfamiliar faces, including both black and white ones. Monitoring the subjects using an fMRI brain scan, they found that the amygdala was activated when subjects viewed black faces, but not when they were shown photos of their own race. Previous studies had found that the more the amygdala "lit up," the higher the person scored on a standard test for racial prejudice. Interestingly, the amygdala was activated to at least some degree, indicating a biased response, even in those test subjects who reported that they had no prejudiced or bigoted views at all, underscoring the automatic and unconscious nature of these responses.

This study was only able to assess the emotional component of prejudice, the negative bias, but not the cognitive component, the stereotypes and false beliefs. Brain scans cannot read our thoughts or beliefs. So, social psychologists developed cognitive testing to assess a person's stereotyped beliefs. This kind of testing involves what are called priming techniques. First they get the subject to think about an out-group by methods such as showing them a photo of an out-group member, called the prime. In a second stage, subjects are generally shown a series of words, some of which represent negative stereotyped traits typically associated with the out-group. The subject may be asked, for instance, to read these words out loud as fast as they can. Prior research has established that if the subject holds stereotyped beliefs about the out-group, they will be able to recognize and pronounce the stereotyped trait measurably faster than they are able to pronounce a neutral or positive trait. Through such methods it is possible for researchers to determine if prejudice is present, even when the subject may not be consciously aware of his or her prejudice.

The fundamental question here is, is there a way to get rid of prejudice? A seminal experiment by Fiske provided a striking and surprising answer to that question. In this experiment, investigators assessed both the emotional and cognitive components of prejudice in a group of subjects, using fMRI scans and cognitive testing techniques as described above. This assessment was repeated under two different conditions, with different instructions.

In one part of the experiment, white subjects were asked to look at photos of black faces and judge whether the person was over twenty-one. This instruction encouraged the subjects to look at the faces on the basis of social categorization, making a quick judgment about whether they belonged in the "over twenty-one" group or the "under twenty-one" group. Like race or gender, "age group," categorizing on the basis of "young" or "old," is one of the socially distinct categories or groups that we instantly recognize in our culture. Viewing the faces in terms of their membership in a group discouraged looking at them as individuals, which would require more detailed analysis of the individual characteristics of that face. Under these conditions, when the white subjects assessed the black faces on the basis of "over or under twenty-one," subjects' racial prejudices were elicited—activating both the negative emotional bias (activating the amygdala based on fMRI) and racial stereotypes (determined by cognitive testing).

In the second phase of the experiment, subjects were encouraged to view the person in the photo as an *individual,* rather than on the basis of their membership in a group (such as an age, a gender, or a racial group). This was done by first flashing the name of a vegetable on the screen, before showing each photo, and asking the subjects to think about the individual in the photo and decide if that person would like the vegetable. This task was designed to get the subject to think about each face as a unique individual with personal preferences and characteristics. Amazingly, and much to the surprise of many researchers, the deliberate intention to view the person as an individual *completely* eliminated the prejudiced response on such a fundamental level that neither was the amygdala activated nor were the racial stereotypes elicited! The prejudice simply evaporated!

This finding utterly overthrew the previous strongly held notion that prejudice is an inevitable feature of human existence, and that we had no power to prevent these "automatic" and "unconscious" responses from occurring. Apparently social psychologists and neuroscientists had grossly underestimated human capacity to see others as they truly are, to see others as unique individuals just like "us," rather than automatically reacting with a danger-alert, responding to unfamiliar people as if they were members of a small tribe of hostile cavemen who would like nothing better than to clobber us with a stone ax and raid our supply of berries and mastodon steaks.

It was astounding! These subjects had already been shown to have racial prejudice to at least some degree. And even if one did not have stereotyped beliefs, it was thought that at least the negative emotional bias against other groups was a deeply ingrained, automatic human response, something beyond our conscious control. But now, it seemed that this fundamental innate human response, a response that was at the root of prejudice, hatred, conflict, and even violence—the Us Against Them response—could be quickly and easily extinguished. In fact, all we need is the deliberate intention to look at others as individuals: "Hmm . . . I wonder what kind of *vegetable* this guy enjoys?"

This technique was so easy to do and so effective, that it led researchers to wonder if things could really be that simple. So they decided to up the ante. Based on previous studies, they had documented prejudiced responses to a variety of common "out-groups": groups based on age, gender, disabilities, or wealth. Like the photos of racial groups, these photos also elicited various automatic emotional reactions. They now decided to try the "vegetable technique" with "extreme" out-groups, highly stigmatized groups in our society such as the homeless and drug addicts.

Their previous work with extreme out-groups had revealed some unexpected findings. Using the same fMRI techniques, they found that viewing the photos of extreme out-groups instantaneously activated an area of the brain known as the *insula*, an area associated with avoidance behavior and feelings of extreme disgust—significantly, in previous studies this pattern of brain activity had been seen in subjects' *responses* to nonhuman objects such as garbage, mutilation, and human waste. The *most* striking finding in this study was that viewing the homeless people's photographs also *failed* to activate a brain region known as the dorsomedial prefrontal cortex (mPFC), an area of the brain that responds to socially significant stimuli and lights up whenever people think about other human beings or themselves. The implication of this finding? Researchers reported the brain's response was "*as if people had stumbled on a pile of garbage.*"

Using the "vegetable method" with the photos of the "human garbage," Fiske was able to reverse the prejudiced response to those photos as well—with the result that the "human being" recognition region, the mPFC, was activated, and the "disgusting trash" response was not activated. Unbelievably simple: "*What kind of vegetable do you think this beggar would like?*" allowed the subject to see a real human being instead of an inanimate pile of garbage.

In addition to helping individuals overcome prejudice against other groups, the principle behind the vegetable technique can potentially help eliminate another widespread social problem that we identified earlier: *stereotype threat.* The salient feature of the vegetable technique is deliberately seeing someone as an individual instead of as a representative of a group. Applying that same principle, University of Colorado psychologist Geoffrey Cohen and his research team conducted a study with enormous implications for our educational system and the racial achievement gap—the well-known finding that, on average, black students lag behind white students in academic achievement. This gap is widely thought to be due to stereotype threat.

In this study, the researchers selected a seventh-grade class comprised of roughly half white students and half black students At the beginning of a semester, the teacher gave every student a list of values (for instance, maintaining relationships with friends or family, working to be good at art, cultivating athletic ability). The researchers then randomly divided the class into two groups. In the experimental group, the teacher asked the students to choose the value most important to them and write an essay explaining why they considered the value important. Students in the control condition were asked to indicate their least important value and write about why this value might be important to someone else. Once students had finished writing, they placed their essay in an envelope and gave it to their teacher. The teacher then continued with the day's normal agenda. The entire procedure took approximately fifteen minutes.

At the end of the semester, Cohen and his colleagues were given access to the official transcripts of all the students. The results were stunning: As expected, on average, the black students did more poorly than the white students; however, the black students in the experimental group improved on average by roughly 25 percent of a grade point, which represented about a *40 percent reduction in the racial achievement gap*.

The results of this study were so shocking, in fact, that they had a hard time believing it. They repeated their study on another group of students—with the same results (the odds of this occurring by chance being roughly 1 in 5,000). The authors of the study theorized that just writing this one essay had the effect of reaffirming the students' self-integrity, enhancing their self-worth, and affirming their individual values. Thus the assignment appeared to buffer minority students against stereotype threat and its consequences.

This is just a preliminary study, of course, but the implications are vast—the achievement gap has been one of the most challenging issues in our society for educators, and no doubt there are multiple causes. But considering the millions of dollars spent every year to try to close this gap, and the countless number of worker hours spent in so many specialized programs to try to reduce the gap, an intervention that takes only minutes could be of immense value—extending far beyond academic achievement.

Our Fundamental Equality

"Your Holiness, to review your approach to overcoming prejudice, you mentioned how we need a variety of methods, such as personal contact, or seeing the others as individuals rather than as mere representatives of a group. But your main method seems to be overcoming our negative conditioning, by challenging and overcoming our false beliefs, such as the inherent superiority or inferiority of one's own or other groups. . . ."

"That's right," he confirmed.

"So, do you have any further thoughts about some specific lines of reasoning that we could apply here to help overcome our negative conditioning or these false beliefs?"

"Yes," he said, "the way to do this is by reflecting on our fundamental equality as human beings. I think the more you increase awareness, *actively promote positive ideals such as the fundamental equality among all people, the less prejudice there will be in a society.*"

"Can you suggest ways that can help us develop a greater appreciation of our fundamental equality as human beings?" I asked.

"For instance," he explained, "modern biology and genetics have powerfully demonstrated how few differences there really are between human beings. *So,* arguments can be made on a scientific basis, pointing out, for example, how on a genetic level these kinds of racial differences, leading to the claims of superiority or inferiority, simply do not exist. Investigating these scientific findings more closely could help. In fact, maybe you could investigate this and include it in our book. There are also concepts in secular philosophy and political thought that emphasize the equality of human beings, such as the concept of natural rights as well as the socialist notion of the fraternity of the proletariat which transcend national boundaries. In liberal democratic systems too, there is the idea that all people are born equal. In addition, there is the fundamental premise underlying the justice system that we are all equal in the eyes of the law. . . ."

"Your Holiness, here you are suggesting really analyzing and reflecting very deeply on our fundamental equality as human beings. I notice that the lines of reasoning you are suggesting are all from the Western perspective. But what about from the Buddhist perspective? Aren't there certain practices that would help create this sense of fundamental equality?" I asked.

"Of course, there is the practice of cultivating equanimity in Buddhism that could help reduce our biases."

"Could you describe that practice?"

"Yes. This meditation practice involves visualizing a friend, an enemy, and a neutral person and then first allowing your mind to react to each of these in your normal way: observing how you feel attachment to your loved one, a feeling of hostility toward the one whom you dislike, and a feeling of indifference or no emotion to that stranger. The next step is to ask yourself, 'Why do I feel such different emotions to these three individuals?' You will find some grounds, like your friend has done this or that for you, has shown you kindness, and so on. But then you begin to investigate, analyze, use your reason, to see if these are valid grounds, if they are reasonable. Analyzing in this way you will discover that the reasons, the basis for calling one person friend, another enemy, or feeling indifference toward the third, are not permanent conditions, and this may change at any moment. Your friend may harm you and may become an enemy, your enemy may show you kindness and become a friend, and the stranger may become a friend or enemy in the future. So, deeply reflecting in this way you will realize that there are no justifiable grounds for discriminating between them in this way and feeling such strong emotions. You will see that these designations or labels of 'friend,' 'enemy,' or 'stranger' are impermanent and subject to change at any time.

"So, Howard, this type of visualization practice helps reduce your biases for or against others, and levels out these extreme fluctuations of emotion that you feel for others. The purpose of such an exercise is to establish a stable basis so you can cultivate the same level of closeness and caring toward all people—the same compassion.

"Of course," the Dalai Lama added, "this practice can be especially powerful from the Buddhist point of view, when we take into account many past lifetimes, so your friend may have been your enemy in the past, your enemy may have been your closest loved one many times, and so on. This is why it is very helpful to have a variety, different lines of reasoning—one line of reasoning may be more effective for one person, another line of reasoning for someone else. But whether it is from a scientific perspective, or from the perspective of Buddhist practice, the main thing is reflecting on these truths deeply, so that it becomes part of your fundamental outlook, and how you relate to others."

The Myth of Race

Well, there's at least one thing that humans are really good at: Our imaginations are endless when it comes to thinking up ways to see ourselves as different from one another. No matter what characteristics we use as a basis to distinguish ourselves from others and separate into groups, those same characteristics can potentially be used as a basis for prejudice, discrimination, or hatred. In today's world we can find prejudices based on gender, nationality, weight, age group, level of wealth, political party, degree of physical attractiveness, religion, and countless other attributes.

In reflecting on the destructive effects of the many forms of prejudice, there is no doubt that racial prejudice is among the greatest sources of human suffering and misery. It is clearly worthwhile, therefore, to take a closer look at racism and the concept of race.

According to the 1990 census, for example, Americans said they belonged to some three hundred different races or ethnic groups. Where are they all hiding? I haven't seen them. Latinos divided themselves into seventy different categories, Native Americans separated themselves into *six hundred* tribes. We say race is biological, yet we pick out a religion and call it a race (Jewish), or we refer to people from the "Irish" race for instance, designating a nationality as a race, or perhaps my favorite, the "Aryan race": that pure master race of Nazis and skinheads. Historically, the Aryan race refers to a variety of Indo-European peoples who lived in Iran, Afghanistan, and India around 4000 BC, in those lands later settled by ancient Hittites, distinguished by speaking the Proto-Indo-European languages. Well, maybe I'm too skeptical, but if I had to guess, I'd bet that not more than 60 percent of the Nazis and skinheads grew up in the ancient Hittite region and speak Proto-Indo-European, fluently anyway, and I'd bet that even fewer know how to read it and write it!

In this chapter we have been discussing how people are born with innate biases, and how we tend to react to other races with a negative emotional bias. But in looking at this issue more closely, *human beings do not have an instinctual bias against other races*. What we do seem to have is the tendency to have a bias against other groups in general, as discussed earlier—those who seem different, those whom we define as *out-groups*. This is not a racial issue. In fact, during the period when evolutionary forces were shaping our fundamental brain architecture, the different races we see on Earth today did not even exist. Different "races" did not appear on the scene until one hundred thousand or two hundred thousand years ago, and by that time the brain had already undergone most or all of its evolutionary changes.

Ever since the Human Genome Project announced its initial results in 2000 in unlocking the sequence of the approximately twenty-five thousand genes, there has been a renewed debate on the nature of race. Three billion different "base pairs" (the various combinations of the four basic chemical units of the DNA molecule, like "letters" of the genetic "alphabet") make up human DNA. Virtually every cell in the body contains a complete set of the two long, twisting paired strands of DNA molecules, broken down into the discrete regions known as genes, each gene containing the recipe to make one or more protein-building blocks. This is the fundamental blueprint of life, carrying the complete instructions to build and run a human body. Unlocking the sequence of these genes was a remarkable achievement, taking over a decade of intensive research, with the collaboration and contribution of scientists all over the world.

This look into the code of life sparked a renewed interest in taking a look at who we are, and what it means to be human and the differences and similarities among different races. It was reported in the popular press that every human being is approximately 99.9 percent the same and there is greater variation in a person's genetic make-up within each race than among the races. This finding leads many people to conclude that humans are so fundamentally alike that the concept of race is out-dated, essentially a myth, a mental projection, at least from the bio-logical point of view. For example, we place such a great importance on skin color in our society, yet the difference between two human beings based on skin color is so small, it is almost nonexistent; in fact, it has been reported, for instance, that white skin is produced by the changing of *one DNA "letter" out of three billion*! We think we know what race is—in fact, "everybody knows"—yet when it comes to really defining it, we are lost. The closer we look for the essence of each race, looking for that *one person* we can point to as an example of the biologically and genetically "pure" race, the more it seems to be in our imagination.

Soon after such findings began to get abroad, as always, some sci-entists began to refute such findings. They pointed out, for example, that there are some genetic differences between populations when one looks at some "alleles," the variations of different genes. Still, the fact remains that there are no clear-cut distinct divisions among races, since you'll always find members of other populations or races or eth-nic groups who carry that "special" allele that is thought to belong to a single population.

Scientific research also reminds us that we are all family—*literally*. We share common ancestors, and our most recent common female ancestor, *of every person alive today,* is popularly known as Mitochon-drial Eve. She lived in Africa around 140,000 years ago (no, she is not the same Eve as in the Bible; as this Eve was not the only woman on Earth, she had contemporary family and friends, and we've inher-ited some of their traits as well). Scientists have traced our ancestry to her as a result of a special bit of DNA, a small strand that is found in mitochondria, little sausage-shaped structures inside cells, the cell's "powerhouse" that produce energy. Most of our DNA is a mix of DNA from both our parents, but mitochondrial DNA gets passed down only through mothers, and it does not change. So, using special calculations, scientists have traced back our common ancestry to one woman.

For that matter, all men are brothers—well, at least men share a common male ancestor, Y-chromosomal Adam, who lived in Africa around 60,000 years ago. This was determined in the same manner using a piece of DNA on the Y chromosome that is passed down only to men, that does not mix with other DNA; it is like a genetic surname that allows men to trace their paternal lineages back through time.

Race may appear to be something concrete, because we can see differences before our own eyes—so few question what it really is. For most people, the tremendous importance people place upon race seems to be plenty of evidence that human beings can be clearly distinguished on the basis of race—it is enough that we seem to intuitively "know" in our gut that there must be fundamental and functional biological differences. But what are these differences?

Scientists have theorized that the different racial *appearances* humans have are derived from certain isolated populations living in a certain discrete geographic location for many thousands of years—the more one lived in hot sunny climates, the more skin melanin we needed to protect us, and the body may be taller or shaped differently to give us more surface area for evaporation. Or if we lived in colder climates with less sun, we needed less melanin in our skin, but maybe we needed shorter, more compact bodies, with more fat to conserve warmth. But it seems tragic to place so much emphasis on something with no more significance than different members of the same family choosing to clothe their bodies differently according to the climate where they were raised.

Continuing with our discussion of racism and prejudice, I said, "Your Holiness, you say how certain positive ways of thinking could be pro-

moted within a society that could reinforce the belief in our fundamental equality and help overcome racism, prejudice. But I was just
thinking how after the human genome was cracked, there was a lot of
press coverage about how 99.9 percent of our DNA, the blueprint for
building the human body, is exactly the same as every person we will
ever meet. To me that was an amazing statistic! I felt that was really
powerful evidence showing how alike we are. (So, on a genetic basis we
are much more similar than we are different, and the difference is neg-
ligible.) Even President Clinton went on TV and mentioned this figure,
and has continued to mention it publicly even after his presidency was
over.

"Additionally, the fact is that these values or ideals such as democracy, equality, and so on, are *already* promoted in our society. Yet, that
awareness does not seem to have such a big impact on society. People
all over the world still exploit each other, fight with each other, and
generally act as if the differences between us are huge, almost as if we
are a different species. So, I'm wondering what else is missing. . . ."

"Howard, I think if you look from a wider perspective, you will find
that the promotion of these values is actually working, is effective. From
the standpoint of human history, there have been great advances in the
world, with greater awareness of these values, the ideals of equality and
so on spreading worldwide. Look at the advances in just the past few
hundred years."

"Well, that may be true," I admitted, "but I don't know, it still seems
that for some people at least, it is very difficult for them to revise their
outlook and perception, to expand the boundaries of those with whom
they identify, to include others as part of 'us,' based on a deep sense of
our fundamental equality."

"Yes, it might be difficult," His Holiness replied, "and even though
in some cases it may be difficult, *I think that it is possible to change.*
Look at your example of America, and the cultural phenomenon in the
United States of the civil rights movement. At one time there were communities that were completely segregated. But in cases where the minority black community was given equal opportunity as a result of this
movement, achieving the same socioeconomic level and living in the

same neighborhoods as the other races, sharing the same community problems and concerns, such as the education of their children, I think there was less division of Us and Them. On the other hand, in those communities in which the black people were afforded fewer civil rights, living separately, there was more suspicion between the two races. So I think this shows that there is potential at least to reduce these kinds of divisions; it is not impossible."

"That's true," I said again. He was starting to convince me. Still, as I was wondering about the potential for genuine change in the most intractable conflicts between racial, ethnic, or other groups, he continued, as if sensing my doubts. "Howard, here we are talking about prejudice and conflict between groups, and this reminds me of a moving story I once heard during one of my visits to Israel. I met some people who were involved in a grassroots peace movement there that brought together children from the Israeli and the Palestinian communities. These children were taught to see the image of God in each other. They practiced reminding themselves that God was in the children of the other side, in the same way that He was in theirs. This was a kind of equanimity practice.

"I was told that whenever there was a renewed conflict, these children who had trained to see God in the face of their fellow children from the other side found it almost impossible to develop hatred towards the other children. They were unable to reduce these children under the generalized category of the 'enemy.' I think this is really wonderful!" the Dalai Lama exclaimed enthusiastically.

"So, I really believe that genuine change is possible," he concluded, "but, of course, change takes time. As we mentioned, these attitudes are based on false beliefs and distortions of thinking, and any change in society must first begin in the individual mind and heart, with a transformation of that person's outlook. This change occurs one person at a time."

Chapter 5

EXTREME NATIONALISM

"WELL, THIS week we have been talking about Us Versus Them divisions, and the dangers of this progressing to prejudice, conflict, and violence. I am just thinking that identifying with one's country or nation seems to be one of the most powerful examples of Us. It seems that following a period of national crisis there always seems to be this resurgence of patriotism and nationalism. Of course a lot of the time this nationalism expresses itself as a kind of vocal patriotism, expressions of support for one's country, a lot of flag-waving, and so on. But historically, the more intense this kind of nationalism, the greater the danger of falling into destructive patterns, and it is not much of a leap to go from a zealous kind of patriotism to overt hostility toward other countries. This kind of thing has acted as a fuel for a lot of conflicts in history.

"So, I'm just wondering, what is your own take on nationalism, its benefits versus the disadvantages or destructive potential of nationalism?"

The Dalai Lama said, "I do not think that nationalism in itself is destructive. Being a member of a particular nation can be a part of a person's sense of identity. So, nationalism can be useful, giving you a sense of belonging, and you can have a sense of pride in your national identity. This is good. I think nationalism is like an instrument or like science—if you utilize science the wrong way, then it could bring disaster. If you use it properly, it brings benefit. So, it is up to us to use it in the right way.

"Now when we speak of nationalism, we are talking about differences based on national identities, a key part of which are differences in cultural heritage and historical background. Each nation has a characteristic culture or group of cultures, a cultural heritage. Of course, there are also geographical boundaries between nations. That is a part of it. But I think culture is the main thing. And, of course, each community must have the right to preserve their own culture, including language, customs, and dress, and so on."

I asked, "You mention the benefits of nationalism and the importance of maintaining a cultural or ethnic identity, but wouldn't you agree there can be disadvantages of nationalism as well, destructive aspects?"

"Here, I would distinguish between a healthy nationalism and extreme nationalism," the Dalai Lama replied. "When nationalism becomes extreme, it can become a dangerous ideology, so powerful that it can incite people to commit acts of aggression. How this can happen we saw very clearly in the tragic story of the Balkans at the end of the twentieth century, with the terms 'ethnic cleansing' and 'Balkanization' entering our everyday vocabulary. What we witnessed in this tragedy was how extreme national identities led to a vicious cycle of violence between the Serbs, the Croats, and the Bosnians. Here was an example of the effects of one's national identity overriding other aspects of people's identity that could otherwise provide a basis for coming together."

"So, as a society, what do you think we can learn from that tragic experience in Eastern Europe?" I asked.

"Clearly one important lesson we need to learn is that people's national identities are very important to them and should be respected.

In particular, what this tells us is that when different nationalities co-exist within a larger group, whether within a federation of countries like with the European Union, or a single country, we need to ensure that the different nationalities are respected and accorded dignity. Of course if you have a diversity of different cultures within one country, in order for all of them to thrive, I think freedom is very important and a good fair constitution, with the rule of law."

At the very moment the Dalai Lama spoke of these issues—free-dom, rule of law, respect for all cultures, all nations—traditional Ti-betan culture, and Tibet's historical status as a nation, was in the grips of a death struggle that would determine the survival of an ancient tradition and heritage. To him, this was a living issue, not a matter of abstract philosophy—terms such as "freedom," "respect for indi-vidual cultures," and "rule of law" were not mere slogans to him, or sound-bites for the evening news. Quickened by an inner passion, and marked by a certain resolute look in his eye, the Dalai Lama's words conveyed a genuine sense of urgency. One sensed that real human suf-fering was at stake, and that the Dalai Lama's dedication to these prin-ciples and the boundaries of his concern were not reserved for Tibetan culture alone but were extended to all cultures on earth. I could not help but be moved.

"Anyway, I think that the tragedy in the Balkans can teach us an important lesson of what can happen when that kind of basic respect is absent. . . ." He paused, then added quietly, "Respect for others' tradi-tions is so important in today's world."

Thinking about a comment I had heard the Dalai Lama make in the past, the idea that real peace was not merely the absence of war, it occurred to me that the mere absence of prejudice was not the same as true respect.

I observed, "Up to this point we have been talking about overcom-ing prejudice, but now it seems we are taking it one step further or be-coming more proactive, talking about cultivating a sense of respect for other groups. The logical question is, do you have any thoughts about how to increase or cultivate a greater sense of respect for other cultures or nationalities?"

"Yes. I think that we have discussed how some individuals may be more educated or have more wealth, and so on, and some may have less, but despite these kinds of differences, they are still all human beings, and worthy of human dignity and respect on that fundamental level. The same principle applies on the level of cultures and nationalities— there may be others who are different, whose way of life or manner of dress you may not understand, but you can still maintain respect and accord them human dignity based on your common humanity.

"But here," he continued, "there's another thing. Something that is very important on many levels: learning to appreciate diversity, really reflecting on its value, investigating its benefits. The more you can appreciate diversity, the easier it will be to respect those who may be different. For example, from the viewpoint of humanity as a whole, I think the variety of cultures, variety of ethnic groups can be enriching to humanity. So the point really is that *in order for the collective humanity to thrive, the individual members of that collective have to thrive.* A good analogy is a garden. In order for a garden to be beautiful and wonderful, there needs to be diversity of flowers in the garden, plants, and the combination of different sizes, shapes, and colors adds to the garden, and each of them needs to thrive in their own environment. Whereas if you have only one type of flower in that garden, in just one collection, it doesn't work. It is the *diversity* that gives a garden its beauty."

The time for our meeting was up. So engrossed in the Dalai Lama's words, I had not even noticed the usual flurry of activity by his staff and attendants coming and going on the veranda outside in preparation to usher one guest out and another one in. But now hovering around the screen door, the signal was given by the Dalai Lama's secretary and I quickly prepared to leave.

As I stepped out onto the veranda, framed by a dense arrangement of purplish bougainvilleas draped over a latticework, I watched the Dalai Lama's next guests ushered into the room to meet with him. It was a small group of men and women, and I noticed that the members of the group represented several different nationalities and all seemed united by their excitement to see the Dalai Lama—an apt ending for our discussion about harmony among all nationalities. As I walked down the driveway to the main gate of the Dalai Lama's residence complex, I enjoyed the lush vegetation of the grounds—thick bamboo trees and bushes, oak, fir and pine trees, wild rhododendrons, and potted flowers of every color in full bloom—purple, yellow, red, orange . . . As I slowly walked down the hill, enjoying the diversity of a real garden while still thinking of the Dalai Lama's garden metaphor for the beauty of a diversity of peoples, I was overcome by a peaceful, hopeful feeling, as if perhaps someday the Dalai Lama's vision could come to pass.

One does not need to look very far into the past to come upon the most horrible examples of the destructive force of extreme nationalism or ethnic prejudice and hatred. The example chosen by the Dalai Lama, the Bosnian War, was not so long ago. Almost immediately after the Republic of Bosnia and Herzegovina declared independence from the former Yugoslavia in 1991, the world began to witness the very worst side of extreme nationalism, as the three traditional ethnic groups living in the region (Orthodox Serbs, Catholic Croats, and Bosniak Muslims) began a fierce civil war based on ethnic nationalism, each struggling to gain political control of the new country or parts of it. By the time the war ended with the 1995 Dayton Accords, more than one hundred thousand people had been killed and almost two million people displaced—the results of a war that laid waste to much of the region, leaving in its wake 60 percent of the homes, half of the schools, and a third of the hospitals damaged or destroyed; along with the destruction of power plants, roads, and water systems; torture; soldiers raping women in front of their families, in public squares, sometimes abusing and gang raping them together, for days or even weeks at a time. All three sides contributed. Serbs were particularly ruthless in their "ethnic-cleansing" efforts, systematically burning down homes, placing men in detention centers where some were tortured or starved to death, using tactics seeking to eliminate members of the other groups living within their geographic regions.

With suffering on such a vast and unimaginable scale, sometimes it is easy to look upon such wars as "world events" and lose a sense of the impact of extreme nationalism in the lives of ordinary individuals. But perhaps the story of three lives would be a powerful example for the tragedy of Us and Them thinking.

In our earlier discussion, the Dalai Lama spoke about the relationship between the individual and the group—how a person could have a strong sense of individual identity, of independence, of confidence and personal strength and at the very same time have a deep sense of belonging in a group. "It's not Me *or* We, but Me *and* We." Here, he extends the same principle to groups: believing in the possibility of many ethnic groups living in one country, each celebrating its own uniqueness, honoring its traditions while at the very same time cultivating a sense of belonging and a national identity.

Such a model, the ideal balance of individual and group identity, was once seen in a group of sixteen- and seventeen-year-old boys, Bosniaks, Croatians, and Serbs, who came together in 1984 to play for the Yugoslavian junior national basketball team, a team that was to become a legend. For four years this group was invincible, a dream team of young players who never lost a game in formal international competition on the court, and who grew up together off the court, forging deep friendships as they traveled together, roomed together, trained hard, and shared each other's lives. Their sense of personal camaraderie and athletic confidence was unshakable during those years, to the degree that the night before their most important game, the 1987 World Championship for Junior Men, they snuck out of their hotel rooms together to spend the night jumping on trampolines. And they still emerged triumphant, beating the Americans at their own game the next day, 86–76.

After winning the world junior championship, many of these young future-NBA stars went on to play for the Yugoslav senior national team. Friendships remained firm between Serbian players such as Vlade Divac or Aleksander Djordjevic and Croatian players such as Dino Radja or Toni Kukoč, who continued playing together through their 1991 victorious European Championship in Rome.

The first sign of the end of the young Dream Team came on the afternoon of the finals of the championship series, just days before Slovenia had declared its independence from the Yugoslav federation. The minister of sport of the new nation had called a young Slovenian guard of the team to tell him if he played that night, he would be considered a traitor to his country.

As the Balkan region soon broke apart and became embroiled in conflict, suddenly new categories emerged. No longer Yugoslavians, the players now had new teams and new labels, Croatians, Serbs, Bosniaks. To many, these labels seemed to eclipse all other aspects of their identity. Bosnian Muslim team member Teo Alibegovic said, "You know, I never knew what nationality anyone was when we were playing with each other. And I bet you they never knew what I was. Well, now we know." The friendships, once thought unbreakable, now seemed to crumble under the pressure.

It was particularly hard for two of the star players, Serbian Divac and Croatian Kukoč, who had become very close friends over the years. Divac had tried to stay in contact with his former teammates, and although they had not entirely broken off contact, he was still deeply troubled by the strained nature of the friendships; he even broke down in tears during a 1996 interview as he spoke of the tragic developments. Kukoč meanwhile reported, "Last summer I visited hospitals to see the wounded. Once you see nineteen-, twenty-year-old guys without arms, without legs, you don't think about basketball."

Fortunately, as the years have passed, a healing has taken place among most of the former teammates, and today these two are friends again, working together in the Balkans on humanitarian efforts and teaching tolerance to children through basketball.

When you see a team like that in action, it is beyond a sport; it can become a metaphor for the height of human potential (like the Boston Celtics' dynasty of the 1960s, led by basketball greats including Bill Russell, John Havlicek, and Sam Jones)! It's the perfect balance, where you can see the highest development of individual effort, individualism at its finest, and at the same time the highest representation of group effort. In these truly great teams, you'll see five separate individuals, each with his own unique talent, each clearly delineated, with their own personality; one might be a great clutch shooter, another tough on defense and shot-blocking, a third a hard-driving scorer. No one man may have it all, but each has developed his own specialized talent, while knowing the strengths of the others, and when they come together, they are in complete sync with a kind of synergy as if they are truly one organism, with the whole greater than the sum of the parts.

I can't think of a more apt description of the Dalai Lama's ideas about the possibility of having a strong individual identity and a strong group identity at the same time, as well as an apt metaphor for the benefits of having a diversity of individuals within a larger whole—whether it is basketball players on a team or ethnic groups within a larger federation.

His Holiness suggested deeply reflecting on the benefits of diversity as a powerful practical strategy to help cultivate respect for those who may be different. While such a team provides both an illustration and a broader metaphor for the benefits of diversity, there has also been a great deal of scientific research providing more concrete evidence of the benefits of diversity, which is worthwhile to review.

The Benefits of Diversity

In his book *The Wisdom of Crowds,* author James Surowiecki opens with the story of an eighty-five-year-old British scientist, Francis Galton, an expert in the science of heredity, who decided to go to a fair and livestock exhibition one day in 1906. He had a long-standing interest in breeding and was curious to see the results of animal breeding that day. The author recounts how Galton came across a weight-judging competition at the fair, in which people were betting on the weight of a fat ox on display, "*after* it had been 'slaughtered and dressed.'" With prizes offered for the best guesses, ultimately around eight hundred people made a guess. While there were a good number of butchers and farmers among the eight hundred contestants, overall they were *a diverse lot,* with quite a few who had no particular specialized knowledge of cattle. Galton figured that even though there were some experts in the crowd, most of the people would have no idea of what the final weight would be, and the average guess was likely to be way off the mark. After the contest was over, Galton borrowed all the tickets from the contest and analyzed them. After averaging all the contestants' guesses to come up with a single figure, representing the "collective wisdom" of the crowd that day, Galton was stunned with the results: "The crowd's judgment was essentially perfect!" After being slaughtered and dressed, the ox weighed 1,198 pounds. The crowd guessed 1,197.

Surowiecki goes on in his book to give example after example of similar stories, and adding scientific theories and studies, demonstrating the basic thesis of his book: "Under the right circumstances," he writes, "groups are remarkably intelligent, and are often smarter than the smartest people in them." He makes the counterintuitive argument that groups of people are better at problem solving and make better decisions than even the top experts in the group.

Of course, we all know how incredibly foolish people can be at times when assembled in crowds, prone to idiocy ranging from witch hunts to unthinkable acts of evil (e.g., lynching). So, the key here is identifying the "right circumstances" Surowiecki refers to, the conditions that allow the wisdom of the group to emerge. The conditions identified by Surowiecki lend support to the Dalai Lama's argument that diversity—whether a diversity of individuals in a crowd, a diversity of cultures within a nation, or the diversity of nations on our planet—can sometimes offer great benefits. Drawing upon many scientific studies, and an abundance of practical examples, Surowiecki concludes that "the conditions that are necessary for the crowd to be wise: diversity, independence, and a particular type of decentralization."

Thus we come to another benefit of diversity: Diversity enhances the *wisdom* of a group, improving our problem-solving and decision-making capacity. With so many problems in the world today, this is a benefit that is not to be dismissed lightly. If a group of people are seeking to solve a problem or come to a consensus on an important decision, a *diversity* of fresh perspectives, new sources of information, and different funds of knowledge all contribute to the wisdom and strength of the group. In a sense, one could draw an analogy to the ancient Indian tale of "The Elephant and the Blind Men," where a group of blind men are asked to describe an elephant. One feels the tail and describes the elephant as being like a rope, another feels the leg and describes it as a pillar, and so on. Acting alone, the blind men are all way off the mark, but if enough blind men were assembled in a group, each contributing to the picture, eventually they would come up with a pretty good description of an elephant.

A key 2004 study at Stanford University directly demonstrated the benefit of diversity in improving the thinking capacity of a group. Researchers Anthony Antonio and Kenji Hakuta divided a group of white students into small groups set up to discuss several contentious social issues, such as capital punishment. Unknown to the students, they were grouped so that all shared the same opinions, based on a prescreening interview. Also unknown to the subjects was that one of the "students" in each group was a "plant," collaborating with the researchers. Half of the plants were black, half were white. In addition, some plants were instructed to agree and some asked to disagree with the others in the group.

In carefully analyzing the content of assigned fifteen-minute pre- and postdiscussion essays, the researchers found conclusive evidence that diversity in these groups had beneficial effects on the thinking abilities of the group members, specifically improving a type of thinking known as "integrative complexity" (IC). IC is a measure of high-level intellectual thinking, roughly involving the ability to look at a problem from a variety of perspectives, and to be able to integrate these various perspectives in coming to a conclusion. IC is valuable in problem solving and decision making. The benefits in the study were found when a group included a member of another race, whether the black student agreed with the majority or not. In the same way, the benefit was found when the group included a member with a different opinion, whether this different opinion was expressed by a black or white "plant."

Considering that this is just one example of the many benefits of diversity, one might reasonably ask, "Well, if diversity is so great, and crowds are so damn smart, why isn't there greater diversity in 'crowds' at all levels in society, with more people naturally choosing to work and live in more diverse environments?"

The answer, as usual, is, well, things aren't that simple; there are many variables in dealing with human behavior. So, despite the benefits of diversity, there's a catch—the group also must be motivated to work together and not let their differences cause bickering or conflict that prevents working together productively. In order to enjoy the benefits of diversity, those from different racial or ethnic backgrounds must first have the opportunity to come into contact with each other, and then must begin to break down attitudes that create barriers among diverse groups.

In order to tackle this problem, it is important to understand that just as there are benefits to diverse groups, there are also benefits to homogeneous groups, such as greater productivity arising from group solidarity and a sense of cohesion. Recent research clearly confirms that people trust each other more, have a stronger feeling of community, lower crime rate, and decreased levels of depression and anxiety disorders when living in more homogeneous communities, or where your group is in the majority. So, somehow we must reconcile the fact that people feel happier when living among those of similar race and ethnicity with the absolute need for a sense of harmony and cooperation among different groups, the need to feel comfortable with those of other races and nationalities in our increasingly multicultural societies. This issue is dramatized in Western society today by the intense debate between those who feel we should celebrate our racial and ethnic differences, seeing nothing wrong with "keeping to our own," and those who argue in favor of greater integration of our multicultural societies, even total assimilation into one big happy human family.

Earlier the Dalai Lama spoke of the need for a greater spirit of community, for cultivating a sense of connectedness, of closer social bonds, but here we can categorize two types of social bonds: One type binds people together within a group, on the basis of common traits such as the same racial, ethnic, or religious background. The second type creates closer social ties between members of different groups, what is often called bridging social ties. Most social scientists today agree that it is the bridging social ties that are badly needed in contemporary Western society, the type tragically lacking in the Balkans among the Serbs, Croats, and Bosniaks. The challenge, of course, is how to build these bridging social ties—how to create a feeling of connection to a wider community while still retaining cultural or ethnic identity.

The studies show that people feel happier if they're with people who are like themselves. *But what does "like themselves" mean?* This seems to be the crux of the problem—a problem that was also clearly identified by the Dalai Lama when speaking about the destructive aspects of Us and Them thinking, concluding, "*We need to promote a more inclusive way of relating to others. That's certain.*" We need to find a way to look at others from different racial, ethnic, or national groups and perceive all of them to be part of a larger, more-inclusive "we."

In this chapter, the Dalai Lama presented some sound strategies to help us overcome the biases, prejudice, and hatred that can act as obstacles to cultivating this "more inclusive way" of perceiving others. In Part Three of this book, we will return to the discussion of how to relate to others in a more inclusive way, showing how this can lead to greater personal happiness as well as help overcome many of the societal problems in today's world. Before turning our attention to those topics, however, events in the world reminded us that there were still some vitally important issues to discuss in our quest to find happiness in our troubled world.

PART TWO

Violence Versus Dialogue

Chapter 6

HUMAN NATURE REVISITED

O N THE morning of September 11, 2001, events were unfolding that were to change the world. As the World Trade Center was collapsing in New York, the Dalai Lama was peacefully asleep in his modest bedroom at his hilltop home in the mountains of northern India. The following morning he awoke at his customary hour of 3:30 AM, briefly shook the sleep from his system, and by 4 AM began his daily ritual as a Buddhist monk, with four hours of prayer and medita-tion. So as the clarion call for a new war was sounding in America, the Dalai Lama sat deep in meditation, the only sound a comforting patter of a light monsoon rain falling on the tin roof of his private quarters, while outside an atmosphere of peace and tranquillity settled over this remote mountain village, still enveloped in darkness at this hour.

Not long after 9/11, I returned to the Dalai Lama's home in Dharam-sala to resume our discussions. It had been almost a year since we had last met in this room, and it seemed that nothing in the room had changed in the interim. In fact, nothing had seemed to change in that room during the two decades that I had been visiting there: It had the same spacious, peaceful feeling, the same quality of openness created by the large windows, one side facing snowcapped mountains, the other side facing the lush Kangra Valley extending far below. The same Thangkas, Buddhist scroll paintings of the goddess Tara, framed in colorful silk brocade, hung on the pale yellow walls. The same floor-to-ceiling relief map of Tibet covered one wall, and the same Buddhist shrine adorned with fine Buddhist icons, statues, ritual bowls and butter lamps, remained where it had always been. Even the Dalai Lama's simple upholstered chair and the matching sofa on which I sat, both arranged around a large, deep red lacquer coffee table, appeared to be the same.

No, not much had changed here, I thought, as I looked around the room. In fact, as the decades passed, as far as I could tell, the only visible changes had occurred in the adjoining room, one reserved for guests waiting to meet with the Dalai Lama—as the years passed, the room's walls had filled with more and more awards, honorary university degrees, honors, medals, and plaques.

But the world outside had changed. In the intervening months since my last meeting with the Dalai Lama, the terrorist attacks of September 11 had occurred—and once again world events reminded us of the cruel and horrible things that human beings can do to one another.

We embarked that morning on an investigation of the darker side of human behavior, the acts of violence, the hatred, the atrocities that human beings can inflict upon one another. In our last series of discussions we had investigated the origin of the dualistic Us Versus Them way of thinking that can give rise to prejudice and conflict. Now we turned our attention to the more aggressive forms of human behavior, seeking to understand the causes of violence. In attempting to trace the causes of these acts of evil to their source, we began with a fundamental question: Are violence and aggression simply part of our basic human nature?

Is Our Basic Nature Violent?

"That morning," the Dalai Lama recounted, in speaking of 9/11, "after my meditation, my attendant, Lobsang Gawa, came into my study and informed me that the World Trade Center in New York had been attacked. He told me that the buildings had completely collapsed!"

"What was your first reaction?" I asked.

"Disbelief. I thought, This can't be true! I thought someone was telling me a story. So I turned on the BBC World Service radio and listened as they covered this. Then I switched on the BBC World Service TV and I watched these planes crash into the buildings and the buildings collapse in flames. Then I knew it was true. I saw the people's desperate attempts to avoid being burnt alive, jumping from the windows. So sad! Such destruction! It was unthinkable. Unthinkable."

"So what was your second reaction, after you got over your disbelief?"

The Dalai Lama shook his head sadly. "It created a powerful reminder of the destructive potential of human beings. Such hatred! It is almost beyond imagination. I then prayed for all the innocent victims and their families."

Thinking back to America's reaction to the attack that day—one of outrage, a swift, forceful determination to bring the perpetrators to justice—I asked, "Well, when one considers the terrible suffering that those terrorists and people like bin Laden have brought upon thousands of innocent people, that human beings can do this to one another, doesn't that sometimes undermine your basic belief in the goodness of human beings, of human nature?"

"No," the Dalai Lama responded, without missing a beat, "not at all. Because even though such horrible acts like this are committed by a handful of human beings, I remain firmly convinced of the basic goodness of human beings, and at the fundamental level, our nature is gentle and not violent."

This was not the first time we had spoken of basic human nature. I thought back to the very first time we had discussed this topic, more than a decade earlier.* I recalled his direct, penetrating look and unequivocal tone as he had said, "*It is my firm conviction that human nature is essentially compassionate, gentle. That is the predominant feature of human nature.*" His views on this topic had apparently not changed.

---

* *The Art of Happiness* (New York: Riverhead Books, 1998).

Despite my prior awareness of the Dalai Lama's essentially positive view of human nature, I was still a bit surprised by the unwavering tone of complete conviction when he said that the events of September 11, still so fresh, had not shaken his belief in the fundamental goodness of human beings. Even directly confronting the cruel and senseless murder of thousands of innocent people did not give him a moment's pause, and in fact his belief seemed to be stronger than ever. Wanting to understand where his strength of conviction came from, I asked, "Well, when we see the brutal, terrible things people do to one another, how can that not have any effect on your belief in the fundamental goodness of human nature, of human beings, which even includes the perpetrators of atrocities like September 11?"

The Dalai Lama thought for a moment. "Perhaps one thing is that I look at such events from a wider perspective. When such things happen we often tend to look for one person or a group of people to blame. But I think it is wrong just to look at one individual or group of individuals and isolate them as the sole cause. If you adopt a wider view, you'll see that there can be many causes of violence. And there can be many factors contributing to such events. So many factors. In this case, for example, I think religious belief is also involved.

"So if you reflect on this event more deeply," he explained, "you realize that many factors contributed to this tragedy. To me, this reinforced one crucial fact: It showed to me that modern technology combined with human intelligence and guided by negative emotions—this is how such unthinkable disasters happen."

"Can you elaborate on what you mean by that?"

He replied, "You see these terrorists must have had tremendous, almost unimaginable determination to sacrifice their own lives to commit such an act. That could not happen without forceful emotions, negative emotions. That provides the motivation. But then motivation alone, negative emotions by themselves, do not produce such events. If you think about it, you realize that a lot of planning must have gone into this attack, months if not years of careful planning. For example, it was calculated so the planes were full of fuel. These precise plans require the use of human intelligence. And then they need the means to accomplish such an act. In this case aircraft were used, a result of modern technology. So this is what I mean.

"You know," he continued, with a sigh, "in reality, so many factors contribute to such horrible acts. For example, these individuals were motivated by hatred. In fact, when I first saw the building collapse on September 11, I thought, Hatred—that's the *real* culprit!"

"Your Holiness, I can understand your view how there may be all these factors contributing to these acts of horror. But the fact is that ultimately it comes down to an individual or a group of individuals inflicting acts of violence and suffering on other human beings. So don't you think it is possible that, setting aside all these complex factors and causes that you mention, some people are really just evil, that their nature is evil?"

Shaking his head, the Dalai Lama replied, "This concept of evil, even the very word 'evil,' can be problematic. As we have discussed before, it seems like in the West sometimes there is a tendency to see things in absolute terms, to see things as black or white, all or nothing. On top of that, under the influence of mental states such as anger, this tendency becomes even stronger. A kind of distortion of one's thinking, one's perception, takes place. So, as I mentioned, when you think of such events, you immediately seek a target, looking for an individual or group to blame, something concrete that you can direct all your anger and outrage at. And in that state you see things in terms of all good or all bad, see people as good or evil. So from that perspective, you might view a person as purely evil.

"But from a Buddhist perspective, we have no concept of *absolute* evil, in the sense of evil as something which exists independently— something that is not caused by other factors, that cannot be affected by other factors, and cannot be changed or modified by other conditions. 'Absolute' evil has a sense of permanence. So, we do not accept the idea of evil people, in the sense that a particular person's intrinsic nature is one hundred percent evil, and they will remain that way because it is their fundamental unchanging nature.

"Now, within the Buddhist perspective we *do* have the concept of a person acting in an evil way, doing evil things, under the influence of negative emotions and bad motivation and so on—but we see this evil behavior arising as a result of certain causes and conditions. We feel such events can be explainable without invoking a metaphysical force like evil.

"So, basically," he summarized, "if a person commits a very destructive act, you *can* say that act is evil. No question. And *you should always oppose that act, as an evil act.* You must take a very strong stand. And let's say that the person's motivation for the act was hatred. Then you can say that both the *motivation,* and the *action* that it leads to, are evil because of their destructive nature. But we still cannot view *that individual* as 'an evil person,' intrinsically and permanently evil, because there is always the potential or possibility that a new set of conditions will come into play and that very same person may no longer engage in the evil behavior."

"Well, I can understand what you are saying," I said, "but if you look at that act as arising from a variety of causes and conditions, and view the perpetrator as just under the sway of all these other factors, and that these factors are what really caused the behavior, isn't there a danger of seeming to excuse or condone the person's behavior, as if it is not their fault? It seems that the more you look at the various causes and conditions leading to the act, the more you seem to let the perpetrators themselves off the hook."

"Again," he said, "saying that nobody is intrinsically evil, that evil is a relative state dependent on other factors, does not give someone an excuse to commit these evil acts. Just because you allow for the possibility of one's motivations and behaviors to change in the future, this does not mean that you somehow excuse or condone that act, or that you do not hold them responsible as if they had nothing to do with it."

"Well," I countered, "regardless of whether these horrible acts of violence are the result of identifiable causes and conditions, or they are attributed to evil people, the fact remains that human beings are capable of this kind of behavior; we have preyed upon and inflicted suffering on each other throughout human history. I mean you even mentioned that your second reaction to hearing about 9/11, after you realized it was real, was that it was 'a powerful reminder of the destructive potential of human beings.' And there are so many reminders . . . acts of destruction like the Holocaust, so horrible it defies imagination! I don't know, but it seems that such stark reminders of our destructive potential, our capacity to inflict harm and cause others suffering, might at least give one pause to consider the darker side of human nature."

With a solemn nod he slowly replied, "Yes, when you are confronted with horrors like the Holocaust, it can shake your faith in humanity itself. You know, I'll never forget my first visit to Auschwitz. There were several things I saw there that struck me very powerfully, and one of them was this huge collection of shoes. The shoes of the victims. And what struck me with complete horror and deep sadness was when I saw many small shoes, children's shoes! I felt so strongly for those innocent children. They didn't even know what was going on. I really felt, 'Who could do such a thing?' So, I prayed there."

These last words had been spoken softly, and as his words trailed off into silence, his somber expression led me to wait a few beats before continuing. The Dalai Lama did not believe in the concept of absolute evil. He seemed to have no compulsion to isolate Hitler and his evil henchmen as the sole cause of the Holocaust, directing the full force of his anger and sense of moral outrage at them. Yet when speaking of experiences like his visit to Auschwitz, one can sense in his tone of voice and general manner how profoundly affected he is and one does not sense an absence of moral outrage. This is not a matter of him ignoring the horror of such tragedies, nor is he unaware of the evil things human beings can do to one another. Still, with full awareness of the human capacity for evil, his belief in the fundamental goodness of humanity remains unshaken.

Continuing our conversation, I said, "Your Holiness, I guess my point is that whenever people consider the Holocaust, or similar events on a smaller scale, it not only seems to be a confirmation that there is evil in the world, but it also seems to challenge this benevolent view of human nature."

"Again," he said, "I think it would be a mistake to look at such events, and conclude that these things represent our basic human nature, as if somehow we are compelled to act that way. We must remember that these kinds of situations are not the norm, not representative of ordinary day-to-day life. For example, in Buddhist ethics, we have a list of what are called 'heinous crimes.' These include the murdering of one's own father and mother, creating schism within the community, and so on. But just because these things exist doesn't mean that human beings cannot adopt a moral way of life."

"Yes, that may be true, but . . ."

"Howard," he went on, "I think we should remember that what we are proposing is a mode of behavior that is grounded upon the recognition of the basic goodness of human nature. And with that full awareness, deliberately adopting a way of life to express this. That is our purpose, our goal. So that's why we are trying to educate humanity. We are trying to promote the idea that basic human nature is positive, so there is the possibility to promote our sense of community, our sense of concern. And this is not a religious matter. This is not simply a matter of philosophy either. It is our future. . . ."

As the Dalai Lama spoke, there was a kind of infinite compassion in his tone, as if he saw with utter clarity and great sadness the limitless suffering human beings inflict on one another as a result of ignorance—ignorance of our own true nature, an ignorance that clouds our vision, obscures understanding of our own goodness and vast capacity for kindness, causing us to live in darkness and fear, with suspicion and hatred of one another.

At the same time, the Dalai Lama's compassion never seemed sentimental or fatalistic. In fact, it seemed to be matched in equal measure by a kind of resoluteness, a bold determination to educate others to his best ability, to help them see themselves who and what they truly are, to see themselves as he sees them, as fundamentally good and decent. Now, once again, the Dalai Lama went on to briefly review some of the same key arguments he had made years earlier, presenting a well-reasoned, careful argument in favor of his view of human nature, based not just on the Buddhist theory of Buddha Nature, but primarily on biology.* He first pointed to the physical and emotional health benefits of compassion and caring and the many destructive effects of hostility and aggression, effects such as cardiovascular disease—then he appealed to common sense and reason, asking: Which "nature" is more suitable for the human mind and body, for the flourishing of human life—aggressive or gentle?

I noticed that he had added more sophisticated examples and exhibited greater depth of knowledge from a scientific perspective than during our first conversations on the topic years ago, now including arguments such as, "According to medical science, one of the most crucial factors for the physical enlargement of the brain during the first few weeks immediately after birth is simple physical contact by a mother, or some other caregiver." But despite the rational nature of his arguments, his manner was far from that of a detached anthropologist, or cold, clinical biologist; in fact, he spoke with a warmth and concern, as if lives were at stake this very minute.

Although the Dalai Lama's view of human nature was profoundly optimistic, it was not a blind optimism, and so like always, tempering his views with common sense and reason, he concluded, "Of course, the basic goodness of human beings doesn't rule out that there will be these destructive acts like we saw on 9/11. We can't expect that every human being will live in accordance with principles reflecting our basic human nature. After all, all our spiritual teachers failed to turn the entirety of humanity into something good. The Buddha failed. Jesus Christ failed. But then to go on to say that since all these great masters in the past failed, we will fail too, so, well then, why bother? That approach is also foolish. We should do what we can."

---

* In Buddhist philosophy, "Buddha Nature" refers to the underlying, basic, most subtle nature of mind. This state of mind, present in all human beings, is completely untainted by negative emotions or thoughts. Buddha Nature, sometimes called the "original clear light of mind," is what gives every human being the potential for enlightenment.

Reassessing Our Basic Nature

Over the past few decades there seems to be a revolution going on in the scientific community in investigating the eternal question of human nature: Is human nature fundamentally aggressive and violent, or kind and gentle? For the past several centuries, a rather dark, pessimistic view of human nature—as innately aggressive, selfish, and territorial—has widely taken root in Western culture, planted by a host of thinkers, ranging from philosophers such as Thomas Hobbes and George Santayana to ethologists such as Robert Ardrey and Konrad Lorenz. However, in recent years, an exponentially growing number of leading scientists have been abandoning this pessimistic view of human nature. On the opposite end of the spectrum from the more traditional, grim view of human nature as aggressive and violent, is the Dalai Lama's view of human nature—one that is characterized predominantly by the positive states of kindness, caring, compassion, even gentleness.

The growing shift toward the Dalai Lama's view lands most thinkers and researchers somewhere toward the midpoint between these two poles: More and more are coming to the conclusion that while we have the neural apparatus that gives us the capacity to act violently, there is nothing in our neurophysiology or human nature that *compels* us to do so. As a result of a massive amount of scientific research in recent years, more and more evidence has been accumulating, disputing the innately violent nature of human beings and suggesting that while we may have the potential for expressing either positive or negative traits, the one that ultimately gets expressed through one's behavior—whether one acts with kindness or violence—depends largely on training, conditioning, and our situational circumstances.

Of course, while many individuals are moving closer to the Dalai Lama's view of human nature, the question is far from settled among modern scientists, and among the general public the aggressive view of human nature still remains deeply entrenched. So, what is the truth?

In this case, actively searching out the truth about human nature may reveal a bleak, perhaps almost hopeless, picture. The facts are difficult to dispute: In the last century alone, two world wars in which virtually the entire planet was engaged; in the first half of the century, the Holocaust; at the end of the century, events such as the Rwandan genocide. Apparently we had learned very little. And violence comes in many forms, not just casualties of war. Domestic violence is the single most common cause of injury to women. Millions around the world are victims of rape, murder, and assault. Such crimes are epidemic in many countries, particularly in the United States. Only twenty years after World War I, "The War to End All Wars," our planet was again engaged in worldwide warfare. The death toll in World War II: seventy-two million, soldiers and civilians.

After the final defeat of the Axis powers, there was a spirit of genuine optimism. The world had a chance to start anew, a chance to solve disputes through alliances and organizations like the United Nations. That was the hope. But the reality? Fifty years after World War II, a study published on the NATO website reported that during those fifty years, there were 150 armed conflicts, with an estimated 25 million to 30 million dead, not including deaths due to famine or disease or other indirect effects of the conflicts. And how many days without war during this fifty-year period? How many days of peace on earth? *TWENTY-SIX DAYS!!!*

With "truths" like these, aren't we essentially compelled to conclude that human nature is fundamentally aggressive?

Fortunately the answer to that is, No!

If we follow the Dalai Lama's customary recommendation to deliberately investigate human behavior from a wider and more comprehensive perspective, looking at the interplay of events that may contribute to any given situation, and examine rates of aggressive, violent behavior of our species from a long-term perspective, a very different set of facts emerges, presenting an entirely different picture of humanity: According to researchers, during the age of hunter-gatherer societies, *30 percent of the male population died by violent means,* at the hands of others. What was the percentage during the bloody twentieth century, even with the wars, the genocides, the constant warfare? *Less than 1 percent!* And as the new century and millennium has dawned, this rate has continued to fall dramatically. In looking for additional supporting evidence of this trend, Harvard psychologist and author Steven Pinker has noted that even in the worst locations the murder rate today is *twenty times lower* than it was in indigenous societies.

Over the millennia there have always been ups, downs, and cycles in the rates of human aggression and violence; but the direction is absolutely clear: The tendency toward violence and murder is slowly declining, leaving open the genuine hope that the Dalai Lama may be correct about human nature after all.

We do not need to compare the conduct of those living in modern Western society with our prehistoric ancestors in order to find convincing statistics showing the predominance of human kindness over human cruelty. In 2004, for instance, an extensive survey conducted by the National Opinion Research Center found that American adults perform an average of 109 altruistic acts a year. Multiplying this figure by the adult population at the time reveals that there were 23,980,000,000 acts of altruism performed in America that year! The same year, the FBI reported an estimated 1,367,009 violent crimes of all types, nationwide. Doing a bit of calculation reveals an inspiring statistic: For every single act of violence in America that year, there were roughly 17,540 acts of altruism!

Comparing this stunningly positive statistic with the selfish and aggressive view of human nature widely promoted in our society, it isn't surprising that most of us have a somewhat skewed view of human nature. For example, according to the FBI, from 1990 to 1998, the national homicide rate in America dropped 32.9 percent. During that same period, homicide coverage on the network news *increased* 473 percent! This is not by accident. From an evolutionary perspective, there are reasons why we are much more interested in watching acts of violence on TV than acts of everyday kindness. We mentioned earlier how our brains evolved to scan our environment for danger or threats to our survival, endowing us with what some call our catastrophic brains, which are hardwired to be excellent at picking up on what is *wrong* in the environment—but pretty lax on noticing when things are going *right*. With our attention and interest naturally drawn to acts of violence more than acts of goodness, it is unlikely that the network news will suddenly adopt a new programming policy, accurately representing human nature, by covering 17,540 stories on altruism for every one story on violence.

It is up to us to make a special effort, actively investigating and observing our world, looking for evidence of human kindness and the positive side of human beings. One of the most powerful and compelling bits of evidence is a startling study that emerged in the aftermath of World War II. The staggering figure of seventy-two million casualties in that war was the result of many different methods of killing: bombings, torpedoes, land mines, extermination camps, and the aftereffects of war, such as starvation. But among all these methods of killing, perhaps the closest indicator of innate human aggression is the willingness of individual soldiers on the battlefield to kill fellow human beings, the enemy soldiers. Here is one of the few instances of legally sanctioned killing, where violent, aggressive behavior is not only tolerated, it is even encouraged, under conditions designed to absolve the soldier from guilt—and on top of that, in many cases the soldier's own survival is at stake.

Following World War II, U.S. Army historian Brig. Gen. S.L.A. Marshall conducted a seminal study. For the first time in history, he systematically investigated the firing rates of soldiers on the battlefield. The results were nothing short of stunning. *He found that only fifteen percent to twenty percent of the soldiers were willing to fire their weapons at the enemy in combat!* This figure was confirmed and reconfirmed, with consistent results. This was not due to acts of cowardice, as the soldiers remained in the battle and were often willing to risk their lives to save others. There was no lack of bravery. It was bewildering. After extensive investigation of this phenomenon, the conclusion was clear: *Human beings simply have an innate aversion to killing another human being, even when under threat themselves.* Sadly, this discovery led the military to look into ways to condition soldiers to kill the enemy, and firing rates in the Korean War and Vietnam escalated rapidly. But the original findings stand as a testament to the Dalai Lama's view of a benevolent humanity, where kindness prevails over killing, and gentleness over aggression.

In seeking the truth of human nature, it could be worthwhile to look at the views of an individual whom many would consider to be the single most influential figure in determining the modern view of human nature, at least in the popular imagination: Charles Darwin, whose theories on evolution, natural selection, and "survival of the fittest" revolutionized how we think of ourselves. Many people in society today have only a vague understanding of Darwin's concepts. The notion of natural selection and survival of the fittest has led many to develop a sense that evolutionary forces naturally selected aggressive, strong, territorial, violent human beings, since these are the characteristics that would enable one to fight for scarce resources and survive to pass down their genes.

This notion is far from the truth. In writing about human beings and our evolution in the *Descent of Man,* Darwin states that our strongest sentiments, the attributes at the very *core* of human nature, include our social instincts, sympathy, caring for others, and delight in the welfare of others, the same fundamental characteristics argued by the Dalai Lama! Charles Darwin's views of human nature came from his careful studies of other species, his rich and detailed observations of people, and even his study of his own ten children. In recent years, leaders in the field of evolutionary thought are returning to some of Darwin's original observations, and taking a fresh look at certain human characteristics, such as the great amount of caring involved in raising human offspring. As a result, these scientists are reformulating their view of human nature to become much more closely aligned with the Dalai Lama's view.

Perhaps it may be that, at the end of the day, a given individual's view of human nature as either positive or negative may be a matter of choice—depending on whether he or she chooses to focus on our human history of violence and aggression, or to focus on evidence of human kindness and benevolence. This choice is not simply an academic exercise, a matter of philosophy; it is critically important, with far-reaching implications and effects on both the individual and societal levels. On the societal level, for example, the question of human nature goes to the very heart of our earlier discussion of our sense of community, caring, and concern for others—the Dalai Lama's belief in the possibility of forming and sustaining meaningful interpersonal bonds and community ties is based on his belief that human nature is fundamentally positive.

Our perception of human nature has equally important implications and profound effects on the individual level as well. Ultimately our goal is to find happiness in our troubled world. And there is compelling evidence showing that how we perceive the world around us can affect our happiness. An extensive study of more than eleven thousand Americans conducted by professor of sociology Abbott Ferris at Emory University confirmed what we might intuitively guess: The perception of our world, and by extension human nature, as either good or evil can directly affect our levels of happiness. Ferris found that those who tended to perceive more evil in the world were significantly less happy than those who saw the world, and human beings, as essentially good.

In articulating these profound implications, the Dalai Lama explained, "The difference in one's vision of human nature can mean the difference between living in a world filled with fellow human beings who are perceived as hostile, violent, and dangerous, or as essentially kind, helpful, and gentle. A deep awareness of the essential goodness of human beings can give us courage and hope. On the individual level as well, such a vision of our basic nature can help promote a greater sense of well-being and connectedness with others.

"Even if the objective facts, historical and scientific, did not conclusively support either of the two views," he continued, "from a practical point of view, it is still in our best interest to embrace a more positive view of human nature. After all, we humans have a tendency to make real what we choose to believe, somewhat in the manner of a self-fulfilling prophecy."

Chapter 7

VIOLENCE: THE CAUSES

WHILE THE Dalai Lama and I touched upon a variety of topics during the course of our conversations, there remained a single question that was woven throughout all of our discussions, the question of how to find happiness in our troubled world. Thus, in looking at the various factors that have undermined human happiness throughout history, factors that have caused suffering and misery on a vast scale, there is no doubt that violence is among the primary factors.

Turning our attention to a deeper investigation of violence, I said, "Your Holiness, in trying to determine the causes of the acts of evil or violence in society, you've made the point that you can't just attribute it to the evil nature of the perpetrator and—"

"Yes. That's right," the Dalai Lama broke in. "If you want to get to the root of the problem it is not enough to just attribute the cause to a single individual or group and then just stop there, but rather it is important to understand the deeper causes of these acts of violence. Because to overcome violence you first need to understand what are its causes."

"Well, then at this point I'm wondering if we can start to explore some of these causes. And I guess that the basic question is, do you have any thoughts on what are the causes of violence in general?"

"This is very complicated," the Dalai Lama replied with a slight sigh. "There can be many causes and conditions that can lead to violence and conflicts. You can't just point to one or two factors and say, 'This is the cause.' From a Buddhist perspective we see the nature of reality as interdependent, interconnected, so for any given event or crisis, there are many, many factors that contribute to the problem, on many levels. Each situation has its own unique set of circumstances that have contributed to the problem."

"Well, can you identify some of the different 'levels' you refer to and list a few of the causes?" I asked. Then, hoping to avoid another vague response about how it all depends on the circumstances, and trying to elicit a more concrete answer, I added, "Perhaps you could use the specific case of terrorism or of 9/11 to illustrate what you mean."

"Of course, since we are talking about human problems, these conflicts and violence are created by human beings. So, the root of these problems is in human emotions and ways of thinking, the afflictive emotions—anger, hatred, greed, and ignorance. And there are distortions of thinking that go along with these afflictive emotions. So, that is one level, the *inner factors*. This relates to one's inner motivation, and in this case the motivation of these terrorists may be hatred. But then on another level there may be wider *cultural factors,* such as the values that are promoted in a particular society. In this case, for example, I think religious belief is also involved. So, that is another level. . . ."

He stopped to reflect in silence for a moment, which wasn't surprising, considering the broad scope of the question, then he resumed. "You know, in speaking of the causes of hatred and violence, conditioning plays a very big role. Conditioning can come from many levels. . . ."

"Levels?"

"Yes," he explained; "for example, conditioning can come from the values or messages one receives from the wider level of society, from the leaders, the media, or educational system. Then conditioning can also come from one's family, and so on.

"So, there may be a variety of influences from the particular environment around a person. These terrorists, these individuals, did not act purely for personal reasons. They grew out of communities who may have held long-standing resentments, based on their perceptions of America or the West. Perhaps in the past they perceived America or the West as somehow exploiting other parts of the world. Perhaps they may have harbored what they believe to be legitimate grievances and felt that there was no forum to express their grievances, nobody to listen to their concerns. And gradually these resentments festered, and turned into hatred.

"Of course, individuals may also be influenced by other members of the group they are part of, so the *situational circumstances* is another level. And on top of that, in some cases the violence may even have historical roots—in this case, although the motivation may be hatred, the roots or the perceived roots of this hatred may lie in the past—some going back even to the previous centuries.

"So in reality," he concluded, "if you adopt a wider view, you'll see that so many factors contribute to such horrible acts."

Making a batch of fresh, warm popcorn, families throughout the Middle East settle in for an evening of television viewing. . . .

Tonight on Saudi Arabian TV, we see a talk show with an attractive female host, well made-up, stylishly dressed, wearing the traditional *hijab* headscarf. Speaking in Arabic with the cool, measured, self-possessed "media accent" used by newscasters in every country, she informs the audience that they are going to do something different that day. She speaks of the importance of educating the next generation, and so she is going to interview a three-and-a-half-year-old girl on today's program.

"May God be willing to give our children the same education so the next generation of children will all be true Muslims who know who their enemies are," says the newscaster. She then introduces a toddler named Basmallah, a three-year-old with an angelic face, dressed in a frilly white

shirt and pink-and-white checkered jacket, traditional head covering—
a beautiful child, the very picture of innocence and sweetness.

After asking the child her name and age, the interviewer gets directly to the point. "Do you know the Jews?" she asks.

"Yes," says Basmallah, with the characteristic "baby-talk" pitch and tone of voice, and the charming assuredness of a confident child.

"Do you like them?"

"No!" the child says emphatically.

"Why don't you like them?" prompts the reporter.

"Because they are pigs and apes," she says with a confident, matter-of-fact tone, as if she were a miniature zoologist, literally describing some strange species of animal.

The reporter smiles and nods approvingly, and asks, "Who said this?"

"Our God!"

"Where did he say this?"

"The Koran."

"That's right!" the reporter cries delightedly, charmed with the child's wisdom. "He said it in the Koran!"

The reporter continues. "Basmallah, what do the Jews do?"

Here the child starts to become a little confused. "What?" she asks.

The reporter repeats, "What do they do?"

Clearly a bit of uncertainty creeps into the child's expression, but she still responds: "The Pepsi Company!"

The reporter looks slightly embarrassed, but tells the audience, "Oh, she knows all about the boycott!" Then she continues to press the child. "What did the Jews do to our prophet Muhammad?"

The child takes another stab at the question. "He killed someone!"

Again, the reporter adds the right spin to the child's wrong answer, telling the child, "Of course, our prophet Muhammad was strong and could kill them [the Jews]!"

The reporter continues to press the child to tell what bad things the Jews did, until the child hits on the right story, and with the reporter's encouragement to tell us what "the Jewess" did, the child recites a story about a Jewish woman who poisoned the Prophet's food, concluding the story with " . . . and he said to his companions, "'I will *kill* this woman. . . .'"

At the end of this interview, the reporter concludes, "No one could wish a more devout girl! . . . The next generation of children must be true Muslims!"

This real-life example provides a tragic illustration of the Dalai Lama's point that conditioning can play a role in hatred and violence. It doesn't take much of a stretch of imagination to imagine Basmallah at seventeen years old, a bomb strapped to her chest, filled with rusty nails and screws, walking into an elementary school in Israel or perhaps America, a beatific smile on her face and an ecstatic vision of eternity in Paradise, blowing herself up with as many innocent Jewish children as she can—children who have the innocence she once had on that happy day when she got to wear her pink-and-white outfit and she was praised on national TV for being such a devout Muslim.

The Dalai Lama is unshakable in his belief that acts of human violence and evil are not created simply by a handful of people whose fundamental nature is evil or violent. Recognizing that such acts arise from many different causes on multiple levels, his approach to overcoming the acts of evil and violence in society begins by painstaking investigation of the underlying causes. This view of evil as arising from identifiable causes and conditions is shared by modern science and backed up with a massive amount of scientific research over the past five or six decades. In fact, a series of seminal experiments dating back to the 1960s, conducted by several legendary figures in social psychology, initiated what could be seen as a Golden Age of scientific research investigating the "causes and conditions" leading to evil behavior.

In a way, this Golden Age of research on the causes of evil can be traced back to 1961, to what could be considered the watershed event in the modern scientific investigation of human evil: the trial of Adolf Eichmann, one of the principal architects of the Holocaust, Hitler's Final Solution. As the first televised trial in history, the trial brought to life the horrors of the Holocaust to a stunned audience throughout the world, an audience previously unaware of the extent and magnitude of the atrocities. The trial not only shocked the general public but also led a great many social scientists around the world to turn their attention to this massive act of genocidal evil and ask a fundamental question: How could such events have been possible? It seemed incomprehensible!

At that time a twenty-eight-year-old Yale social psychologist, Stanley Milgram, watched along with the rest of the world as Eichmann, now a middle-aged auto-factory worker, sat in a bulletproof glass box for sixteen weeks, finally on trial after years of hiding, on trial for unspeakable atrocities. Moving very little except for his darting eyes and his thin lips silently twisting and grimacing as if he were trying to get rid of a bad taste in his mouth, Eichmann sat in his box, often appearing rather disinterested as dozens of his victims described his vicious brutality and unimaginable horrors. He generally remained expressionless while witness after witness recounted how Eichmann had gone about his work with dedication and zeal. To all charges, he merely shrugged and replied, "What is there to admit? I carried out my orders."

To many people, one of the most surprising and troubling aspects of this trial was Eichmann's commonplace appearance, bland affect, and extraordinary *ordinariness*. He appeared to be an average, unremarkable-looking man in a plain dark suit, balding, gray-complexioned, and wearing horn-rimmed glasses. Rather than a sadistic monster of unparalleled dimensions, an inhuman anomaly of nature, he seemed to be more of a colorless functionary, a bureaucrat, a man of average abilities. Political theorist and writer Hannah Arendt, who was covering the trial, was so struck by these features that she characterized Eichmann as the embodiment of the "Banality of Evil."

Following this trial closely, Milgram was intrigued by Arendt's observations and was gripped by a persistent question: Was it really possible that Eichmann's infuriatingly banal claim, "I was just following orders," was truly responsible for the systematic extermination of six million Jews?

Feeling a compelling personal need as a Jew, along with a compelling professional interest as a scientist, Milgram was determined to find an answer to this perplexing question—a question that led to one of the most influential, controversial, and troubling experiments in the twentieth century.

The experiment began as a group of paid volunteers, told that they were helping science find new ways to improve memory, were randomly divided into the roles of Teachers and Learners. Learners would memorize a list of associated words while Teachers would administer the testing. In reality, the Learners were not randomly chosen subjects at all—they were actually "plants"—actors working secretly in confederation with Milgram, the experimenter.

The Teachers were told that their responsibilities were to verbally indicate correct responses and, more significantly, to immediately deliver an electric shock to the Learner for wrong responses—beginning with 15 volts. The current was increased by 15 volts for every wrong answer, up to 450 volts. The control panel of the impressive-looking electroshock machine was labeled with thirty switches, ranging from SLIGHT SHOCK to DANGER: SEVERE SHOCK—and finally, at 435 and 450 volts, simply the ominous markings XXX.

The Teacher watched as the Learner was taken into an adjoining room, strapped into an "electric-chair," and connected to an "electric-shock generator." Before starting, the Teacher was given an unpleasant 45-volt "slight shock," just to demonstrate what the electric current felt like. The Teacher and the Experimenter then moved to an adjoining room where they could verbally communicate with the Learner through an intercom, but not see him.

The "Learner" answered the first few questions correctly, but soon began to make mistakes. After a few voltage increases, he started to complain about the shocks. (Of course, all the Learner's responses were carefully scripted, and he was not being shocked in reality.) As the intensity of the shocks increased, step-by-step the Learner's responses escalated from an initial grunt or moan to frantic banging on the wall, shouting "*I can't stand the pain, let me out of here!*" to screams of agony and even vociferous complaints about a heart condition. At around 300 volts the Learner banged on the wall vigorously, refused to answer any more questions, and demanded to end the experiment. The Experimenter merely reminded the Teacher of the rules: Failure to respond counts as an error—he must continue. After that, the only responses to questions were screams of pain. At 375 volts there was a final loud scream of pain, a desperate banging, and suddenly all responses stopped—nothing but dead silence after that. However, a lack of a response was treated as an error, and the Teacher was instructed to continue until reaching the final 450 volts.

If the Teacher wished to stop the experiment, the Experimenter assured him, "I'll assume all responsibility," reminded him of his agreement to assist in this research, and "prodded" him to continue with increasing intensity, ranging from "Please continue" to "You have no choice, you *must* continue!" If the Teacher still wished to stop after four "prods," the experiment was halted. Otherwise, it proceeded until the Teacher administered three successive maximum 450-volt shocks.

Now, prior to conducting the experiment, Milgram polled both senior psychology students at Yale as well as a wide sample of his professional colleagues, asking them to predict how many subjects would continue shocking their fellow volunteers all the way to the maximum 450-volt current. The students predicted, on average, only around 1 percent. The psychiatrists, experts in predicting human behavior, estimated one-tenth of 1 percent—limited only to a few truly sadistic, pathological, or "evil" individuals, like Eichmann.

The predictions were wrong. *Two-thirds of the Teachers continued to the very end!* Two-thirds of the subjects—ordinary, decent people—continued to shock volunteers like themselves while listening to shrieks of agonizing pain, complaints of a heart condition, and even fatal silence, where one might reasonably conclude the other "volunteer" was dead! And this was no fluke: Over the years, this experiment has been replicated countless times in countries all over the world, and rates of obedience in administering shocks to the "fatal" level have remained remarkably similar to Milgram's original study.

This experiment gave many investigators their first glimpse into the psychological conditions that might have led to the atrocities committed during World War II, uncovering evidence of how even decent people might be led to perpetrate "evil" acts of violence and cruelty. These subjects were not sadistic, twisted, or pathological: As Milgram concluded at the time, "*Ordinary people, simply doing their jobs, and without any particular hostility on their part, can become agents in a terrible destructive process.*"

So, what were the "causes and conditions" that led the compliant subjects to essentially torture their fellow volunteers? What was going on here? As it turned out, these subjects did *not* suddenly lose all sense of morality or responsibility—it was just hijacked for a while. Or, more precisely, they simply handed it over to the authority. Milgram theorized that the situation created conditions in which the experimenter was perceived by the subjects to be a "legitimate authority," someone who presumably represented Scientific Advancement and Progress—unquestionably a good thing. These circumstances created a psychological condition in which *the subjects temporarily shifted their sense of personal responsibility to a legitimate authority.* Alarmingly, all that was needed to legitimize this "authority" was a white lab coat, a clipboard, and a cold, clinical demeanor.

In fact, the obedient subjects did not suddenly become uncaring individuals without human decency. All of them experienced some level of distress, often showing signs of tremendous stress, anxiety, and reluctance. But once they transferred their sense of moral responsibility to the experimenter, at that point they saw themselves *merely as an agent acting for the authority.* Psychologically, it was as if they were merely a stand-in, there to act out the experimenter's sense of morality and responsibility, not their own.

Milgram's obedience experiment was so unexpected and troubling that it triggered a wave of other studies and experiments, beginning in the 1960s, seeking to identify the various causes and conditions that create acts of violence and evil. Milgram and others went on to identify many other situational conditions and variables that could affect a subject's behavior and willingness to shock. For example, Milgram found that providing a positive social model—another "volunteer Teacher" (in this case a confederate of the researcher) who rebelled—decreased subjects' compliance to less than 10 percent. On the other hand, making the subject part of the experimenter's "team," part of the group conducting the experiment, resulted in 90 percent of the subjects instructing the "Teacher" (again a confederate) to administer the maximum shock.

Besides obedience to authority, researchers went on to identify many other factors that could affect one's willingness to inflict harm on one's fellow human beings—these other factors, for example, could be related to the nature of the setting, the individual's role in a situation, or conformity to group pressures.

Today, after almost fifty years of research, the body of evidence demonstrating the power of social situations and conditions to alter the thinking and behavior of individuals, groups, and nations is overwhelming. How overwhelming? In documenting the level of scientific support, Princeton University professor Susan T. Fiske reveals, "*The power of social context to influence actions has been proven in approximately 25,000 studies including 8,000,000 participants.*" With such extensive evidence, leading social psychologists seem to be in almost universal agreement with Stanley Milgram, who concluded, "*The social psychology of this century reveals a major lesson: often it is not so much the kind of person a man is as the kind of situation in which he finds himself that determines how he will act.*"

Due to the abundance of authoritative research, most leading social psychologists today take a strongly "situational" view of the origin of evil behavior. On the other hand, the notion that "evil people"—people whose intrinsic nature is completely bad—are the sole cause of evil is still intractably imbedded in the popular imagination in the West. As the Dalai Lama has said, when bad events occur, there is often a tendency to select a few individuals and place all the blame on them. This simplistic idea—that evil people are the "cause" of violence and evil—is unlikely to help us truly understand the nature of violence and evil or find real solutions. This view is about as helpful as a theory that there is an evil little homunculus spontaneously growing inside the skull of an evil person until it pops out of the person's ear at night, fully formed, ready to unleash its evil deeds upon the world.

However, while there is no doubt that situational circumstances can affect our behavior, the idea that evil is simply the result of temporary situational forces or conditions acting upon ordinary healthy people can be another extreme, with a limited scope of understanding. The situational forces and conditions are factors on one level. But as the Dalai Lama points out, there can be causes of violence on other levels as well. For example, during the Holocaust there could have been considerable variation in "evil" conduct: Some concentration camp guards were known to deliberately smash infants to death against a wall while forcing the mothers to watch, force daughters to have sex with their fathers, force women to have sex with horses, throw inmates into a latrine and drown them in feces . . . the horrors are limitless. But not every guard committed such atrocities. Such acts clearly go far beyond simple obedience, beyond what one would expect of situational forces acting on an ordinary, decent person.

To fully understand the origins of evil in those cases, one must look beyond merely the situational conditions and look at the personal level as well, recognizing the role of powerful *inner forces* motivating such acts: pure hatred. Of course, people are not born with hatred, so *broader societal conditions* could play a role here—such as virulent anti-Semitism in this case, acquired from social conditioning, propaganda, education, and other sources.

However, when looking at the causes of violence on various levels, the Dalai Lama began the discussion by pointing out that at the most fundamental level one can trace the roots of violence to the human mind, to the destructive emotions and the distortions of thinking that are linked with these emotions. This was the topic that we now went on to address.

Chapter 8

THE ROOTS OF VIOLENCE

Our Emotions and the Distortion of Reality

Since wars begin in the minds of men, it is in the minds of men that we must erect the ramparts of peace.—FROM THE UNESCO CHARTER

"YOUR HOLINESS, in identifying the causes of violence we have discussed how there can be many causes and conditions on different levels. You mentioned, for instance, some wider causes such as social conditioning, which can make a society more prone to act out with violence. Or, on another level, you mentioned factors such as situational circumstances or the influences of one's particular community or family. These sorts of causes can generally be considered external factors. But you began by saying how the roots of violence can be traced to the human mind, our destructive emotions, and distortions of thinking."

"That's right," the Dalai Lama affirmed.

"So now I would like to turn to some of the internal factors, the emotions and characteristic ways of thinking that may play a role here."

"Yes. Good. Perhaps one of the most crucial things to recognize is at the root of much of human conflict and violence are certain destructive states of mind. For example, when you are under the influence of negative emotions like anger, hatred, fear, extreme attachment, and greed, this tends to open you up to mental projections and distortions of thinking which obscure you from truly understanding the reality of the situation, and this can lead to greater conflict."

"Regarding these negative emotions, I can certainly understand how critical it is to address these in order to get at the roots of violence," I agreed. "After all, emotions like anger and hatred are at the very core of violence, and emotions like fear are inextricably bound to these kinds of problems—in fact, fear is not only a pervasive state of mind in today's uncertain world, as a result of things like the threat of terrorism, but it also plays a role in the generation of violence. For example, aggression is one way people might react to fear.

"But as far as your suggestion that we don't see reality clearly in conflict situations, I'm not entirely sure about that," I argued, "because in one sense, when you look at conflict situations, you might find one or both of the parties *are* looking at the reality. I mean the 'reality' is essentially the same thing as the objective facts. And you can have conflicts in which the parties are looking at what happened, objectively, and reacting based on that. For example, a suicide bomber deliberately blows up and massacres babies and schoolchildren. Or, on an individual level, maybe someone is harmed by another, assaulted, or maybe someone was robbed or cheated or whatever. The victim may react with anger and violence perhaps, but at the same time they still may be looking at the very real, objective facts, of what the other person did, how many people they killed or whatever—I don't think there is necessarily a distortion of the reality of the situation. In other words, sometimes the reality of the situation is that it is an ugly situation. That's the reality."

"Well, Howard, these situations can be very complicated, which is why, if we are discussing these things, sometimes it is best to take things on a case-by-case basis. But anyway, what you are saying may be true. But in your example, although the person may be looking at the objective facts, still they may be looking at only *some* of the facts, only *part* of the full picture. While the evidence they may be looking at may be true or accurate, looking at only some of the facts and ignoring others represents a kind of distortion of the full reality. In any situation there are many levels, many aspects, many causes and conditions related to a particular event—and to see the *true* reality, one must take into consideration *all* the key facts."

"That's true," I admitted.

"So," he went on, "if you really examine these conflict situations involving violence, I think you'll often find that people do not see the problem realistically. A kind of *narrowing of vision takes place,* as if seeing the problem through a certain kind of mental filter. And one thing that seems to be true is that strong emotions lead to unrealistic thinking. In fact, all of the afflictive or destructive emotions have the potential to become obstacles to seeing reality clearly."

"This link between distortions of thinking and destructive emotions reminds me in a way of cognitive psychology, which is based on this idea," I observed. "For example, it is well recognized that certain distorted or irrational ways of thinking can lead to depression. So, I'm just wondering—you mention how destructive emotions can lead to distortions of thinking, but do you feel that it works the other way as well? In other words, do you think that distortions or misperceptions in thinking can lead to disturbances of emotions—and can create or contribute to anger, hatred, fear, greed, and so on?"

"Oh, yes. It works both ways," he said. "In fact, hatred and all the afflictive emotions are based on a distortion of reality; they are states of mind that arise on the basis of misperceiving the reality of the situation. . . ."

"For example?"

"For example . . . I had a firsthand personal experience of seeing how this unfolds. In the seventies I visited the Soviet Union and I noticed how even the ordinary people there genuinely believed that the West hated them so much and that they were ready to attack at any time! As I had already been to Western European countries by then, I knew that this was not true—it was a complete distortion of reality. But the perception of the West as a real threat made them a legitimate object of hatred."

Something about his example seemed to miss the mark for me. "I don't know, Your Holiness, it seems that your example involves fear and hatred arising from a factual error, a mistaken belief about the West's motivations and intentions. But here we are talking about destructive emotions and distortions of thinking as causes of violence. And somehow it seems to me that the problem runs deeper than a mere error in facts, that the afflictive emotions and distortions of thinking are a cause of violence on a much broader and more fundamental human level. . . ."

Nodding in agreement he said slowly, "Yes, that is true." Then in a methodical, analytic way, the Dalai Lama went on to explain. "For instance, one way that human beings are different from other animals is that we have this wonderful human intelligence. This intelligence can be used in wonderful ways, constructive ways. But at other times, it can get us into trouble. So, for example, as compared with other animals we humans have a much greater capacity to plan for the future. We also have a highly developed memory, the capacity to think about long past. Well, in many conflict situations you may find people reacting based on events that took place in the past, sometimes even many centuries ago. They are unwilling to look at the reality of the present situation, clinging so strongly to conditions that are no longer even present. This represents a kind of distortion of thinking, a narrowing of one's perception. . . ."

"In what way do the destructive emotions relate to this kind of distortion of thinking?" I asked.

"For example, hatred is the most powerful fuel for these situations. Anger is a component of the feeling of hatred, but hatred seems to have another component—it encourages a clinging on to a past event, some kind of perceived wrong. This creates a grudge, and a desire for some kind of vengeance. So, sometimes I mention that hatred prevents you from moving on—it chains you to the past. In fact, a key premise on which the concept of reconciliation is based is not to react with strong anger to events that have already passed."

As the Dalai Lama spoke, I could not help but think about the virtually infinite capacity of human beings to hold on to past grievances. It seemed to have no limit. Later, after returning home from Dharamsala, I began to notice, for instance, how in committing atrocities in the twenty-first century, Islamic extremists routinely dwell on events that happened many centuries ago as part of their justification for murdering innocent civilians today. Although I had not paid much attention to it before, I began to notice the common practice among Islamic terrorist groups and militants of regularly referring to the Crusades to stir up hatred and violence, using the term "crusaders" to refer to all Western nations as well as all Christians. . . .

In fact, many Islamic leaders have become very skilled in evoking the past to accomplish their own ends. Slobodan Milošević, for example, the Serbian leader later to be charged with crime against humanity and genocide, marked his emergence as a powerful political force by committing an act that was sure to trigger an emotional response and stir up hatred among the Serbs. He deliberately went to Kosovo to give a rousing speech at the site of the Battle of Kosovo Polje, the spot where the Serbs were defeated by the Ottoman Turks in 1389. By playing upon deep-seated Serb fears of defeat and subjugation, he could strengthen his own power, and later push people to commit acts that they might otherwise have refused to do.

The Dalai Lama points out how historical issues will often play a role in large-scale violent conflicts, issues that evoke destructive emotions such as hatred and fear—one or both groups reacting in the present based on being hurt or wounded in the past, reacting based on historical threats to their existence, conditions that now exist only in the imagination of the combatants. As destructive emotions such as hatred and fear take root in a society, infiltrating the collective psyche of the population, judgment becomes infected, making the population more susceptible to decisions based on distorted thinking, exaggeration, and lies—and more vulnerable to manipulation by leaders or government propaganda.

Later in this chapter we will point out how the destructive emotions not only cause changes in our way of thinking but also cause characteristic changes in our body. Researchers have recently discovered how hormones such as epinephrine (adrenaline), which are released when we feel fear can cause stored memories to become much more vivid, much stronger, and more tenacious memories than nonemotional memories. Of course, this makes sense because fear functions to alert us to threats or dangers, and it is adaptive to store away strong memories of things that are a threat to one's existence. But when the widespread fears engendered by war, terrorism, atrocities, and even genocide become stored in the collective memory of entire populations, they also become stronger and more tenacious—which is why it is so easy for leaders to manipulate the public by evoking these historical memories, why Osama bin Laden constantly refers to "crusaders," why Slobodan Milošević went to the site of the Battle of Kosovo Polje to stir up ethnic fears and hatred.

Thus, using rhetoric to stir up fear based on these historical events, leaders can manipulate populations to travel down a path to war, to terrorism, to genocide—no evil is beyond the scope of those driven by the intoxicating cocktail of fear, hatred, and prejudice. Such violence can even become part of an endless cycle passed down from generation to generation, with fear causing aggression and violence, and violence creating more fear, which in turn causes more violence.

Recognizing that ultimately the only way to prevent such violence is to uproot it at its source, we continued our investigation, tracing the development of violence back to its origins in the human mind, to destructive emotions and distortions of thinking.

"You know, Your Holiness, when discussing the roots of violence on an inner level, it is easy to see how the negative emotions can lead to violence—not only emotions like anger, hatred, and fear, but emotions like jealousy and greed are often behind acts of violence as well.

But just as there are a variety of negative emotions that can be involved in violence, there may also be a variety of ways that our thinking can become distorted, different ways that our perception can become narrowed. For example, you just mentioned one way—the tendency to focus narrowly on the past, so we lose sight of the present reality and the future. I'm wondering if you can discuss some of the other ways that our thinking or perception can become distorted."

"Yes," he replied. "Now this is very important. *This narrowing of perspective, for example, can be associated with failure to see the situation in a wider context, and the inability to adopt a long-term perspective. This can limit our ability to find the most appropriate solution to a problem. Of course, the tendency to see things in absolute terms, as black or white, which is common in the West, is something we have discussed in the past. These tendencies often lead to inflexibility in one's point of view and the failure to see any possible middle ground. There can also be a lack of willingness to look for common interests in a situation where we are trying to resolve conflicts through dialogue.*"

Becoming more and more animated as he discussed the various types of distorted thinking, he explained, "I think one of the most dangerous manifestations of this kind of narrow perspective is our tendency to oversimplify and generalize, which is particularly common in times of crisis. I remember at one press conference I was asked whether I saw what happened on September 11 as an indication of a fundamental clash of two civilizations. So, I asked, 'What two civilizations are you talking about?' He answered that one was Western Christian civilization and other was Muslim civilization. So I immediately told him, 'Absolutely no!' that is not how I see that event. To me, bin Laden is an individual, he is an Arab person, and also he is a Muslim, yes, but at the same time he cannot stand for the entire Islamic civilization. To me, what happened on September 11 was to a large extent a consequence of a particular individual and his group's actions and their motivation, their resentment and hatred. So it does not represent a clash of civilizations!"

As always, the Dalai Lama's clarity of mind and reasoning were flawless. But sadly, I thought, there are always others who don't agree:

"In a war of civilizations," Osama bin Laden has said, "our goal is for our nation to unite in the face of the Christian crusade.... This is a recurring war."

The Dalai Lama continued. "I think this 'clash of civilizations' is very dangerous language. If we start seeing conflicts in the light of a clash of civilizations, then we will start believing that civilizations are inherently in conflict with each other, thus we will begin to behave consistent with that view—making it more difficult to identify with the other groups."

Sighing, he went on. "But it seems that people will have this tendency to generalize and to oversimplify things. And I think that one of the key elements of this oversimplification is, as I mentioned, a distortion of reality. In this case the distortion mainly involves a kind of exaggeration—exaggerating the nature and scope of a particular event, for example, but also the dangerous tendency to exaggerate our differences, as opposed to what ties us together.

"In fact, you'll find this kind of thing everywhere. Here in India, for example, sometimes you may have some violence take place within a community. But instead of focusing on resolving that particular situation and dealing with the specific individuals responsible for the act, some Hindu leader may proclaim, 'Look, this is what the *Muslims* do to us *Hindus*! Or, some Muslim leader may equally say, 'Look at what the *Hindus* are doing to *us*!' And the moment they overgeneralize and exaggerate in this way, it evokes a different kind of response, creating unrest within these communities. I feel that this is not good, it's absolutely wrong. Actually, it is a kind of manipulation."

Suddenly he began to chuckle. "You know, speaking of our tendency to exaggerate, this reminds me of a story. I remember once an elderly lady from western Tibet came to see me and she was telling me about her experience of Chinese persecution. Of course, what she was telling me was a very serious and tragic matter, but as she told her story, her tone and manner became more and more exaggerated, until by the end of the story, she exclaimed, 'And we were all imprisoned, and we all *died*!'" The Dalai Lama laughed. "I mean, here she was standing right there in front of me, and in this really exaggerated tone, telling me that she had died!"

His laughter faded as he said, "More seriously, I think that actually there is one other way that this tendency to oversimplify and generalize can be very dangerous. Now sometimes you will see that leaders, whether political or religious, like to use certain simplistic labels like 'This group is evil' or 'That group is evil' to stir people up. There can even be a kind of deliberate manipulation. I think this tendency to see things in black and white, as all good or all bad, can really lead to so many problems."

"Problems such as . . . ?"

"If you view the person as intrinsically evil, as a permanent and unchangeable part of their nature, there would be a greater tendency to see getting rid of the person as the only solution. In Buddhism, where we recognize cause and effect, and understand that there are particular causes and conditions that lead the person to act in a negative or destructive way, and thus recognize it can be a temporary condition, it opens up the potential to change."

He continued. "So, basically, if we are looking at the dangers of this kind of labeling people 'evil,' I see two main dangers. First, when you characterize someone as intrinsically evil and explain their behavior on that basis, it prevents us from looking deeper into the real roots and causes of that behavior. It can even result in deliberately avoiding the real problem. When this happens, unfortunately we will fail to learn how to effectively prevent similar acts in future. That is the cost. By blaming Hitler as the evil force behind all the atrocities committed during World War II, for example, there might be a tendency to not look for other causes, so one could ignore the role played by the German people and political and cultural conditions of the society during the Nazi period.

"The second main danger," the Dalai Lama continued, "is when the label 'evil' is applied to an individual or group of people, it naturally sort of demonizes that person or group. *Once this kind of perception takes root, a process of dehumanization takes place.* They are seen as subhuman. And if we no longer see the person as a human being, as someone like ourselves, then we have no common ground. They are seen as subhuman. *And without common ground, there is no basis for empathy to arise. The end result of this is that it opens the door to justifying any injustice done against them, any horror, any atrocity, even genocide."*

Shaking his head, he sighed and added softly, "You know, Howard, when it comes to the afflictive emotions and the distortions of thinking that accompany them, these can become the source not only of violence but of so many problems. We find that these distortions of thinking, that kind of narrowing effect on our thinking or perception, can manifest in so many ways to cause misery and undermine the basis of our happiness."

"Well, Your Holiness, now that we have sort of diagnosed the problem, identified these destructive emotions and the distorted, narrowed ways of thinking as the root cause of violence, we can go on to talk about the cure tomorrow, how to deal with the negative emotions and overcome the narrowed ways of thinking."

"Very good," said the Dalai Lama, with a warm, open smile. "So, I'll see you tomorrow."

As it turned out, while we did end up examining one critical emotion—fear—in great depth that week, it would be quite some time before we returned to a discussion of how to overcome negative emotions and the distorted, narrowed ways of thinking that could act as both a cause and as a result of negative emotions.

The Dalai Lama points out that the roots of violence can ultimately be traced back to our destructive emotions and their capacity to distort our perception of reality. In order to understand the role of negative emotions and distortions of thinking as causes of violence, it can be helpful to briefly review what are emotions, why we have them, and why they are associated with distortions of thinking. First, although we categorize certain emotions as negative or destructive, it is important to remember that every human emotion evolved for a constructive purpose—from a broad evolutionary perspective, all emotions were designed to help us survive and reproduce. The emotions evolved to prepare us to deal very quickly with the vital events in our lives. The English word "emotion" comes from a Latin word expressing the idea of "movement," and the emotions in general are highly effective mechanisms for getting us to take heed of a situation and move us in a direction that is important for our welfare and survival. The "destructive" emotions in general were actually designed to help us to immediately react to dangerous or life-threatening situations and respond in a way that will increase our odds of survival. They tell us that something "bad" has happened or is about to happen, and suggest a particular course of action. In fact, they *strongly* recommend a certain course of action. Of course, emotions also have other useful roles—particularly in communication, where they help communicate our inner state to others, through characteristic facial expressions or body postures. In recent years there have been some new theories about the functions of positive emotions as well, which we will explore later on.

As we discussed earlier, the basic anatomy of the brain evolved during the Pleistocene epoch, a period when our environment was likely to produce far more potentially deadly situations than today. The basic negative emotions—e.g., fear, disgust, anger, sadness—evolved as very efficient solutions to dealing with the recurrent problems that our remote ancestors faced. Each of these emotions have their own adaptive function. For example, fear helps us respond to threats or danger; disgust, with its primal urge to expel, was designed to help us avoid contamination or reject potentially toxic foods; anger helped prepare us to fight or attack, of course, but can also serve as a signal or warning when something is thwarting us; and sadness likely encouraged us to take a necessary time-out to regroup after a loss, to be cautious, to conserve our energy, and no doubt it also elicited help from others. Thus, each emotion has its own purpose or objective, so each one is associated with its own characteristic way of feeling, thinking, and acting that are custom-designed to help us accomplish those objectives.

Since most of these negative emotions were designed to help us deal with critical or life-threatening events, where a fraction of a second could make a difference, they had to get us moving very quickly and decisively. In these kinds of dangerous situations there is no time to consciously analyze the problem in depth, so the emotions kick in even before the information is fully processed in the neocortex, the thinking center of the brain. As we mentioned earlier, the manufacturing site of the negative emotions is in the brain's limbic system, in structures such as the amygdala, which is responsible for producing emotions such as fear or hostility. The unpleasant-feeling tone of a negative emotion may not be very fun, but it serves us well by calling our attention to what is going on, making us attend to the business at hand and "moving" us toward dealing with the situation. The sense of imminent doom that characterizes the emotion of fear, for example, may be quite uncomfortable, but it is that discomfort which assures our full attention, encourages us not to dawdle, and galvanizes us to take preventive action.

Of course, emotions are not just associated with a "feeling"; each of the emotions is also associated with changes in our way of thinking and characteristic changes in the body. Messages sent out along neural pathways from the limbic system to the neocortex can influence our ways of thinking. There are also complex connections between the limbic system and other parts of the brain as well as various organs in the body. Messages transmitted along those neural pathways or circuits can cause rapid changes throughout the entire body. In regard to these physical changes, each negative emotion is associated with a specific "action tendency," a series of physiological changes that mobilize support for specific actions—actions that are meant to prepare us to respond to danger or help assure our survival.

To better understand this process, we can use "fear" as an example. Fear is our protective mechanism that alerts us to danger, particularly life-threatening situations, and like other emotions it prepares us to quickly respond in a way that will help assure our survival. So, how does it do this? After our sense organs perceive the potential threat, the sensory information is sent to the amygdala, which first makes sure we feel motivated to take some action by creating the unpleasant feeling of impending doom. Then it gets our body ready to act: Instantly messages are sent out through hardwired neural circuits, making direct contact with target organs in some cases, and in other cases stimulating glands to release chemical messengers such as hormones, which travel through the bloodstream to other target organs.

These messages cause a cascade of events throughout the body, all preparing the body to do what it needs to do in order to survive: Heart rate and blood pressure rise, preparing us for action. Breathing speeds up, delivering more oxygen. Muscles tense. Perception sharpens. Sweat starts to break out, in case the body needs a little evaporative cooling after a hard run. Stress hormones such as adrenaline or cortisol surge through the body. These hormones act to enhance essential functions, directing the flow of blood to the muscles, particularly big muscles of the legs or arms, preparing us to run or fight. They mobilize our stores of energy by releasing glucose from the liver for quick energy, and even cause changes in the blood platelets to make sure blood clots quickly if the body is injured. At the same time, messages are sent to shut down nonessential functions, temporarily suspending activity of the digestive system, reproductive system, or immune system—after all, if you are being chased by a homicidal maniac with an ax, your brain figures that maybe the moment isn't the best time to be taking a break for a little afternoon sex, or digesting a nice meal and storing some fat for the winter, or doing a bit of internal housekeeping by making some antibodies to fight an infection.

These physiological changes are often called the stress response or fight-or-flight reaction. They can help prepare us for a general defensive action or more specific kinds of behavioral responses depending on the nature of the danger. Such responses could include escape, or aggression if the person cannot escape. Freezing or immobilization is another potential response to fear, which would be appropriate if one is about to go over a cliff, or if the best means of survival is concealment, and in some cases this may even inhibit the attack reflex of some predators.

We can see how these physical changes associated with the negative emotions can be quite useful in the life-threatening situations they were designed for. However, in a sense these changes can be seen as having a limiting or "narrowing" effect on our behavior. These "action-tendencies," the preprogrammed physiological changes in the body associated with the emotions, are urging the person to take a particular course of action, such as fight, run, vomit (i.e., with the emotion of "disgust"), etc. You can still choose any action you want—although the emotion of fear, for example, may prepare the body to escape, you are not *compelled* to run away, and may still decide to sing an aria or lie down and take a nap. But one's course of action here is "narrowed" in the sense that the body is "primed" for a more limited and specific course of action.

Of course, in addition to the physical effects, the negative emotions can also have effects on our ways of thinking. The combination of effects on the body and mind are sometimes called the thought-action tendencies. The Dalai Lama pointed out that the negative emotions tend to distort our thinking, having a kind of "narrowing" effect on our perception, just as they have a narrowing effect on our behavior. Thus, we can say that the negative emotions have an overall narrowing effect on our thought-action tendencies.

The essential question is, how do the negative emotions and their narrowed ways of thinking, which cause us to distort and misperceive reality, lead to violence and destructive behavior? After all, that's the Dalai Lama's main premise here. To answer this, it is helpful to first take a closer look at the specific changes in thinking caused by the destructive emotions.

Scientific research has provided evidence confirming that negative emotions in general tend to have a "narrowing" effect on our thinking. This makes sense if we look once again at the reason why the negative emotions evolved. In life-threatening situations, our odds of survival are the greatest if we are able to use all of our cognitive resources to deal with the problem at hand—if you focus all of your attention, all of your brain power and thinking capacity, on how to survive that particular situation at that very moment. So, by its very nature, your thinking and perception are narrowed in those situations—limited to the problem at hand, focusing on the present moment.

Now, in these dangerous situations, where even a fraction of a second can make a difference, speed and decisiveness in dealing with the situation are critical. To maximize our survival, there's no time for the brain to send information upstairs to the higher thinking centers of the neocortex, taking time to analyze our situation, deliberate, and consciously decide what is the best course of action—instead, we are automatically programmed to react using some of the more primitive brain mechanisms that we discussed earlier in the context of prejudice and stereotyping. Your brain will want to quickly categorize what you are dealing with, relying on simple binary categories, "black or white" thinking—safe or dangerous, and so on. This kind of thinking will conserve your cognitive resources, assure that you act quickly and efficiently, and so on, but this comes at a price: You'll focus your thinking on the threat in front of you, increasing your odds of survival, but at the expense of long-term thinking. The black or white thinking will allow you to react quickly, but at the expense of seeing the "gray areas."

These types of distortions will limit your awareness of any wider issues involved in the problem that you are dealing with. Unfortunately, this kind of thinking hijacks reasoning, logic, and critical thinking by largely bypassing the centers of higher thinking in the brain. This explains why the changes in our way of thinking caused by the negative emotions limits our ability to find solutions to our problems. It explains why this kind of thinking prevents us from finding common ground or compromise positions when attempting to successfully resolve our conflicts without resorting to violence—both of which were concerns expressed by the Dalai Lama during our discussion.

These kinds of "narrowed" thinking are common to all the negative emotions, but as we mentioned, each of the negative emotions was custom designed to help deal with a particular type of danger. So, in addition to the *general narrowing effects* of negative emotions, *each of the negative emotions has its own specific distortions of thinking, specific effects on a person's judgment and decision making* that can be distinguished from the rest of the negative emotions. Since each emotion is associated with a specific way of judging what is going on, and a characteristic tendency to make certain kinds of choices or decisions, this can be seen as another kind of distortion, or narrowing of thinking.

The characteristic distortions of thinking caused by anger are well documented, and can serve as a good example of the more specific narrowing and distorting effects of negative emotions. Extensive research has confirmed the Dalai Lama's observations that when angry people think about a situation or person, or when they seek to solve a problem, they tend to oversimplify facts, think very quickly and superficially, and come to quick judgments. Their thinking is thus narrowed, or limited, by filtering out details and avoiding deeper investigation or analysis. This can be distinguished, for instance, from the distorting effects of sadness, as sad people process information by *focusing in* on details, and they may engage in more extensive analysis, but they filter out the bigger picture, and may selectively focus on information that reinforces their sad mood.

When making decisions, angry people also tend to have an underlying feeling of certainty about their facts or opinions, which can lead to a feeling of confidence and optimism but also can impair their ability to be objective or rational.

These tendencies can be traced back to anger's most basic function—when we are frustrated or thwarted in achieving a goal, anger kicks in to remove the obstacle. The cause is seen as something external that we must fight against or overcome. So, for example, this general orientation toward dealing with some kind of threat or obstacle is associated with the tendency to see external agents as the cause of the problem, and with the characteristic tendency to blame others whenever anger is elicited. In fact, studies have shown that the mere experience of anger can automatically activate ways of thinking that lead to prejudice.

These characteristic ways of thinking also cause angry people to become more punitive when given the opportunity to inflict harm on others. For example, in one study, anger was induced in a group of subjects, then later they were asked to evaluate a series of fictional court cases, having nothing to do with the issue that made them angry—the angry individuals tended to blame the defendants much more and to recommend harsher punishments.

This experiment also pointed out another very problematic aspect of the destructive emotions: The effects on one's thinking and behavior tend to persist, and left unchecked, they will carry over to other situations having nothing to do with the original event that triggered the emotions. There has been a large body of scientific evidence showing how one's subsequent judgment or decisions can be influenced by a negative emotion—even when the individual is unaware of this. Studies have been done on employees in workplace settings, for example, showing how a subject's anger seeped over to his judgments of co-workers and acquaintances, such that angry participants were less trusting of these individuals, even though they had nothing to do with the reason for the person's anger. In such cases, until the emotion is resolved, there will be a tendency, or "cognitive predisposition," to see subsequent events through an unconscious perceptual lens—where the person will interpret events in a distorted way, which will of course influence their judgment and decisions.

In our discussion, the Dalai Lama explained how destructive emotions can cause changes in thinking that tend to distort and obscure reality. He explained how some of these common distortions of thinking, such as lack of awareness of long-term consequences of our actions, black or white thinking, failure to look at the wider issues contributing to a problem, and so on, are the source of much human misery and suffering. In discussing the link between destructive emotions and distortions of thinking, he also pointed out another critical issue: Not only can destructive emotions cause distortions of thinking, but distortions of thinking can also cause destructive emotions; it can work both ways. This is highly significant, because if factors like social conditioning, propaganda, manipulative leaders, or situational circumstances act to distort one's thinking and perception, under some conditions this may generate or intensify destructive emotions such as anger and hatred, with potentially disastrous results.

In identifying this potential cause of violence, the Dalai Lama brought up the example of using rhetoric such as "good and evil," which encourages people to oversimplify and distort reality, to manipulate people to act aggressively or violently. In fact, that has been a common strategy used by leaders of all kinds throughout history in every corner of the world. In the hours following 9/11, for example, as the American government scrambled to identify the perpetrators of the atrocity, and Osama bin Laden was discovered to be the culprit, Americans were desperately calling for information about this unknown figure. In response, President George W. Bush said, "The only thing I know about him for certain is that *he's evil!*"

Now, one would guess that there might be a few things that the president would immediately want to know about bin Laden, a few useful facts to share. And bin Laden wasn't unknown to U.S. government law enforcement agencies at that time, and had been on their radar screen even during the previous administration. But all Bush knew for certain was that the man was "*evil.*" Apparently that was all we really needed to know.

In the coming days, the world would hear about al Qaeda, which Bush also characterized as "evil." Not long after that, we learned that al Qaeda was being supported by the Taliban in Afghanistan. The Taliban were now "evil." As the weeks passed, President Bush's language suddenly became much more liberally peppered with the rhetoric of Good and Evil—a fact later confirmed by a University of Washington study carefully analyzing his speeches both pre- and post-9/11. And so the evil grew—by the time of the president's State of the Union address only four months later, entire countries had been added to the list: Iraq, Iran, and North Korea had become "*an axis of evil.*" This is the type of rhetoric that leaders will often use to mobilize popular support for a war—wars such as the invasions of Afghanistan and Iraq, which followed the terrorist attack of September 11.

At the end of our conversation, the Dalai Lama pointed out how our destructive emotions and distorted ways of thinking can cause immense suffering and misery. Because of this, it is critical to develop strategies to reduce our destructive emotions and correct our distortions of thinking. But before turning to a broader discussion of the antidotes to our negative emotions and distorted ways of thinking, our conversation first took a detour to more closely investigate how to deal with one specific negative emotion—an emotion of critical importance in relation to the many problems of today's world.

Chapter 9

DEALING WITH FEAR

"YOUR HOLINESS, we have been talking about the roots of violence, tracing it back to human emotions and ways of thinking. In this context, I think there is one emotion in particular that is critical to explore in greater depth: fear. Aside from hatred and violence, I think fear is perhaps the greatest destroyer of human happiness. In fact, among all of the negative emotions, I would guess that fear is responsible for the most human suffering, particularly in its capacity to create violence on a wide scale—probably more significant than even anger in that regard, since wars are based more on fear than anger. And it can become a vicious cycle—not only does fear have the potential to create violence, but violence in a society of course creates fear. In fact the goal of terrorism is to create terror, not just harm others with violence.

"So I'm wondering if you have any thoughts about how to deal with the kind of fear that can take root in a society following events such as 9/11," I asked. But then as an afterthought, I added, "Well, come to think of it, the scope of our discussion doesn't need to be limited to the fear of terrorism. Because the thing I'm really wondering about is how to deal with fear in general, no matter what its source—for example, there can be widespread fear during times of economic or financial uncertainty or crisis, and so on."

The Dalai Lama replied, "Yes. I think that if you really want to develop the most effective way to deal with that kind of fear, you need to begin by identifying the different categories of fear, so you can apply the appropriate method of dealing with each one. . . ."

"Different categories in what sense?" I asked.

"One category is fear that is valid. Realistic fears, where there is a real threat or danger. The appropriate response to this legitimate kind of fear is to have a sense of precaution and take active measures to protect yourself, to whatever extent is possible."

"You know, Your Holiness, this reminds me that we have been addressing the destructive nature of fear, but of course fear and anxiety can also have a positive function. I mean that from a biological and evolutionary perspective, the fear center in the brain was designed as an alert system, to warn us of life-threatening or dangerous situations."

"That's true," he agreed. "In fact, besides bringing about a more cautious or vigilant attitude, there may be other positive functions of fear, depending on the circumstances. For example, you might view a fear of terrorism as destructive from one perspective, but on the other hand, that kind of fear might even bring a community closer together, making you feel more appreciative of your neighbors. That's a possibility."

Suddenly chuckling, he commented, "So many possibilities! It seems that human beings' thoughts, conceptions, and perspectives have no end!"

"Of course," I pointed out, "this alert system in the brain switches on the fight-or-flight response in the body—preparing the body to either run away and escape or to act aggressively, in order to assure our survival. But one problem is that in the modern world, most of us are not regularly encountering life-threatening situations—yet our brains are still acting as if we are."

"Yes, exactly," he said, "which brings us to the other category of fear—unrealistic or unreasonable fears. These are fears based on exaggeration, mental projection, and false beliefs. This can be very common, because like the other negative emotions we discussed, fear also has a strong potential to distort reality and obscure our understanding of the situation in the correct way.

"*So, the main approach here is to investigate the conditions giving rise to the fear, investigate to what extent the threat is real and imminent, or an unrealistic projection based on exaggeration and distortion. We need to be able to recognize at what point a reasonable fear becomes unreasonable, the point at which our emotional reactions become excessive and counterproductive, rather than being an appropriate response to danger.*"

"Of course," I said, "even if an individual is able to distinguish real from exaggerated or imaginary fears, one is still left with the need to find ways to cope with real fears. I mean, how do you deal with a valid fear based on very real dangers, and yet there are no precautions you can take, nothing you can do? For example, in the U.S. following 9/11, the government broadcast a terror alert system, where the level of danger was indicated by color codes, such as yellow, orange, and red. But even if the level of threat was high, there was really nothing a person could do about it. It just created an atmosphere of fear."

"Now this can be a little complicated," he said. "I think that in general in situations where a person is experiencing fear, even when there is some real threat there, a kind of distortion of reality will take place, and this fear will very often exaggerate the perception of danger. So, in this case the alert system may have created the impression of increased danger everywhere throughout the country. Now, our basic approach to fear is first investigating the reality of the situation. So, as real as the danger may be, if one investigates the level of danger in your particular place, you might discover that the level of threat might not be the same throughout all of America—it might not be as great in certain rural areas, for example. Then one can respond according to the reality of your situation. I think that even a slight element of exaggeration can contribute to greater fear. So, this approach can at least reduce or eliminate whatever component of fear that is caused by one's imagination through exaggeration or distortion of reality. So, I think that the greater your awareness of reality, learning to distinguish between real and imaginary or projected fears, becoming more aware of how you may exaggerate or distort reality, the more effective you will be in dealing with fear."

Having already discussed the evolutionary basis of the destructive emotions, we can understand the reasons for the narrowing effect of the negative emotions. Like the other negative or destructive emotions, fear has its own unique kinds of distortions or narrowing effects on our thinking or perception. Specifically, as the Dalai Lama pointed out, fear creates a strong tendency to oversimplify and overgeneralize. This is not surprising, of course, since if there is any time that we might want to make quick judgments about what we are dealing with, quickly labeling a particular person or situation as belonging to a broad general "category," one that we are already familiar with, it is at a time when our life may be in imminent danger. And, in these life-or-death situations, where our existence is threatened, immediately simplifying what we are encountering, considering only the bare essentials—e.g., is this good or bad? and then getting the hell out of there if it is bad—is a pretty good game plan.

We can see how it was adaptive to generalize, even overgeneralize, in our remote past as a species—e.g., if we see a snake, it will help us survive if we quickly put this "animal" we're perceiving into the "snake" category and either running away or beating it with a club rather than take the time to consciously analyze the snake's markings to determine if it is poisonous or harmless. People who failed to categorize and label snakes quickly were likely to be bitten, and not likely to survive to pass down their genes. On the other hand, if one saw a vine or curved stick that resembled a snake, and one mistook it for a snake and jumped back quickly, i.e., if one "overgeneralized" and too quickly put that object in the "snake" category and mistakenly felt fear, then it would not hurt anything—the person would still survive. So we are set up to overgeneralize to begin with—to see sticks as snakes, and sometimes feel fear in response to illusions or distortions of reality.

In the modern world, however, we aren't generally dealing with snakes and sticks, and the influence of these kinds of distortions of thinking can be profound. The Dalai Lama mentioned, for instance, how fear can lead us to exaggerate dangers. This has been confirmed with an unusual experiment on emotions after 9/11, conducted by researchers at Carnegie Mellon University. Unlike most scientific studies, which often use small numbers of subjects, drawing them from the most handy fodder for scientific experiments—university undergraduate students—this study used a representative sample of one thousand Americans of all ages and backgrounds, measuring their emotional responses only days after 9/11 and then again several weeks later. The study revealed, first, that the media can have a strong influence on which emotions people experience—stories that showed people in Islamic countries cheering with joy after 9/11 elicited anger, and stories showing anthrax-laden letters going through the U.S. mail system elicited fear, as one might expect. The research also suggests that either anger or fear can be elicited by other means, such as leaders using certain kinds of rhetoric.

But the study also revealed how these emotions can cause distortions of thinking—such as exaggeration. *The investigators found that individuals responding with fear tended not only to greatly overestimate the danger of themselves becoming a victim of terrorism within the following year but also led them to overestimate other kinds of threats and dangers* (although consistently estimating themselves to be at less risk than the average American). In fact, researchers feel that fear likely fueled the sense of pessimism that contributed to the national economic downturn after September 11. Even though fear tended to cause people to embellish the true degree of threat, it led to the call for tighter security in the United States and a greater willingness to give up certain freedoms in the name of "security."

So, we can see that the propagation of fear within a society can have widespread effects on individual behavior as well as public policy. Fear can lead to horrors beyond imagination, since it can be a major factor in mobilizing populations to support wars, genocidal actions, and atrocities of all kinds. As we have seen, fear arises from our most primitive urges resulting from activation of the amygdala. The primitive brain mechanisms involved here include simplification, generalization, and Us and Them categorization—all prime ingredients for stereotyping. Now, when strong superior/inferior divisions and hatred are thrown into the mix, all it takes is for some leader or government propaganda to plant the idea that our existence is *threatened* in some way by the "inferior" group, to trigger the type of fear that leads to mass violence.

Some years ago, a politician was explicit in describing the use of fear: "Of course the people don't want war," he said, "but after all, it's the leaders of the country who determine the policy, and it's always a simple matter to drag the people along whether it's a democracy, a fascist dictatorship, or a parliament, or a communist dictatorship. Voice or no voice, the people can always be brought to the bidding of the leaders. That is easy. All you have to do is tell them they are being attacked, and denounce the pacifists for lack of patriotism and exposing the country to greater danger. This method works in any country."

The politician who said this was Nazi leader Hermann Göring, speaking in his cell during the Nuremberg trials to a U.S. forensic psychologist. This was part of Göring's rebuttal to the psychologist, who said that one difference between democracies and dictatorships is that in the United States of America, for instance, only Congress could resolve to declare war.

Fear evolved as our danger-alert system. It served our ancient ancestors well, helping them deal with the everyday dangers they were most likely to face. Fear still serves us well in dangerous or life-threatening situations. But at the same time, fear can get us into serious trouble— the fact is that sometimes the human brain isn't very good at reacting with fear to the right things, with disastrous consequences. Designed for an earlier period in human evolution, in the modern world fear is often activated in response to the wrong thing, at the wrong time, under the wrong conditions.

Experiments in which subjects have been conditioned to react with fear to photos of various objects (both living and inanimate), by first pairing the photos with mild electric shocks, have shown that the human brain has hardwired neural circuits that are more easily conditioned to fear snakes, spiders, or heights—common dangers our ancestors were likely to have trouble with—than harmless things like birds or butterflies. Unfortunately, our brain anatomy and neural circuits have not caught up with the modern world. We have a predisposition to fear snakes, spiders, or sharks, but not cigarettes or cars, which kill far more people but have not been around long enough to create fears that come prewired into the human brain. Studies have shown that our brains react to modern objects that are truly dangerous—e.g., guns, knives, or sticks of dynamite—the same way they respond to butterflies.

We become easily conditioned to fear all sorts of things that are not inherently dangerous, sometimes based on false beliefs and sometimes lies. As we saw in the discussion of prejudice, we are generally still programmed to react with fear when encountering those of other races or social groups, which has been a source of endless suffering in today's interdependent and multicultural world in which cooperation with other groups is essential for our survival.

As we've seen with our great human memory and imagination, we can be manipulated to react with fear in response to events that happened centuries ago. When we respond to things with fear based on false premises and beliefs, there is no limit to the human tragedy that can result.

Thus, because we can no longer trust that fear will always faithfully protect us from danger—and in fact because of its potential to cause disaster; our potential to be manipulated by fear; the potential for fear to arise based on distortions of reality, exaggeration, and lies; the potential for fear to undermine human happiness; the potential for it to rise up and destroy us—it becomes critical to remain vigilant. We need to use our human reason, judgment, and critical thinking to monitor our fears, to assure that we look at our fears realistically, as the Dalai

Lama suggests, to react with fear based on real threats rather than on imagination, exaggeration, and lies.

※

"Your Holiness, in view of the potential for fear to arise on the basis of imaginary or exaggerated threats, and the potential for fear to cause violence, I agree with your recommendation to first investigate to see if our fear is based in reality or not. And then if we find that we are exaggerating the level of danger, then this will decrease the level of our fear and reduce the potential for violence...."

"That's right."

"But still, my question is, how should people respond when there really *is* pervasive danger in their society? What about places like Israel, for instance? There have been periods where the Palestinian terrorist attacks seem to occur almost on a daily basis, with the terrorists deliberately targeting public areas, places where people go to shop or eat, specifically and deliberately killing and maiming innocent civilians, families, young couples, babies...."

"In this case," he said, "the danger is real, very real. And if you are living under such situations of danger, then your fear is valid and an appropriate response...."

"Well, that's my question: How does one deal with this feeling of pervasive fear in one's daily life? You can't totally stay home. You have to go out and live your life, but there is this underlying fear."

"There is no easy answer here," the Dalai Lama admitted. "Life sometimes presents dangerous situations. I think the very first place to start when learning to cope with such situations is with your basic outlook, recognizing that life will never be completely trouble-free, never totally danger-free. That you must accept. So, dangerous situations come up at times. For example, in the area where I live in India, recently there was a real indication of danger involving a conflict between Pakistan and India. Now the reality is that in a war, Pakistan would definitely be easily defeated. India, being a much bigger country, has an army three times the size of that of Pakistan's 250,000. India has more than double the strength, so naturally Pakistan will be defeated. Given this military reality, it is quite possible that out of desperation and with no room for moral or ethical consideration, Pakistan may choose to use their nuclear weapons against India. Delhi, being the capital, will most probably be on the top of the list. As the situation escalates, other bombs could be dropped, with radiations reaching Dharamsala, where I live."

He was speaking in such a matter-of-fact tone that I could not help but ask, "So, weren't you afraid when there was an escalation of tensions between those two countries?"

"Howard, living without fear under such potential dangers actually can be dangerous."

"Yeah, but what can a person do about it? The people in Dharamsala have no control over who is sending the nuclear bombs. It's not like, 'Okay, I'm going to be cautious, I'm going to avoid being hit by a bomb if we're attacked!'"

He replied, "Under such circumstances, you simply have to accept the possibility of something occurring. The community of Dharamsala cannot pick up and move elsewhere."

"Maybe the whole community can't move, but individuals can...."

"Some of my Indian friends from Delhi suggested that Dharamsala is very dangerous because of its proximity to Pakistan and therefore I should move and stay in Delhi. But I felt that suggestion was even more silly because Delhi could even be more of a target than Dharamsala. In the past when there were conflicts between India and Pakistan, I used to go down to the South Indian Tibetan settlements, but now because of their proximity to Bangalore, which is a very important metropolitan city, that option isn't particularly viable either," he said.

"Still, there must be options for you or others...."

The Dalai Lama replied firmly, "Dharamsala is my home. There is always some risk. One cannot remove all danger from life, that's just reality."

Feeling that he avoided my question about how to dispel valid fears, or perhaps hoping for a more concrete method or response, at least something more encouraging than "Life is tough," I took another stab at it.

"I'm just wondering, can you think of any other situations where you felt afraid?"

"Yes, at times I have felt some fear," he said candidly.

At my urging he went on to tell me about a time when law enforcement officials had uncovered some evidence indicating that he may have been in some physical danger from a few violent, radical members of an organization. It was a bit difficult for me to imagine him suffering from fear or anxiety, so I asked, "So, did you experience the normal symptoms of fear, like a feeling of nervousness, and so on?"

"Of course, as a human being I did. However, it did not affect me very much. For example, it did not disturb my sleep, not even for one night, or my appetite. Still, I was aware of the possibility of some danger."

"So how did you resolve that fear?" I asked.

"Now here, once again, that was a case of a valid fear. There was the possibility of some threat to my life, so there were some credible grounds for fear. As we mentioned, with the category of fear based on mental projections or false perception of reality, you can dispel the fear by adopting a more accurate understanding of the situation. But in this case it was the type of fear where there was a legitimate concern. So you need to prepare yourself for that possibility. So, here, of course, as a response to this we had the authorities take security concerns much more seriously and be more vigilant."

As I was hoping to explore with him an approach to dealing with fear that could be used by those of us who do not have security staff, I pressed on. "You know, I'm still wondering if there is an approach to dealing with the kind of fear that has a valid basis, but where there may be no immediate steps one can take to reduce the threat. Something to help one carry on with one's day-to-day life, without being inhibited by fear."

He said, "In this case, one can remain poised and remain vigilant, but other than that there is not much that can be done. . . ."

Perhaps sensing my dissatisfaction with his answer, he laughed, and added, "Well, Howard, I suppose there always might be some individuals who simply are not reflective enough to have any fear. Those who remain ignorant, oblivious to dangers, and go happily about their lives, fearless. . . ."

"Oh, you mean the lucky ones?" I joked.

"That's right, those lucky ones!" he repeated, laughing.

I felt he must have more to offer, knowing his ability to maintain such a positive state of mind in all circumstances. He seemed to speak of the possibility of his own and others' destruction without a trace of worry in his voice or manner, with a sense of complete fearlessness and acceptance, but without a sense of giving up, as if he were at peace with the idea, but with a tone of compassion, not an uncaring tone. Surely, I thought, that kind of attitude did not come about spontaneously; there must be an approach to cultivating it.

I decided to take another tack, become more concrete, still in hopes of some solution, some insight. "Well, let me ask you this: Has anybody in Dharamsala ever spoken to you about their fears of the nuclear war?"

"Yes."

"And what did you tell them? What did you advise them, when they came to you and said they were worried about the possibility of nuclear war?"

"I talked to them and told them that I, too, shared their concerns."

Still somehow unable or unwilling to accept his response, I continued to press on as if he had some kind of magic solution he had not yet revealed: "Well, when people came to you, your friends or family, and they expressed to you their fears about this nuclear war, isn't there anything more you can tell them other than sharing their concerns? I mean . . . is there anything you can say that would help relieve their fears or anxieties? No words of comfort you can give them?"

He shook his head sadly and with utter resignation quietly said, "There is not much. In any case, Howard, we mustn't forget that often what gives people comfort and assurance is the act of sharing their fears with someone they love. That can be very important."

As the shadows lengthened outside the Dalai Lama's room, it was clear the hour was growing late. The Dalai Lama's secretary and his attendants were waiting outside the door. The session was over for the day.

In discussing an approach to dealing with realistic fears, based on legitimate threats, the Dalai Lama begins with the simple act of accepting that some degree of danger is a natural part of human existence. This idea is one that he had frequently brought up in the past as a general strategy to deal with virtually any kind of problem or form of human suffering. He had explained in the past how our fundamental attitude about problems and suffering can affect how we cope with these things when they inevitably arise. Accepting suffering as a natural fact of human existence allows us to focus more on finding a solution to the problem, and less on feeling that life is unfair, that one is unfairly and unreasonably singled out for misfortune, becoming less caught up in the drama of the "victim" role.

But in this context, I was looking for a strategy to deal more specifically with realistic fears, and I found his advice in this case to be quite disappointing! With an air of resignation, at least as it seemed to me at the time, he had nothing to offer except the simplistic advice to talk about one's fears and concerns, sharing them with others. As a practical and effective method to reduce one's fears, I had a hard time swallowing the idea that merely sharing one's fear with others could have much benefit. Of course, I thought, it is always nice having others with whom one can talk. But as a method to help combat fears and to deal with legitimate threats, it seemed to me that the result of sharing your fear with another could just as easily be that instead of reducing your own fear you increase the other guy's fears, so now you have two people feeling fear, instead of one. How could that help?

In thinking of his advice as being perhaps shallow, there were a few things that failed to occur to me. For example, when treating psychotherapy patients in the past, I had noticed that some patients reported that they felt much less anxious and much better after just one or two sessions in which essentially all I had done was listen to them, nod my head, and offer the brilliant and insightful remark "Uh, huh . . ." Often I'd disparagingly dismiss these quick improvements as simply a "flight into health," a phenomenon long recognized by psychotherapists in which the patient gets much better very quickly after simply talking about their problems, which therapists sometimes interpret merely as a kind of denial mechanism, a way of avoiding digging deeper into their painful issues. But more recently some theorists are seeing this phenomenon in a new way, as representing legitimate improvement. And besides that, sharing one's fears and anxieties in psychotherapy can in itself sometimes provide powerful relief of at least one layer of worry or anxiety simply by the patient discovering that they are "normal," that others share similar worries, that they are not unique or alone in their fears. From that perspective, the suggestion that sharing one's fears may help relieve some of the fear, even in truly dangerous situations, suddenly didn't seem to be such a weak strategy.

Initially the Dalai Lama's suggestion to talk about one's fears and share them with others as a strategy to overcome very real fears in seriously dangerous situations had struck me as having the same level of sophistication as a fortune cookie. I suppose I had been disappointed because up until then every one of his theories and views had been supported by scientific evidence, and feeling that this advice was well below par, I didn't expect to find the same level of scientific validation. However, in looking at the act of self-disclosure from other perspectives and in greater depth, I found that quite a different picture began to emerge.

In fact, scientific literature provides ample evidence that simply sharing one's fears and concerns about traumatic events and dangers can be of tremendous value. Social psychologists at universities all over the world have conducted studies to investigate the most effective methods of dealing with fear after both natural and man-made disasters—after earthquakes, war in the Persian Gulf, terrorist attacks in Israel, tragedy in Bosnia—and have come to some conclusions about the most effective ways to cope in situations where one may not have control over wider events. The consensus, supported by clinicians in psychology and psychiatry, points to the importance of simply connecting with others and sharing one's concerns.

Research has shown that self-disclosure fosters social bonds, which in turn reduces individual stress as well as encourages others to do the same, which can take root in a society to reduce more widespread social tension. There is a wide body of evidence showing the legion of benefits from social bonds and a sense of closeness, from physical-health benefits to its direct effects in increasing feelings of well-being and levels of happiness. Studies confirmed what is readily apparent to most of us during times of crisis: People naturally open up to others and social boundaries dissolve as people strike up intense conversations with not only family and friends but also often with total strangers—in supermarket checkout lines, elevators, or bus stops. This results in feelings of solidarity, which can be a powerful antidote to collective threat. In fact, studies have shown that simply being with others and creating a sense of togetherness can reduce our feeling of fear, even when the level of danger remains the same.

In studying the positive effects of talking about traumatic events, researchers looked at the aftermath of events such as the 1989 earthquake in Northern California, the Persian Gulf War, or the Oklahoma City bombing, and have identified several predictable stages that communities go through in coping with highly stressful or traumatic events. They found that three or four weeks after the event people freely discuss the event, openly talking with anyone about their experiences, and as a result they generally cope relatively well. However, from around the fourth through the eighth week after traumatic events, people often feel that they should be getting over it by that time and stop talking about the event as much. The problem was that most people still thought about it a lot and still wanted to talk about what had happened, but didn't feel like listening to others' stories. A few weeks after the 1989 earthquake, for example, people in the Palo Alto area started wearing T-shirts reading, "Thank you for not sharing your earthquake experience." So, this conflict between the need to talk about the disaster and the unwillingness to listen to others talking about it often leads to a surge of widespread stress, health problems, irritability, arguments, and in some cases even an increase in the rate of aggravated assaults in a community. Finally, an "adaptation phase" generally occurs from eight to twelve weeks after the event, and by the end of that period the majority of those affected by the trauma have returned to normal—reminding us once again of the tremendous resilience of human beings.

In identifying the benefits of talking about one's fears, a study at UCLA identified another fascinating phenomenon: *Merely labeling the emotion of fear reduced it.* In studies using fMRI technology, researchers showed subjects a series of photos with faces displaying different emotions and asked the subjects to verbally identify the emotion. When the subjects named "fear," the brain scan showed activation of an area in the prefrontal cortex that is thought to exert dampening or inhibiting effects on the amygdala (the fear-generating area) and a reduction of activity in the amygdala!

The power of disclosing one's inner thoughts and feelings is so great, in fact, that even if a person has nobody to talk to, simply the awareness, articulation, and labeling of one's negative thoughts and emotions appear to have substantial benefits, both physical and mental. Experiments have shown that fifteen minutes of writing about one's thoughts and feelings about adverse or traumatic events can reduce stress and help people cope. In one experiment, one group of subjects wrote about their most pressing personal problems, while another wrote about a trivial topic, for just twenty minutes on four separate occasions. Those who disclosed thoughts and feelings suffered from fewer illnesses during the period of the study than those who did not. In another study, blood samples were taken of subjects who disclosed and those who did not disclose. The "disclosure" subjects had more helper T-cells, an essential component of the immune system. The researchers theorize that writing about the events helps the individual put the experience in the wider context of their lives, acting as a kind of "broadening" exercise, which can provide substantial benefits, which we will explore further in a later chapter.

It is clear, of course, that sharing one's experience, one's hopes and fears, with another person is not a panacea for conquering all fears and anxieties, nor is written disclosure. In practicing self-disclosure with another individual, opening up to someone else, not everyone has the opportunity or privilege to share their feelings with someone like the Dalai Lama. So, one needs to practice common sense, revealing what is appropriate, with a sensitivity to the context—taking into consideration what is being said and where, when, to whom. Still, with a measure of common sense, as the Dalai Lama suggests, the simple act of sharing one's inner experience with other human beings has tremendous power for dispelling fear and giving inner strength.

When we sat down the next day, I began, "Your Holiness, we had spoken yesterday about the idea of this pervasive fear that seems to be increasing in today's world. For the people living here in India, there's the threat of nuclear attack, threat of terrorist attack for the people living in the States, and of course in Israel it's a way of life! You never know when or where these events might happen—there's just this underlying fear. And you sort of implied that on some level there is not much you can do about that kind of valid fear, when it's not on the level of one's projection or imagination.

"Of course you are absolutely right about that, and yet I can't help but still feel there might be something else; I still do not feel totally satisfied with your response that there is nothing we can do about this fear other than to share it with others. So, before we move on to other topics, I'm just wondering if there is anything we have left out in terms of methods to help us come to terms with fear."

"Yes," he said, "for example, there is always Shantideva's approach, which you and I have discussed in the first *Art of Happiness* book. In brief, Shantideva [the great eighth-century Indian Buddhist teacher] suggests that we analyze the situation and repeatedly reminds us: *if the problem is such that there is a solution, there is then no need to worry about it.* In that case we should focus on finding that solution. *If, on the other hand, there is no possible solution, there is no point in worrying because you cannot do anything about it anyway.* So when you approach a situation with that kind of perspective, then even if you do confront tragedy, you have a greater chance of dealing with it. So, that may be helpful in some situations."

"Of course," I observed, "I realize that there can be many different kinds of fear, different levels. 'Fear' can encompass a spectrum of different mental states that can become progressively more intense and disabling, ranging from a tendency to worry about life's daily events, to a chronic diffuse sense of anxiety to full-blown panic attacks with physical symptoms to episodes of sheer terror. The type of fear a given individual will experience not only depends on the nature of the situation but also is generally determined by a combination of individual biological, psychological, and environmental factors."

"That's right," the Dalai Lama agreed. "So, we need a variety of approaches to deal with the various kinds of fear or the different contexts."

"Well, if we are talking about individual fears and anxieties, on a personal level, you're right that many approaches may be needed, which could include assessment of the person's physical condition, medical illnesses, mental illness such as clinical anxiety disorders, and various treatments that could include attention to diet and exercise, medication, psychotherapy, and particularly cognitive behavioral techniques. As we've discussed in the past, although written in the eighth century, Shantideva's rational approach to dealing with worry is very similar to modern cognitive techniques. In fact, parts of Shantideva's text reads as if it comes straight from a modern textbook on cognitive-behavioral techniques, where reason, logic, and analysis are used to challenge and actively refute our automatic negative thoughts.

"But the context I'm talking about here," I reminded him, "is the kind of situation where there are valid fears related to wider problems and dangers in society, the kinds of wider dangers or threats that one has no control over, in contrast to the more specific problems in one's personal life that a person may be worrying about. So, I'm wondering if you have any further thoughts about dealing with those kinds of fears."

"So, with those kinds of fears . . ." he repeated, taking a moment to reflect, "of course for religious believers, their faith can always play a role in helping them deal with these situations with less fear."

"That's true," I said. "In fact, I'm glad you brought that up. There's a large body of scientific evidence clearly establishing the tremendous benefits of religious faith in helping individuals cope with crises and traumatic experiences and so on. But what about those who don't adhere to a particular religion?"

"Now, taking another look at this, we can see a very important principle: A person's underlying outlook and motivation can certainly affect how he or she responds to life's adversities, threats, or dangers," he replied. "For example, an attitude of kindness and compassion brings a sense of self-confidence, an inner strength. That will reduce fear. In fact, you will often find cases where there might be two individuals in the very same dangerous situation, yet one of them copes much more effectively than the other—here it's one's outlook that could make the difference. In fact, an individual's response to a dangerous situation and ability to deal with fear can often depend more on the person's outlook and personal characteristics than on the nature of the situation itself."

"You know, Your Holiness, that reminds me . . . I remember a case history of a patient I was treating for post-traumatic stress disorder years ago when I was practicing psychiatry. He had gone to St. Croix with his girlfriend and another couple when Hurricane Hugo hit the island. He had a really traumatic experience and was still experiencing symptoms a long time after the event. Anyway, in one session he asked me to meet with his girlfriend and the other couple. There were four people who were all very much alike, with the same backgrounds, ages, and so on, and all four had shared the exact same experience during the hurricane, with all four feeling real fear at the time. But the thing that struck me was that even though they had all gone through the same situation, the same external circumstances, each one of the four responded to those circumstances in a completely different way, in terms of the level of fear they exhibited, how well they were able to cope both during and after the experience, and so on.

"So, your comment about different people responding to the same situation in a different manner reminded me of that story. It really illustrates your point that often it is not so much the nature of a threat that dictates our fearful response and behavior, but how we perceive and interpret that threat. And of course, as you point out, our basic outlook on life, including our religious beliefs, can have a big effect on how we respond to dangers and so on. So, in view of this, can you give me some other examples of certain outlooks or points of view that might help reduce fear?"

"Other outlooks," the Dalai Lama repeated. "Yes, another factor that is relevant here that can influence people's response to a looming threat is the degree to which they are aware of their own impermanence. Generally, in our day-to-day life, most people become so engrossed in their everyday activities that they do not give much thought to the idea that one day we may die. So, without much reflection on this fact, we tend to have an underlying sense that our life will go on and on, that we will be around forever. The stronger you cling to this notion, the more intense the fear will be when there is a threat to that existence."

"You know, Your Holiness, I'm just sort of thinking out loud here; I guess the main point at issue here is that you never know what the future is going to bring, that violence or even death could erupt at any time. We often have no control over that. But I'm wondering if there is a way to transmute one's fear, to use it in a positive way. For example, maybe we could think about our own mortality, and use that to value every moment we have right now, think about our priorities in life, and live every day to its fullest."

The Dalai Lama nodded enthusiastically. "Yes, that is very possible.. ... And in fact there are Buddhist meditations where the emphasis is placed upon being mindful of one's own mortality and contemplating the inevitability of one's death. The main significance of that is to really create a sense of urgency, recognizing the preciousness of this human life. One of the effects of this kind of meditation is that you will take very seriously whatever moment you happen to have now, since there is no guarantee that it will last forever. So the whole purpose of that meditation is to utilize your life in the most effective way, put all your effort to make the present moment most meaningful, not simply to engage in some morbid thoughts about your own death.

"That's why in the Buddhist scriptures there are constant admonitions to reflect upon the transient nature of things—not just of one's own existence, but of the entire universe! You know, there is a beautiful passage in one of the scriptures where it says that even the very Earth that we live on, the elements of water, fire, in short, the entire universe—nothing will remain, not even in the form of dust, millions of years from now. If that is so, why wouldn't our very fragile individual existence also come to an end? Such contemplations create a more expansive outlook that can help reduce the likelihood of reacting with intense fear. In fact, there are similar ideas in modern cosmology and astrophysics, where they have calculated how our Earth and all the planets in the galaxy are definitely moving toward a collision course and eventual annihilation in the very distant future. So once you have that kind of basic recognition of the transient nature of all existence, then that may actually have an impact upon your attitude toward your own impermanence, which could at least take the sting out of your intense fear."

The Dalai Lama spoke of death, the universe, the movement of planets and galaxies, wherein a billion years was the blink of an eye. It was so familiar to him it sounded like someone describing the layout of the home in which he grew up. Perhaps that shouldn't be so surprising, considering that his lifelong daily meditation practice included a meditation preparing him for death. But as he made these concepts seem to come alive—setting our transitory, fleeting, little human lives against the backdrop of the eternal expanse of time, the infinite reaches of space—somehow things began to look a little different. How? I'm not sure. But I was no longer dissatisfied with his advice about how to deal with fear, for one thing.

There is no question that the world today is filled with dangers. Genuine danger, a legitimate threat to our safety, evokes fear—that's natural.

The Dalai Lama points out that it is foolish to live without fear; after all, healthy fear has a protective function. But the fundamental question remains, with so many conflicts in the world today, with so many man-made threats that could erupt at any time, so much uncertainty, where financial markets could collapse at any time, how can we go about our daily lives without allowing fear to sap our capacity for joy, undermine our sense of confidence and optimism about the future, or even paralyze our lives?

Of course, as the Dalai Lama continuously cautions, there are no easy answers and no single key to resolving widespread fear in a society, particularly the brand that can undermine human happiness, freedom, and lead to conflict and violence. But he gives us an approach that can set us in the right direction, an approach that is completely congruent with the findings of modern science, so that the convergence of the two approaches offers genuine hope for the future.

From the scientific perspective, of course, scientists have had ample opportunity to conduct studies on fear and conflict in communities and societies all over the world—looking at patterns of human behavior in Israel, Northern Ireland, the Balkans, and so many other regions, places where life is uncertain and fear is familiar, in regions torn with conflict. Researchers have accumulated enough evidence to identify effective strategies to deal with fear as well as reduce the cycle of fear and violence, methods that parallel the Dalai Lama's views.

This approach begins with awareness. As we have seen, fear can be preconscious, we can react with fear before we are even aware of it, so becoming aware of our fears brings it into the realm of reason—on a biological level, this means transferring control over our responses from the primitive amygdala to the more advanced prefrontal cortex, where we can modify our more primitive blind urges with the higher brain functions of reason, critical thinking, and a wider, more long-term perspective, tempered with human kindness and compassion. Part of this process of awareness involves identifying the customary situations that tend to trigger fear, and actively investigating the various ways we normally express and resolve our fears. It isn't difficult—all we need to do is observe our own behavior.

Cultivating greater awareness of our fears can be a very powerful strategy—in fact, we have seen how merely consciously labeling the emotion we are experiencing as "fear" will reduce it. But cultivating greater awareness is just the first step in the Dalai Lama's approach. With full awareness of the importance of overcoming fear, at least the destructive varieties of fear, the next step involves applying antidotes to fear, the specific strategies or techniques to reduce fear and stress.

Of course, when we are talking about fear and anxiety in response to dangerous or threatening situations, actively working toward reducing the danger or threat can be a legitimate approach, even if it is only in small steps. But of course if one has no control over the external threat, and if there are no practical steps one can take to reduce the danger, then one needs to turn to internal strategies to deal with the fear.

Reminding us that there is never just a single approach to overcoming human problems, how we need multiple weapons in our arsenal to combat destructive emotions such as anger, hatred, or fear, here the Dalai Lama begins with a few approaches, including sharing one's fears with others, cognitive techniques (including Shantideva's formula), or calling upon one's religious faith.

In speaking of different approaches to reducing fear, the Dalai Lama also mentioned how our underlying attitudes and outlook can affect how we deal with fear—beginning by adopting a fundamental or basic outlook that recognizes and accepts that there may always be some degree of danger in life, that this is part of life. He also points out that the way an individual perceives a threatening or dangerous situation can make a big difference. And, *even more important, an individual can deliberately change how they perceive a threatening situation, which can be an effective way of reducing fear.* In Part Three I describe to the Dalai Lama an experiment in which a group of subjects were able to reduce their stress when they viewed a task as a challenge instead of a threat. All it took was a deliberate change in outlook, in which they perceived the task in a new way.

Finally, in looking at all these various ways to reduce fear and anxiety, particularly in situations beyond one's personal control, investigators generally like to point out an important feature of human nature: Humans have a tremendous capacity to adapt, a process called habituation, the same process in the brain that is responsible for the fact that you do not "hear" the ticking of the clock that seemed so loud when you first got it, or the noise of traffic outside your window that seemed so loud when you first moved to your apartment. In the same way, our level of fear and anxiety will naturally tend to diminish as we get used to new conditions—even conditions where there may be some threat. In one study in Israel, during a period of regular Palestinian terrorist attacks on public buses, investigators found that aside from other coping strategies an individual might have, simply riding the bus more often was associated with a reduction of fear and anxiety.

Fear can have effects on the individual, group, and societal levels. Conflicts, wars, and widespread acts of aggression and violence can be the results when fear takes root. When dealing with conflicts you'll find that when an undercurrent of fear continues to run through one or both sides in a conflict—which generally involves fears for one's safety, security, or continued self-identity—as long as the other side is seen as a threat in some way, a conflict will never be resolved. This is the core problem in many cases of intractable conflict. To make matters worse, the violence in such cases can be particularly difficult to eradicate due to fear's inherent tendency to distort thinking, exaggerate one's perception of the threat, destroy reason, and narrow one's point of view.

Eliminating the factor of fear will go a long way in resolving many conflicts. This is why addressing the fears of each side is becoming an increasingly important part of conflict resolution. This approach involves negotiators seeking to help the parties identify, articulate, and finally understand their own underlying fears, as well as those of their opponents. As the parties begin to identify exaggerated and distorted fears and they begin to see reality more clearly, a feeling of trust will often begin to grow, which can become the beginning of finally stopping the cycle of fear and violence. From there the parties will start to find solutions that they never saw before.

Finally, the attempt to deliberately try to understand another's fears can become the basis for *empathy*, for trying to "put yourself in another's shoes." And at the same time, sharing your own fears with the other side opens up the possibility that they can empathize with you as well. As we will see in the final chapter of this book, empathy is one of the primary keys to overcoming conflict, violence, and prejudice—the solution to so many human problems, with unparalleled transformational power.

By the end of the week in Dharamsala, it felt as if we had covered some solid ground. As I listened to the Dalai Lama that week, I felt that a clearer understanding of both the origins of violence and the nature of our destructive emotions was beginning to emerge. The Dalai Lama had also gotten me to take a fresh look at our basic human nature— not something that I routinely thought about—as well as reflect on the sources of human evil. Finally, I felt that he had shared some good practical strategies, including a useful approach to dealing with fear.

At the end of the week, I also reflected on our previous set of discussions in Dharamsala. I felt that series of discussions had been equally as fruitful, resulting in a deeper understanding of prejudice and ways to start to transcend Us and Them thinking. Not only that, but the very first issue he raised, identifying the growing loneliness and alienation in our society and the erosion of our sense of community, our sense of connectedness, was something that I had never even given any thought to, but once he mentioned it, it was as if a veil had fallen from my eyes—not only did I see evidence of it everywhere, but its importance to human happiness seemed to be undeniable, and I wondered how I had never noticed it before.

As productive as I found our conversations to be, however, I wasn't entirely satisfied. It still felt to me as if something was missing. Of course, one missing piece was easy to identify: While we had traced the roots of violence to the destructive emotions, I felt we had not adequately investigated strategies to deal with them, to overcome them. But there was something else, another missing factor that was more difficult to identify. I felt that the main objective of our discussions, exploring the Dalai Lama's views on finding happiness in our troubled world, was being addressed. He clearly had been speaking directly about various human problems or issues that could affect the happiness of both individuals and societies. His views seemed sound, as always, and his practical advice useful. Finally, after some reflection, I sensed what was causing my dissatisfaction. It seemed that we had been tackling problems or issues piecemeal, bit by bit, but so far they seemed like a collection of topics. So far there didn't seem to be any kind of overriding approach or strong unifying theme or framework that could be used as a guideline to help keep us on course toward both greater personal happiness and a better world. Of course, this was not meant to be our last meeting, so I remained hopeful that eventually things would fall into place.

PART THREE

Happiness in a Troubled World

Chapter 10

COPING WITH A TROUBLED WORLD

A COUPLE OF years had passed since our last series of discussions in Dharamsala. Taking place not long after 9/11, those conversations had focused on themes related to aggression, violence, and fear, the darker varieties of human conduct. Since that time we had seen the invasion of Afghanistan, with the toppling of the repressive Taliban regime, and the invasion of Iraq, with the overthrow of Saddam Hussein. And it seemed there was always some kind of violence breaking out, in one region of the world or another, on a small scale or large, for a short duration or on a protracted, ongoing basis. There seemed no end in sight for the use of violence to resolve conflict. The world did not seem much closer to realizing the Dalai Lama's vision of a world where we felt connected with others, at ease no matter whom we were with, where our fundamental goodness and gentleness reigned, a world largely without violence or fear, except perhaps a few inevitable skirmishes between people here and there. Yet he remained hopeful. The century was still young. There was still time for such changes to occur.

But with so many problems in today's world, I wondered, how did he

maintain hope? What sustained his optimism? And against this backdrop of challenging societal problems and the multitude of stresses of
everyday life, each of us has our own personal troubles as well. So, we
were faced with a fundamental question: How can we find happiness in
such a troubled world?

The Dalai Lama was in the United States on another speaking tour,
this time in Tucson. During the intervening period since our last full
series of discussions in India, we had continued to meet intermittently
but we had shifted to other topics for a while, speaking about issues related to economics, wealth, lifestyle, greed, consumerism, the rich and
the poor.* I had accompanied him on some additional speaking tours
as well, but with his schedule booked solid during his foreign tours, it
was generally not the appropriate time to request meetings for in-depth
discussions of complex topics.

Tucson was different, however. It was here, in my own home state
of Arizona, where we had conducted our first conversations about human happiness so many years before, discussions that were eventually
chronicled in *The Art of Happiness*. This was his first return visit to
Arizona. So, after more than a decade, here we were again, still exploring the theme of human happiness. The Sonoran desert setting, amid
the rocky hills, towering saguaro cactus, and the subtle fragrance of the
desert shrubs, evoked a feeling of nostalgia. Somehow it felt right that
we continue our discussions here, a place that was a reminder of the
cycles of life, ever-changing cycles that revolved around an unchanging
core—the perennial question of how to find happiness.

The Dalai Lama had a full day ahead of him. Aside from a brief
lunch in private in his hotel suite, virtually every minute of his time
had been booked solid. That week he was giving a series of teachings
on one of his favorite Buddhist texts, the *Bodhicaryavatara*, written by
Shantideva. Long teaching sessions scheduled every morning and afternoon left little time for other activities. Usually, whatever few spare
minutes he had in between public or private events would be filled

---

* These discussions will eventually appear in one of the remaining volumes of the Art
of Happiness series.

with brief private audiences. In this case, however, because of my local ties, the organizers of the Dalai Lama's visit to Tucson had graciously helped facilitate some longer blocks of time for us to meet, after his breakfast in the mornings or following his teachings in the late afternoons.

I arrived at his hotel suite quite early in the morning for our first meeting. Not exactly a "morning person," I had barely finished my first cup of coffee, and was still struggling to see in color. As I entered the living room of the suite, the Dalai Lama emerged from the adjoining bedroom with a quick step and a warm smile, greeting me alertly and in great spirits. As per his usual travel routine, he had been up since 4 AM, had spent more than three hours in meditation and prayer, and had finished his simple breakfast of traditional Tibetan *tsampa*. This was his best time of day.

We opened with a little preliminary general conversation as he kicked off a pair of worn rubber flip-flops and settled into a cross-legged position, barefoot, in an oversize upholstered chair. Although by Arizona standards the early autumn temperature was a welcome reprieve from the brutal summer, the Dalai Lama, who generally doesn't like hot weather, commented on the desert heat as I sat down on the sofa opposite him, pulling out my notebooks. As I set up my tape recorder on the coffee table in front of us, we spoke for a few moments about his being back in Tucson after so many years. But with so many questions that I wanted to cover, very shortly we resumed our long-standing conversations, picking up where we left off in Dharamsala.

Quickly penetrating to the very heart of the matter at hand, the question of how to find happiness in our troubled world, I began. "You know, Your Holiness, when you think of all these problems in the world, problems which undermine human happiness—violence, terrorism, prejudice, poverty, and the gap between rich and poor, the environment, and so on—and think about how vast these all are, sometimes it all seems so impossible.... I mean, with so much suffering in the world, the possibility of people finding genuine happiness seems to be so remote sometimes."

"Howard, now one thing—we have been talking about human happiness on the level of a society. And on this level the external conditions can have some impact on the happiness of those living in that society. So, we need to work on overcoming the many problems in today's world. We need to make an effort to change things in whatever way we can, even small ways, so that social conditions are created that can promote greater happiness for all of the members of that society. That's important. That's our responsibility. But when we talk about promoting human happiness, we need to address this on two levels: internal and external. So, we need to work toward solving the external problems, but at the same time, we need to find a way to cope internally, on an individual level, so we can maintain personal happiness in the face of the world's problems."

"So, at this point, then, I'd like to shift to the individual level, and explore ways to find happiness despite the world's problems," I said.

"Very good," he replied.

"But you know," I sighed, "with so many problems in today's world, so many stresses and difficulties in daily life, sometimes it seems that the best way to deal with it all would be to just ignore everything going on around us, or become a hermit or something. But that can't be the solution."

"Yes, the world does have many problems," the Dalai Lama agreed. "But one does not need to withdraw from the world to find happiness." He stopped for a moment to reach for a mug of tea on a side table, then resumed. "You know, this question actually reminds me a little bit of one time in Germany when the interviewer asked me if I thought that stress was a congenital characteristic of the modern world, of modern society."

"What did you tell him?"

"I told him no! In fact, if that were true, then we'd all have to run to a place without TV, without communications, without any modern conveniences, and without such good food!" the Dalai Lama replied. "To me," he continued, "wherever such a place might be, I don't think that would necessarily be a pleasant, stress-free place to live! So, states like stress and anxiety are internal states, whereas the conditions of our society are external—they don't directly create our stress. *Stress and these negative mental states have to do with our own response to those conditions,* and show a certain lack of ability to cope with our environment.

"So, if you reflect you'll see that much of our suffering in life is caused not by external causes but by internal events such as the arising of disturbing emotions. And the best antidote to this inner disruption is enhancing our ability to handle these emotions, and learning how to cope with our environment, the negative situations, and so on."

"Just to clarify," I asked, "when you refer to 'handling these emotions,' are you referring to learning how to regulate our emotions, or more specifically, working on overcoming negative emotions such as anger, hatred, greed, jealousy, discouragement, and so on? In other words, are you referring to the process of training the mind?"

"Yes," he affirmed. "In the past, you and I have spoken about this training of the mind, or what I sometimes call inner discipline, as a method of cultivating greater happiness, so I think . . ."

Hoping he wouldn't dismiss this topic because we had already spoken about it in the past, I quickly cut in. "Yes, we have spoken about this, but I think this is a great place to start today! Because in one series of meetings in Dharamsala a while back, we were discussing acts of evil and violence, and we had traced the cause of this to its roots in the negative, destructive emotions. Well, in those discussions we spent some time on the specific negative emotion of fear, but we didn't get to a deeper discussion of how to deal with the others, or the negative emotions in general. I wanted to return to that topic, so today it would be great to have a little general review of overcoming the negative emotions! It never hurts to do a little review of important topics," I argued. "And besides, in the past we discussed this only in the context of personal development, but now we are discussing these issues in a different context, within a wider framework or awareness of societal factors, too."

With a subtle smile on his face, a smile confined mostly to his eyes, I think maybe because he was pleased at my enthusiasm to stick with this topic, he agreed to my request, saying, "OK. To review, then, this training of the mind involves cultivating positive states of mind and overcoming the negative states of mind, the destructive emotions, or what are known as the afflictive emotions. As we have discussed in the past, according to Buddhist theory, the positive mental states are those which lead to greater happiness. The negative or destructive emotions cause disturbances within our mind, destroying our mental happiness. These afflictive emotions lead to greater suffering. From the Buddhist point of view, we consider these positive mental qualities to be antidotes to the destructive or afflictive mental states—as you strengthen the positive emotion, there will be a corresponding reduction in the influence and force of the negative emotion. So, within Buddhist practice there are certain positive mental factors that act as specific antidotes to their corresponding negative or afflictive emotions—for example, patience or tolerance acts as an antidote to anger, compassion or loving-kindness as an antidote to hatred, and factors such as contentment or modest desires act as antidotes to covetousness and greed, and so on.

"Oh, one other thing," he added after a pause; "here we are talking about this inner discipline. But as I usually mention, this inner discipline needs to be linked with ethical discipline, acting in an ethical way. As you reduce destructive emotions, you need to also work on overcoming the destructive behaviors that go with them, which can also lead to misery and suffering. So, as you develop these positive mental qualities, the inner changes need to be translated into your behavior, into how you interact with others. That is important."

Perhaps one day the world will widely adopt the principles of nonviolence, when the stupidity of prejudice and cruelty of racism will largely be a thing of the past, when poverty and hunger have been eradicated, basic human rights are afforded to all, and social conditions promote human happiness and flourishing. Someday perhaps. When that day will be is uncertain. But one thing that *is* certain is that societal change takes time. So we are left with the question of how best to cope with the problems of our world and still remain happy, a question that the Dalai Lama began to address that morning. So, we returned once again to the level of the individual, exploring the inner approach to happiness as we had done here in Tucson so many years before. But now, we addressed these questions in a wider societal context. And now, scientific research had much to say about the validity of the Dalai Lama's approach to happiness, evidence that was lacking at the time of our first discussions.

As I listened to him begin to outline his general approach to coping with life's adversity and remaining happy, I was astonished by the parallels with the very latest scientific discoveries. In the intervening years since the publication of *The Art of Happiness,* I had closely followed the new developments in the scientific study of happiness and positive emotions, and I now began to see how some of the key scientific findings served to shed new light on the Dalai Lama's approach, which was of course based on ancient Buddhist principles and practices.

In discussing how positive emotions act as antidotes to our negative emotions, the Dalai Lama was reviewing some of the fundamental principles of the Buddhist approach to happiness. This approach is based on the idea that once our basic survival needs are met, happiness is determined more by the state of our mind than by our external circumstances, conditions, or events. Further, from the Buddhist point of view, we can deliberately cultivate happiness by training our minds, by reshaping our outlook and attitudes. From this perspective, we can cultivate happiness much like developing any other skill, through training and practice.

The practice of training the mind begins with familiarizing ourselves with all the different kinds of mental states or emotions that we might experience in our daily life, then classifying them as positive or negative according to whether they ultimately lead to greater happiness or suffering. Thus, emotions such as compassion, kindness, tolerance, forgiveness, hope, and so on are recognized as positive emotions. These emotions are not only linked with greater happiness from the Buddhist perspective but also there have been hundreds of scientific studies in recent years showing that positive emotions have beneficial effects on one's physical health, mental health, relationships, and overall success in life, including career success and financial prosperity.

Of course, there are also many emotions and mental states that can lead to greater suffering: hostility, hatred, extreme anxiety, jealousy, greed, dishonesty, prejudice, etc. These are called negative emotions, although in our discussions we have at times used various other names interchangeably—such as destructive emotions, disturbing emotions, or *Kleshas* in Sanskrit, which is sometimes translated as "afflictive emotions" or "delusions." While the terms "positive emotions" and "negative emotions" are commonly used, these categories are not limited to what we would conventionally define as true emotions—for example, honesty, tolerance, or humility are included among the positive emotions, while dishonesty or lack of self-discipline may be seen as negative emotions. But whatever terminology one chooses to use, the key Buddhist principle here is that the negative emotion and its antidote are fundamentally incompatible, and one cannot experience both at the very same instant—the positive emotion acts to dispel the negative emotion, just as switching on a light will dispel darkness. So, as one gradually cultivates the positive emotion, increasing its force, there will be a corresponding reduction of the negative emotion, just like pouring cold water into hot water—as you pour in more cold water, there is a corresponding reduction in the water's temperature.

In the past decade, new scientific evidence has emerged to prove the validity of this Buddhist principle in some surprising ways. For example, in a seminal experiment conducted by Dr. Barbara Fredrickson, one of the world's leading researchers on positive emotions, along with colleagues at the University of Michigan, anxiety and stress were induced in a group of subjects by telling them that they had only minutes to prepare a speech that was going to be viewed by their peers and evaluated. As one might expect, levels of fear and anxiety instantly shot up, along with the physical stress response, including increased heart rate, increased blood pressure, peripheral vasoconstriction, muscle tension, and so on. After eliciting this stress response, the subjects were told that the speech was canceled and they would not need to do this. Whew! Experimenters then broke the subjects into four groups, inducing a different emotion in each by having them watch film clips known to evoke amusement (a "high-arousal" positive emotion), contentment or serenity (a "low-arousal" positive emotion), sadness (a negative emotion), as well as a neutral control group (evoking no change in emotion). The investigators found that subjects who were feeling the positive emotions recovered much faster from the effects of the anxiety than the control group. Investigators discovered, for example, that the heart rate and blood pressure of subjects with positive emotions returned to normal much more quickly than the control group did, while the "sad group" took longer to recover than the normal controls—leading Fredrickson to propose a new theory about the function of positive emotions. Calling her theory the Undoing Hypothesis, she proposed the idea that positive emotions serve to "undo" or counteract the mental and physical effects of negative emotions: in other words, the idea that *positive emotions act as antidotes to the negative emotions!*

This has direct implications for the Dalai Lama's belief, expressed to the German interviewer he mentioned, that modern society does not automatically have to cause stress. Of course, there is no question that the general state of the world and the conditions of modern society can be highly stressful. One widely recognized fact among scientists is that from an evolutionary perspective, the human body and brain were designed for the Pleistocene era, not modern industrial and technological society. We evolved in small groups on the vast savanna, not in giant sprawling metropolises, with people piled layer upon layer on top of each other in high-rise buildings jutting hundreds of feet in the air. Our bodies and brains were not designed to sit in gridlock traffic, horns blaring all around us, having nonstop meetings all day, last-minute presentations to make, being bombarded with constant sensory stimulation from movies and entertainment, e-mails piling up with no time to reply, as well as TV and radio reporting round-the-clock coverage of all varieties of natural and man-made disasters. Even ten minutes of watching the news can make one's stress level soar. And studies have shown that even the background noise around us, that we tune out and don't even notice, places demands on our nervous systems that we were not built for.

The result of all this is often a chronic low-level stimulation of our stress response, pumping out stress hormones in ways that our bodies were not designed for. These stress hormones were designed to take quick, decisive action in one intense burst of effort, and then go back to normal; they were designed to deal with threats from dangerous predators and aggressors, not to worry for months about some approaching exam, financial stress, or job loss. Our stress-response system was designed for a quick battle with a saber-toothed tiger, not a long drawn-out battle in divorce court. What's good for your body in a short-term crisis can be very harmful over long periods. The long-term activation of the stress-response system or the chronic overexposure to stress hormones may alter the operation and structure of brain cells that are critical for memory, as well as cause a multitude of health problems. Then, on top of this kind of chronic background stress of modern life, we must also contend with adverse situations that upset us, evoking negative emotions such as anger or anxiety, associated with sharp peaks in the stress response, the fight-or-flight reaction.

Fortunately, as the Dalai Lama suggests, there is a way to overcome these chronic and acute stress reactions—and as Fredrickson's experiment shows, our positive emotions can act as antidotes, reversing the negative effects of the stress response. Of course, this brings us to a fundamental question, the key question: *Can we learn to regulate our emotions, bring them under voluntary control?* And here we are talking about a method of producing sustained increase in positive emotions, not just a brief transient experience of positive emotion from watching a film clip.

As our conversation continued, the Dalai Lama went on to answer this question.

Continuing our discussion of cultivating happiness by training the mind, the Dalai Lama explained, "Another thing—in addition to the specific antidotes to the negative emotions, there is also a general antidote. As you know, within the Buddhist tradition, we consider all of the afflictive emotions to be rooted in ignorance—misconception of the true nature of reality. Therefore, the antidote to ignorance, known as the Wisdom factor, or generating insight into the true nature of reality, can be seen as a general antidote that can eliminate all of the negative emotions at their root.

"Also," he added, "regarding these positive and negative emotions. Again, from the Buddhist perspective, we say that the positive emotions have a valid foundation, based in reality, while the negative emotions lack this valid foundation and are generally based on misperception or distortion of reality. For example, compassion for another person is based on the recognition that the other person, like yourself, wants happiness and does not want pain and suffering. This is a valid perception, part of reality. On the other hand, with an emotion like hatred, you will find that it is usually based on the perception of the individual as 100 percent negative or bad, as if that is the person's permanent, unchanging nature. That is a distortion of reality, since if you investigate closely, everyone will have some positive quality, and they will also have the potential to change."

Familiar with these concepts from having attended many of his public talks as well as our private conversations, I nodded, then steering the conversation back to what I considered to be more practical matters, I said, "Well, for right now, leaving aside things like valid foundation or permanently rooting out all negative emotions, the main point here is developing the ability to cope with our environment, adversities, and the stresses of daily life and to find happiness. So, if positive emotions are the antidotes, then the logical question is how to cultivate them . . . and I guess that, basically, the main question here is how can we learn to cope with . . ."

Anticipating the rest of my question, the Dalai Lama continued. "So I think *to a large extent one's attitude and perception play a key role here. One thing is sure: How we view the world around us, how we view others, and how you interpret your circumstances and the events going on around you can definitely affect how we might respond to our environment, our world, and its problems. This is our fundamental outlook. And I think this is directly related to our ability to cope with problems and maintain happiness.* So, we need to pay attention to this level and develop an outlook and attitudes that give us strength and can help us cope."

"Well, Your Holiness, I guess that I keep asking the same sort of thing, over and over again"—I laughed—"but I'm wondering if you can suggest some more specific or concrete methods to help us cope. For example, how exactly does one go about developing an outlook that can give us strength?"

The Dalai Lama laughed. "And I keep saying over and over again, the solution is, *'Be realistic!'* This being realistic . . . I guess it seems that this is almost like a mantra to me, ' . . . realistic approach . . . realistic approach . . . ' when dealing with problems. For example, in our struggle for Tibet's freedom, as you know, I've always advocated a realistic approach which involves forgoing our demand for full independence, and instead seeking genuine autonomy. Some of my Tibetan critics who insist on full independence are known to have stated that they find my phrase, 'realistic approach,' to be a source of great annoyance!

"*So, anyway, I think the underlying basis for the kinds of attitudes and outlook that is most helpful for coping is realistic thinking, a realistic approach.* This involves investigating and increasing awareness about the reality of the situations around us."

Although we had discussed this critical issue of realistic thinking in different contexts in the past (the last time in the context of destructive emotions), this morning another thought occurred to me, an objection that I felt some people might raise in response to his position.

"Well, I'm not sure everyone would agree with that," I objected. "I think that some people might claim that the more aware we become of all these problems in the world, the more realistic our thinking becomes, the more we investigate and look into things, the greater the likelihood of discovering all sorts of problems we were unaware of. We might discover that our society offers more problems than solutions, and so on. I'm not sure if that will make us happier, more content, or rather make us just feel more overwhelmed, more distressed and dejected. I mean if I'm concerned about the problems of nuclear weapons and investigate and find out 'the reality' that there's still missile silos all around the area where I live, that's not going to make me sleep any better at night. (Or, if I become more 'aware' of 'the reality' of global warming or something, that is more likely to depress me rather than make me happier.)

"Again, it is a matter of perspective," he said, "and adopting the proper perspective—because such a discovery could also have the effect of increasing one's sense of urgency about the problem, and stimulate the drive to join a group or become more politically active or take some action to try to do something about the problem.

"By recommending this approach of realistic thinking, of increasing our awareness and coming closer to reality, it is very important to understand what is meant by this 'realistic outlook.' For example, I am not suggesting that one look only at the world's problems, or the reality only of the negative aspects of the situation. That is only part of the reality. *A truly realistic approach looks at all angles and facets of any situation*—and this would include both good and bad, not just bad. Life always consists of problems, but also moments of goodness, too. *So, I think the fundamental basis for developing this realistic outlook or attitude is to see things from a wider perspective. If you analyze, investigate, you will find that there are many ways of looking at a problem.* For example, instead of looking only at one's immediate circumstances, sometimes it can be helpful to take a long-term view.

"So, generally speaking, here we're talking about a more balanced view, a more complete view. This is a more realistic view. It involves developing a flexible kind of thinking that is able to see a situation from many angles. *I think in the past we have discussed how the destructive emotions tend to distort reality and narrow our perspective. So, in overcoming negative emotions we need to counter that by adopting a broader and more holistic perspective.*"

"Your Holiness, you are saying that there are different ways of seeing things realistically, from a wider perspective, and that this can overcome negative emotions and help us cope with life's problems."

"That's right."

"So, can you describe one of these ways, and explain how it would help us cope?"

The Dalai Lama was silent for several moments, then said, "I think one can begin with one's very attitude about problems and suffering in general. . . . I think that if we have a realistic attitude and understand that problems are naturally bound to arise in one form or another, it's a simple fact of life, we will be more effective in coping with the problems when they arise. "

"How will this help us cope with problems more effectively, rather than depress us?" I asked.

"For example, with this attitude we won't be so surprised when problems come up—we will be better able to face our problems directly, with less fear, less tendency to avoid or pretend they are not there. We will be able to put our energy into trying to come up with a solution, rather than expending energy by always feeling it is unfair, getting angry and upset that we have this experience, or looking for some single individual or institution to place the blame and then directing all our anger towards that 'source' of all our problems.

"Of course, having the proper attitude about suffering is only one thing. We also need to find other ways to see things from a wider perspective, investigate different approaches of perceiving our problems from different angles, discover an outlook that can help us cope when troubles arise, but an outlook that is based in reality."

One morning two men were driving to a very important business meeting, and they were running really late. On the way to the meeting they got a flat tire. Needless to say, the passenger got really upset about this, but he noticed that the driver remained completely calm and undisturbed by the situation, and immediately just set about changing the tire. As they were changing the tire, the passenger became more and more agitated each minute, but the driver just kept working, still totally unflustered. So finally the passenger couldn't help but ask, "We're going to be so late, how can you be so calm about this?" And almost cheerfully, the driver answered, "This is number three!" Unsatisfied of course, the passenger asked him to explain, and he said, "Many years ago, when I first started to drive, I read a statistic giving the average number of flat tires that motorists will have during their driving years. So,

right then I just decided to expect my fair share of flat tires, which
by the way still has not reached the average, and at the same time
I realized that no matter when or where I got my blow-outs, I
could be sure that when it happened it would never be convenient.
I figured that was just part of the normal costs of having the con-
venience of driving, like paying for gas or oil. So, this is just one of
my fair share of flats, that's all."

Long ago someone told me this story, and while the precise origin
of the story has gradually faded from my memory, the story has stuck
with me, surfacing in my mind from time to time, when I begin to feel
that daily events are conspiring against me. This story illustrates the
principles discussed by the Dalai Lama that morning, showing how accepting problems as a natural fact of human existence can help reduce
unnecessary agitation and negative emotion. It also illustrates the more
general principle, showing how a "realistic outlook," based on looking
at the problem from a wider perspective, can help us cope.

Step by step the Dalai Lama continued to reveal a powerful approach
to finding happiness in our troubled world, an approach to coping with
the problems of daily life without being overcome with hopelessness,
discouragement, or fear. Having mentioned how, from the Buddhist
perspective, positive emotions could act as specific antidotes to negative states of mind, he now went on to identify an all-purpose remedy, a
general antidote that can completely eradicate all negative emotions by
overcoming their root cause, our fundamental ignorance. "Ignorance"
in this context does not mean merely a lack of information or knowledge. Here the term refers to a fundamental lack of awareness of the
underlying true nature of reality, which is known as Emptiness. It im-
plies a more active kind of misperception or misapprehension of reality,
a gap between how things appear and how they truly exist. According
to Buddhist theory, the direct perception of the ultimate nature of reality, the "Realization of Emptiness," purifies the mind from all negative
tendencies, and results in a state of Enlightenment, in which one is
freed from all suffering, and liberated from *Samsara,* the endless cycle
of birth, death, and rebirth.

This is a tall order; according to Buddhist scriptures it can take countless eons of lifetimes to achieve such a state! So, the obvious question is, how is this relevant to those of us who are not Buddhist practitioners, or those who do not want to wait countless eons of lifetimes for happiness? How does this apply to those of us struggling to cope with our troubled world and find a measure of happiness and peace?

According to Buddhist philosophy, there are two levels of reality, ultimate reality and conventional reality. The ultimate nature of reality, as we have mentioned, refers to the concept of Emptiness, and the direct perception of Emptiness comes about as a result of spiritual realizations. Conventional reality refers to day-to-day life, our commonsense reality, accepting the reality of everything that appears to be real. *In the same way, we can refer to two levels of happiness.* In one of our conversations years ago, the Dalai Lama once referred to Enlightenment or Liberation as "the highest happiness." That is ultimate happiness. The goal of the Art of Happiness series is much more modest, but still not always easy: the achievement of greater day-to-day happiness and life satisfaction. This is conventional happiness.

With this last piece we can return to the ideas expressed by the Dalai Lama in our discussion and begin to fit everything into place. As we have seen, the Dalai Lama's approach to finding happiness in our troubled world is a "realistic approach," developing a "realistic outlook," which involves "investigating and increasing awareness about the reality of the situations around us." Here, he is referring to conventional reality. It is a kind of all-purpose method of dealing with everyday problems, coping with adversity, cultivating positive emotions, and overcoming the negative emotions that are the cause of so much of our suffering in life. Thus, we can see direct parallels on the two levels of reality: awareness of the ultimate nature of reality *Emptiness* leads to "ultimate happiness," and greater awareness of the conventional reality of everyday life leads to conventional happiness. Both can be seen as general antidotes to negative emotions and states of mind, with the "ultimate" antidote completely eradicating all negative states of mind, and the "conventional" antidote (which is what we are exploring here) eliminating or reducing negative emotions and states of mind enough to enjoy a happy life.

Finally, in drawing parallels between the Dalai Lama's method of overcoming negative emotions (and achieving happiness) and the latest scientific studies on happiness, we can add one more recent scientific theory about positive emotions. Earlier, we saw how Fredrickson's Undoing Hypothesis provided evidence for the concept of positive emotions acting as antidotes to the negative emotions. This can parallel the Buddhist concept of "specific antidotes," how each negative emotion has a specific positive emotion that can act as an antidote. As it turns out, Barbara Fredrickson and colleagues have also developed another highly influential theory that can act as a parallel to the Buddhist concept of a "general antidote" to all destructive emotions. Her theory, the Broaden and Build Model of Positive Emotions, also helps explain why the Dalai Lama's method is so powerful and effective.

Up until the last decade the vast majority of scientific research on human emotion focused on negative emotions. As a result, neuroscientists and evolutionary psychologists developed coherent theories about why negative emotions evolved, explaining how they helped our remote ancestors survive. From an evolutionary perspective, the negative emotions made good sense. But when looking for the reason why we have positive emotions, seeking to identify how *they* were adaptive from an evolutionary perspective, how they helped us survive, things didn't make a lot of sense. Unlike the negative emotions, which were each associated with specific "thought-action" tendencies that urged us to act in ways that would help us survive, the positive emotions didn't seem to be urging us to do anything in particular; they only maybe told us, "Hey! This is *good*—just keep doing what you're doing, and don't change anything!" It was easy to see how physical pleasure, linked with enjoyment of food or sex, played a role in survival and reproduction, but the adaptive value of the many other positive emotions was largely a mystery.

The *build* part of the Broaden and Build theory proposes that the negative emotions were designed to help us survive when we were in danger, while the positive emotions were designed for those times when things were safe, and their purpose was to build physical, intellectual, and social resources that we could use in the future, which would enhance our odds for survival. These are the emotions associated with invention and discovery, of thinking of new strategies to gain resources and ways to adapt to our environment. And these are the emotions that help foster social bonds that pay off in the future, when things may be difficult and we need to turn to others to help us. As human beings evolved and lived longer, it certainly paid to think about the future and build up a few resources that we could cash in on at a later time.

In one of the original experiments demonstrating the "broadening" effect of positive emotions, Fredrickson and her colleagues gathered a group of test subjects, divided them into groups, and evoked a different emotion in each group by having them watch short film clips that elicited a particular emotion, such as amusement, anger, or fear. She then assessed the effect of the emotion on the participant's ability to think broadly or narrowly, to see either the "big picture" or to focus in on small details. She did this in various ways. In one experiment, for example, she used a "global-local visual processing task"—she showed them a diagram of some geometric shapes, the "standard" figure. Then she showed them two other diagrams and asked them to judge which of the two comparison figures is most like the standard one. Neither choice was "right" or "wrong"; one comparison figure resembled the standard in its overall shape, or "global configuration," and the other one resembled the first more in its fine details, or "local elements." The results showed that those who were feeling positive emotion were much more likely to "see the big picture" and choose the figure that resembled the overall shape. Those who were feeling neutral or in a negative mood were more likely to show a narrower thought pattern, focusing on the small details. Since that original experiment, Fredrickson and others have conducted many similar kinds of experiments conclusively showing some of these fundamental differences in thinking between those in a positive mood and those in a negative mood.

Another investigator, Alice Isen from Cornell University, one of the true pioneers in research on positive emotions, has investigated the effects of positive emotions on thinking for more than two decades, accumulating extensive evidence demonstrating their broadening effects. In one study, for example, she induced a positive feeling in a group of subjects and had them perform some word-association exercises. She would give them a list of three words, for instance, "mower," "foreign," and "atomic," then ask them to think of a word that relates to all three (answer: "power"). She found that the subjects who were feeling happy did significantly better than the control group. Her original research using this method was designed to study the effects of positive emotions on creativity, but in conducting experiments such as these it also became clear that positive emotions help people see things from a wider perspective, as opposed to the narrowing effects of negative emotions.

With this as a background, if we now take another look at the Dalai Lama's "realistic approach," suddenly we find that his words begin to take on a familiar ring! The primary technique or method he recommends for cultivating this realistic outlook is looking at adverse situations from a wider perspective, from different angles, looking at the "big picture," adopting a long-term perspective, cultivating a flexible way of thinking that allows us to see things in new ways, and so on. This is precisely the type of thinking that investigators have associated with the positive emotions through recent experiments.

Here a critical question comes up. The research shows how our positive emotions or feelings of happiness generally act to broaden our perspective and outlook. The Dalai Lama suggests the opposite—that cultivating a broader outlook, a wider and more realistic perspective (using one's capacity for reason, analysis, logic, etc.), is an effective approach to coping with our troubled world and maintaining happiness. So positive emotions may *lead to* this type of outlook that the Dalai Lama is talking about, but is the opposite true? In other words, does deliberately cultivating a broader outlook, seeing one's problems from different angles and so on, lead to *more* positive emotions?

In a word, *Yes!* Studies done by Fredrickson and others have shown that it is a two-way street: Positive emotions lead to broader thinking, and the practice of broader thinking leads to positive emotions. The result is what investigators have identified as an "upward spiral," where the more one practices broader thinking, the more positive emotions and happiness one will experience, which will in turn lead to a broader outlook, and so on.

There seems to be no doubt that looking at situations from a broader perspective can help us cultivate more positive emotions and can help us cope with daily problems more effectively. Of course, there are certain positive emotions or states of mind that are of particular value and importance when dealing with some of the more serious and intractable problems in the world today: hope, optimism, and resilience.

Thus, the following morning we turned to these critical topics.

Chapter 11

HOPE, OPTIMISM, AND RESILIENCE

Hope

SPRING IS the season of hope. And every spring, as Chicago Cubs fans fill Wrigley Field for the baseball team's opening game of the season, there is the same sincere conviction in every heart: "This is the year! This year they will win the World Series!" And every autumn, when the chill returns to the air and the days begin to grow shorter, with their dreams of a pennant shattered, there is one thought in every heart: "Wait till next year!" And what is it that inspires the fans to crowd into the stadium the following year, once again crying, "This is the year!" *even though their team has not won a World Series since 1908?* It is hope.

Hope is one of humanity's most valuable inner resources. And it was hope to which we now turned our attention.

"Your Holiness," I began, "you know, yesterday you had mentioned the benefits of accepting the fact that problems and suffering are bound to arise in life. I was just thinking, however, that despite the potential benefits of adopting this starkly realistic outlook you were speaking about, in view of all the problems going on in the world, things can sure seem discouraging sometimes."

"That's why we need a variety of approaches," the Dalai Lama replied, "and different ways of looking at our problems. For example, even if we are thinking about some of the larger or more serious problems in society, issues like the environment and so on, and feeling a sense of distress or helplessness, if one looks at this from a wider perspective, you can see that many of these problems are caused by our human intelligence, misuse of human intelligence, without being counterbalanced with human values, a good heart. For example, our intelligence has led to developing these modern technologies, but without a sense of human responsibility, technology can cause disasters. But if certain problems are caused or created by our human intelligence, then the same intelligence can be used to find the solution, if the will is there, guided by the proper motivation."

"Well, even if it is possible to find solutions, I think many people might still become discouraged because the problems are so complex, and progress in overcoming them seems to occur so slowly."

"That's why I think it is so important to cultivate an attitude that allows you to maintain hope. Hope can make a great difference in how one responds to problems and difficulties."

"So, since hope is so critical in today's world, I'm wondering if you can talk to me a little bit more about it, and how to cultivate it."

"Yes. . . . Now about hope . . . I think from one perspective one could say that our very existence is sustained by hope. You see, as we have discussed many times, the most fundamental aspiration of all human beings is to seek happiness, to overcome suffering. We may go to bed at night confronted with many problems in our lives. But we go to bed hoping we will wake up the next morning!" He chuckled, then continued. "And then the next morning, in a way, it is hope that motivates us to get out of bed and carry on with our lives—the hope that we will eventually be able to achieve our aspiration for happiness, the hope that somehow we will be able to overcome the obstacles. And we may have other more specific kinds of goals in our lives, and it's hope that allows us to continue working toward those goals. So our lives are very much kept alive by hope."

With this in mind, I asked, "Can you tell me how you yourself have sustained an underlying feeling of hope, in the face of the challenges of the Tibetan situation that remain essentially unresolved right up until the present day?"

"Yes. Here we have been discussing this approach of adopting a wider perspective, and that can be tremendously helpful in maintaining a feeling of hope in dealing with the Tibetan situation, because the more narrow one's view, the more hopeless it might look. If you look at it only in a limited context, looking only at the recent events and the current situation, we have struggled for fifty years, but so far our efforts have not brought success.

"But if you broaden your perspective, and look at the situation from a global perspective, then you might see some basis for hope. After all, the entire world is changing, and there is no reason why China should be an exception. Just a couple decades ago, who would have predicted the collapse of the Soviet Union? In fact, today's China is very different from the China twenty years ago. In the case of Tibet, if you look only at the past Chinese policies, you might not see the potential for much hope. But with a wider perspective you might discover there are changes taking place within the Chinese society itself, especially among the common people who are beginning to show more interest in Tibetan culture and Buddhism. Even among the Chinese people you can see a growing number of supporters and those who show greater sympathy for the Tibetans. So, here again you can see that the wider one's perspective, the greater the possibility for hope.

"Even with respect to the large-scale transfer of ethnic Chinese population into Tibet, which raises serious fears among the Tibetans that this might reduce the Tibetans to an insignificant minority in our own country, one could even envision a potential for a change in policy. One could imagine that without governmental incentives for the Han Chinese to move to Tibet, the population transfer not only might stop, but in fact, some of the current Chinese residents of Tibet might choose to return to their original home, where the altitude and the climate might be more suitable. So anything is possible."

Thinking about the inner strength and enormous sense of purpose that would be required to maintain hope after decades of failure in dealing with the Chinese, I asked, "Were there any other factors that have helped you maintain hope in addition to adopting this wider perspective?"

"This approach has been useful in helping maintain hope," he replied, "but in my case there can be many factors at play. For one thing, I find refuge in my Buddhist practices. For example, there is one passage that I repeat every day, which sustains me, provides a great source of strength, and prevents me from losing hope. . . ."

"You mean your favorite passage from Shantideva?"

"Yes," he said. Then, reciting the passage with a tone of freshness as if reciting it for the first time, he said, "*As long as space remains, As long as sentient beings remain, Until then, may I too remain, And dispel the miseries of the world.* So, here, this stanza helps me shift my perspective, creating a much more expansive vision, looking at the situation in a wider context. So, if you perceive the situation against the backdrop of the expanse of time, along with the recognition that change is inevitable, that impermanence is one of the inevitable characteristics of existence, then one can see that anything is possible.

"Of course, this is primarily a Buddhist approach," he reminded me. "You need to keep in mind that one of the reasons why stanzas such as this one from Shantideva are so powerful for me is that, when I recite them, there is a whole system of beliefs behind it. This includes a belief in the theory of rebirth, the idea of innumerable eons, and so on.

"I think that in general whether one is a religious believer or not can make a big difference in one's ability to cope. And here, I think each of the world's major religious traditions have made a contribution, each with its own ideas or practices that help give believers a kind of inner strength, and prevent them from sinking into hopelessness or despair when confronting the problems of the world. Of course," he added, "from a secular perspective, one may find these ideas difficult to accept."

"Actually, Your Holiness, there's a lot of scientific evidence to back you up, showing the benefits of faith in increasing one's overall happiness and in helping one cope with life's adversities or traumatic events. And this is a topic that I'd like to explore with you in greater depth at some point later on. But for right now I'd like to stick to more secular strategies.

"So, I'm wondering . . . you mentioned how reciting Shantideva's stanza helps give you a more expansive or long-term perspective, but there's a system of Buddhist beliefs behind that. But I think that even from a secular perspective, without that system of beliefs, a person can still appreciate the value of a wider, long-term perspective."

I pondered for a moment. "So, I'm wondering if there are additional ways to develop that more expansive vision but without resorting to thinking about innumerable eons and rebirth and so on. . . . Here I'm trying to think of a specific example related to the topic of sustaining hope."

Suddenly a thought occurred to me. "Oh, this might be an example: Let's say that a person is working on a difficult task, something that seems almost impossible, hopeless. . . . Like, for instance, let's say that a researcher is working on a cure for disease, but of course it is so complex it might seem almost hopeless. Instead of being overwhelmed by the unlikelihood of that person discovering a cure, let's say that he or she may deliberately spend time thinking along the lines of, 'Yes, this task is very difficult, I may not accomplish it myself. But if I make just one small contribution, one small step, then another researcher can build on that, and someone else can then build on their work,' and so on. If the person looks at it from that perspective, then it will not seem so hopeless; he or she will have hope that eventually the cure will be found. Could that line of reasoning act as a substitute, replacing the idea of rebirth and innumerable eons?"

"That's right! That's right! Very good!" the Dalai Lama cried. "That's a very good example. Because, in fact, if you look at the history of modern science and where we currently are, you can see the effects of the contribution made by individuals from different directions and generations. So one person made a contribution and another person came later and built up on this. Another person came and built up on that. So you can look at just the last century and see where science has evolved to a stage where the pioneers of modern science would have never even dreamed of!

"So, Howard, I think that this is in fact a kind of complementary idea, and the kind of reasoning you suggest can be helpful in developing a more long-term perspective that might be useful in sustaining hope, especially when addressing various problems in society or achieving any difficult long-term objective."

"Can you think of any other factors or strategies to help sustain hope, other ways to look at a problem that will give one strength to keep going without falling into discouragement or hopelessness?"

"So, other factors . . ." he repeated softly. "You know, Howard, in maintaining hope and determination in pursuit of a noble objective, generally I feel that it is *crucial to have a clear recognition of how worthy your objective is, the value of the objective. That's the important thing*. Recognizing that your objective is worthy, for example, one that involves others' welfare or the general well-being of the community, helps give you the determination to pursue it. And then when things become difficult, simply reminding yourself of the value of your objective can help sustain hope and courage. You may be really struggling with a difficult problem, for example, but if you can remind yourself that future generations of your family or friends will reap the benefits if you are successful, then this will help sustain your efforts and not give up. *In that case, then whether or not that objective can be realized in your lifetime is not really important*. For example, if you look at the lives of such great spiritual masters as the Buddha and Jesus Christ, the missions that they set out to accomplish were not confined to their own lifetime."

"This idea of 'having a worthy objective,' " I asked; "do you think this is related to having a sense of meaning and a higher purpose in life?"

"Yes, this may be related," the Dalai Lama replied. "Although what I mean here specifically is the need to appreciate the value of the objectives you wish to pursue, it is also the case that when an individual has a sense of purpose in his existence that transcends the narrow personal concerns, this provides one a source of strength and the ability to withstand adversities and hardships. So, if a person's goal or objective is linked to their sense of meaning or higher purpose, then this can make a big difference in strengthening their determination."

To most observers looking at the current situation in Tibet, the Dalai Lama's dream of genuine autonomy and freedom for his people, even without full independence, seems hopeless. It seems inconceivable that the Chinese leadership would suddenly do a complete about-face, and stem the tide of the Han Chinese pouring into Tibet, abandoning their apparent plan of diluting the Tibetan population to such a proportion that they become a small minority in their own country.

Despite this, for the past fifty years the Dalai Lama has struggled ceaselessly, working tirelessly to achieve greater freedom and human rights for the people of Tibet, doing his best to educate others, making appeals whenever or wherever he can. And for fifty years he has met with nothing but failure. At every step, no matter what he does or whom he meets with, as soon as his presence becomes known anywhere in the world, formal protests and informal complaints are bound to be lodged by the Chinese government, exerting whatever pressure they can to bully and intimidate whoever meets with him. This has happened again and again, with ruthless and maddening monotony. For fifty years. But he has not lost hope.

Clearly, the Dalai Lama has mastered the Art of Hope, and in our discussion that morning he explained how he has managed to do this. Using the Tibetan situation as an illustration, he revealed how his "realistic approach" could be used to cultivate hope. The general strategy or main technique that we were discussing that week involved looking at a situation from a broader perspective or from different angles. As we mentioned, this strategy has a broad range of applications in cultivating positive emotions, like hope, as well as reducing negative emotions and in helping us cope with life's difficulties in general. In the scientific literature, this strategy is sometimes called reframing or reappraisal.

In showing how he applies this method to the Tibetan situation, the Dalai Lama began by looking at the situation more broadly along two dimensions: time and space. Looking from a broader time frame, he took a more long-term view of the situation. And looking more broadly from the "space" dimension, he viewed the situation not just from the standpoint of the local conditions and circumstances, but rather he expanded his perspective to view the situation from a wider global context, looking at the changes throughout the world.

As our conversations unfolded that week, the Dalai Lama went on to reveal additional ways of looking at problems "more realistically" or from a "wider perspective." And in this discussion, he added one of the most important ways of reappraising or reframing an adverse situation or problem: finding some greater meaning or higher purpose associated with the situation. As the Dalai Lama suggests, the more one's goal is "linked to their sense of meaning or higher purpose," the easier it will be to draw strength from one's goal, and increase one's determination to overcome any obstacle in life.

Earlier we mentioned how positive emotions can help us cope with adversity, acting as an antidote to the stress response associated with emotions such as anxiety or anger. Summarizing the scientific evidence on this subject, Barbara Fredrickson has said, "Positive emotions are linked to more effective coping, marked by finding positive meaning within problems and taking broad perspectives on those problems." Looking at the data from others' work as well as her own experiments, she has concluded, "Finding positive meaning may be the most powerful leverage point for cultivating positive emotions during times of crisis."

Traditionally, the most common way of finding meaning is through one's spiritual or religious beliefs. In our discussion, the Dalai Lama was completely open in identifying how his Buddhist beliefs and practices have played a powerful role in helping him cope with adversity.

Finding some positive meaning in adversity not only enhances positive emotions in general, but also can strengthen the specific positive emotion we are addressing here: hope. In fact, the positive meaning one derives from religious faith is probably the greatest single source of hope throughout history, from which countless people have drawn strength, inspiration, and courage.

There is no question that having purpose and meaning is one of the surest sources of human happiness in general, in addition to its role in helping us maintain hope, sustaining a person through adversity, suffering, tragedy, and the darkest periods of life. As we have seen, religious faith can certainly provide a sense of meaning, but purpose and meaning can also be found in many ways besides religious faith. The Dalai Lama advises that when one is facing adversity or obstacles in the pursuit of one's goals, one way of increasing hope and strength to carry on is to remind oneself of the value or greater benefit of your objective, reflecting on its worthiness, such as how it may contribute to the welfare or well-being of others. This is essentially a method of finding positive meaning, and an effective strategy to help strengthen hope that can be used by religious and nonreligious people alike.

Referring to studies conducted by herself and others, Fredrickson has said, "With or without the infusion of religion, people can find positive meaning in daily life by reframing adverse events in a positive light, infusing ordinary events with positive value, and pursuing and attaining realistic goals." As our conversation continued, the Dalai Lama's practical advice correlated perfectly with modern scientific theory in discussing the importance of setting realistic goals.

SETTING REALISTIC GOALS

"Your Holiness," I continued, "I think you have come up with some good practical advice about how to cope with problems without becoming completely overwhelmed. I'm just wondering if you can think of any other factors that could be helpful as we pursue our goals in life—factors that could help prevent us from becoming too discouraged as we come up against obstacles?"

"Yes. Another thing. We have been speaking about the usefulness of having a realistic outlook, and I think that as you set about to achieve some goal, it is important to investigate how realistic and feasible it is, to see if your goal is possible to achieve or not. How well prepared you are right at the very start can make a difference. As Shantideva points out in his *Guide to the Bodhisattva's Way of Life,* before you embark on a venture, first examine it properly to see whether or not you can do it. You shouldn't plunge into it hastily. I think that just the clear awareness that your objective is really possible to achieve can help strengthen your hope and determination."

Becoming distracted by my tape recorder for a moment, I lost track and got off track. "Your Holiness, I'm getting confused about one point. You mentioned that one factor to help sustain hope is this kind of single-pointed determination to pursue your objective, based on your recognition of how valuable or worthy it is, regardless of whether it can be achieved in this lifetime. Now you are speaking of the need to set a realistic goal, making sure that the goal is practical, that you can actually achieve it. So, in a way, it seems that—"

Not waiting for me to complete the thought, he replied, "Howard, here we're generally talking about two different things—the global level and the individual level. So in the case of the global level, tackling wider societal problems and so on, even if our objectives don't get achieved in one individual's lifetime or one generation, it's still worth pursuing. But in the case of an individual's personal needs, then one's goals should be practical and achievable. So there's no conflict. It's two different contexts."

Having clarified the point, he went on. "Of course, developing a realistic outlook does not just involve determining whether your objective is possible or not possible. It also involves a kind of active assessment of the possible challenges that might arise in the pursuit of that goal. If right at the start there is a clear understanding that some objectives may be harder to realize and some can be realized more easily, if people are already aware of that distinction and accept it, and if you discover that your particular objective may be harder to realize, then you'll expect that there are bound to be some problems in the pursuit of that. And if people are already aware of this fact, then when they encounter adversity, they are much better prepared. There is then less risk of losing hope. Whereas if from the beginning you totally ignore the fact that obstacles will arise, then when you encounter even a tiny impediment, you lose hope and you react in an exaggerated way."

The Dalai Lama views hope as an essential factor in helping us sustain our efforts when we encounter obstacles and setbacks in our lives, helping us persist in finding solutions to life's challenges, a view supported by many scientific studies. Because of its tremendous value, hope has been a subject of intense interest to psychologists involved in the positive psychology movement. When investigating hope, most researchers classify it as one of the positive emotions, although there is not universal agreement. Some may see hope as more of a thinking process or a kind of character trait. But no matter how one classifies hope, there is no question that it can be a key ingredient in coping with a troubled world. In addition, as a positive emotion, like other positive emotions in general, hope can make a direct contribution to the sum total of one's happiness. And as if this was not enough, studies have found hope to be associated with a wide array of benefits for one's physical and mental health. Hope has been associated with better academic and sports achievement among students, and adults high in hope have stronger relationships, greater success at work, and increased likelihood of attaining their goals in general.

In view of all the benefits that hope brings, it isn't surprising that over the past decade or two there have been many new theories about the nature of hope and how to increase it. Some of these theories have garnered a bit of attention. Most have been discarded. But one psychologist in particular, Charles Richard Snyder, at the University of Kansas, was very influential in this field, making a major contribution to our understanding of hope. Before Snyder's theory, it was felt that hope was a kind of undifferentiated wish or sense that the person can achieve their goals. Snyder thought of hope as a goal-directed thinking process, consisting of two components working together: *pathways* thinking and *agency* thinking. Pathways thinking involves having a game plan on how to achieve your goals. Agency thinking involves the will or motivation to carry it out. Snyder believes that both of these types of thinking must be present in order to maintain hope and that they reinforce each other.

Looking at the Dalai Lama's approach to cultivating hope from the perspective of Snyder's theory, we can easily see how his method contributes to both agency and pathways thinking. Successful agency is the person's sense of determination to accomplish your goal, the feeling of being motivated to get going initially, and to keep going once you start, even if it is difficult. The Dalai Lama suggests that when hope falters, one way of renewing your strength and courage is to deliberately reflect on the value and importance of your goal, since "recognizing its value helps give you the determination to pursue it." This is essentially a way of increasing agency, of strengthening your motivation and determination.

The Dalai Lama advocates having realistic expectations and awareness of your capabilities while setting practical and achievable goals as well as anticipating potential obstacles, which will contribute to pathways thinking. Pathways thinking includes having a sense that there is a clear path to achieve your goals, that there is a practical way to meet your objectives. It would seem reasonable to assume that the Dalai Lama's "realistic approach" to accomplishing goals would certainly tend to foster pathways thinking, and thus strengthen hope. Incidentally, while the popular image of people with high hopes is a kind of blind optimism, of false hopes, the opposite appears to be the case: Research shows that high-hope individuals are actually often quite realistic.

Pathways thinking is also associated with the underlying feeling that you have the ability to find new ways to achieve your goals even if obstacles happen to arise, that you can always find a way to solve the problem, or to think up a plan to meet your objectives. Thus, the more creative you are, the stronger your capacity for problem solving is, the more confidence you will have that you will be able to find a "pathway" to overcome difficulties and accomplish your goals. The Dalai Lama's approach can help enhance this aspect of pathways thinking as well. As we saw earlier, the Dalai Lama's realistic approach to coping with problems involves looking at situations from a wider perspective. This will increase positive emotions, which will increase broader thinking in return, resulting in the upward spiral in which broader thinking and positive emotions continue to reinforce each other.

There is substantial evidence that the increase in positive emotion resulting from this upward spiral is associated with a broader mind-set that helps an individual see problems in novel ways, "broadening" their scope of action, opening up new ways of doing things—new "pathways" to achieving their goal. One experiment illustrates this principle beautifully. In this classic experiment on creativity, the researcher places on a table a box containing candles, matches, and some tacks. The subject is asked to attach the candles to the wall in a way that they will burn without dripping candle wax on the table or floor. The problem is solved if the subject empties the box, tacks it to the wall, and uses it as a platform or candleholder on which to place the candle. This requires a "broadened" type of thinking that sees the box in a new way, not just as a container. Studies have shown that boosting a person's mood or inducing positive emotions ahead of time will increase the likelihood of finding the solution. Thus the increased creativity and capacity for problem solving that results from these techniques enhances pathways thinking—i.e., finding new "pathways" to achieving a goal—which will strengthen one's capacity for hope, even when faced with challenging conditions.

So far, there seemed to be a uniform, almost elegant, correlation between the Dalai Lama's views and the most recent scientific theories and findings, a correlation that continued as he broadened his exploration of hope.

Optimism

"One very important factor for sustaining hope in general is to have an optimistic attitude," continued the Dalai Lama. "If you adopt a pessimistic attitude right from the start, this will be a true failure. Because your attitude will be something like, 'Nothing will work.' "

"Would you consider yourself an optimistic person, particularly in view of the difficulties faced by the Tibetan people as well as the troubles in the world?" I asked.

"Oh yes, definitely," said the Dalai Lama with a chuckle.

"Well, Your Holiness, you are a firm believer in looking realistically at a given situation. And realistically, sometimes situations are pretty bleak. So, wouldn't looking at that optimistically be foolish? Something contrary to the reality?" I asked.

"Not necessarily," he replied. "Optimism does not mean that you are blind to the actual reality of the situation. It means that you always maintain a positive spirit so that you remain motivated to seek a solution to any given problem. And it means that you recognize that any given situation has many different aspects—optimism involves looking at the situation not only from the standpoint of the problem itself, not only recognizing the negative aspects, but also seeking out some positive aspect, some potential benefit, actively looking at the same situation in terms of the potential positive outcomes."

"Well, I'm wondering if you can think of any additional examples of how one might look at problems in terms of potential benefits or positive outcomes, some more concrete examples?"

"Examples, examples, examples!" He laughed good-naturedly. "Howard, you are always wanting these 'more examples'!"

With the evident goodwill that was ever-present in his laugh, a laugh that was always unaffected, guileless, I could never take offense at his gentle chiding. In fact, it made me smile, on the verge of giggling. Besides, he was right. But still, starting to feel slightly defensive I said, "Well, examples are always so helpful in understanding how to apply the various principles or techniques that you bring up. And besides that . . ."

I didn't need to go on.

"OK," he said agreeably, quickly relenting. "More examples . . ."

Just as the Dalai Lama was about to continue, he suddenly had a brief coughing fit. I had seen him in Europe several weeks earlier, where he had developed a sore throat and intermittent cough. Although he was receiving good medical care and had just started on antibiotics, I couldn't help but feel concerned about the persistence of his symptoms. Despite getting on in years, however, only the most severe debilitating illness could induce him to cut back on his intensive teaching schedule.

Reaching into my pocket, I offered him a lozenge.

"Thank you," he said, and as he put the lozenge in his mouth, he suddenly started to laugh: "Oh! So here you can see here a very small example—right now I have this scratchy, sore throat, a small problem. That is negative. But if you investigate, you see, you can always find other angles. So, looking at another angle, a positive angle, this coughing just brought something *good*—a sweet from a friend! A moment of sharing. It isn't all bad. It is a matter of reminding yourself that despite this problem, there are still positive things in my life.

"So, we have been talking about how a narrow perspective can increase feelings of hopelessness and other negative emotions, and cause us greater suffering. If we have too much self-involvement, a kind of very narrow self-concern, this can limit us and cause problems, exaggerating our suffering. So, in the case of this sore throat, this is not really much of a problem—but if I focus too much on myself and keep thinking, 'Oh, what a problem this sore throat is, this cough is so annoying, why am I afflicted with this?' then this just serves to exaggerate the situation, and then it becomes a problem. If your vision narrows so you focus your attention only on a problem or tragedy, you can even become completely overwhelmed by it, when in fact it is a surmountable problem.

"However, we can prevent this. Broadening our perspective acts as an antidote to that kind of narrow perspective, and there are various ways to do this. One way is by comparison, comparing of your own situation with those who are less fortunate than yourself. This can often make a difference, at least in helping cope with one's personal problems. It puts things in a more realistic proportion. For example, if I am troubled by a sore throat and lots of annoying coughing, I can remember that at this moment there are so many people in the world experiencing problems that are so much more serious, so many people suffering, in real pain—and compared with that, this small problem is nothing. Another way is to take a more long-term view, realizing that yes, this may be a little annoying or inconvenient, but this is just temporary and will soon pass.

"And then, as we discussed before, by remembering that problems and suffering are naturally bound to arise, looking from a different angle you'll realize that, after all, as long as I have this body," he said, slapping one arm with the opposite hand, "it is bound to have a certain number of sore throats. That's the reality.

"So, *all of this* is the reality! So, when crisis strikes, you see, if one looks at that tragedy without losing sight of the overall picture, then one will come to realize the following simple truth. 'Yes, my problem still remains; yes, this is most undesirable, but still it is only a part of my life, only a small part at that.' And this kind of thinking will help you cope better, and deal with the problem more effectively."

"Well, I think your cough-and-sore-throat example is really a good illustration of how to use this method of looking for more positive angles, this kind of reasoning," I said. "So, in coming up with different ways that we can perceive our troubles—"

Now appearing to pick up some steam, he leaned forward as if propelled by his mounting enthusiasm, and continued. "Or, another example . . . remembering that one is not alone in dealing with adversity. When we are dealing with problems, sometimes we have a sense as if we are somehow singled out for this misfortune. This is a kind of narrowing of perspective, as if our world is shrinking, and we may feel alone or isolated. But if we remember that there are others who have gone through or are going through similar things, that we are not alone, and in some cases even reach out for support from those other individuals, I think this can help.

"In fact, no matter *what* difficulty we are dealing with, all of us are part of a society or a community, unless one is living as a hermit in a cave. So, you could deliberately broaden your perspective to be aware of the fact you are a member of society. If we remember this, cultivate it as part of our underlying awareness, we will realize that it may be possible to draw from the resources in the community or society during difficult periods. There is always some sort of protection, comfort, or assistance that can be found if you actively seek it out. There may be people or institutions that can help us that we may not even be aware of yet, but which we can investigate. We are not isolated or alone. So there could be many different types of awareness.

"So . . . *here* are your examples!" He laughed, delivering the line with a sweep of the hand and an almost theatrical flourish, as if he were a magician who had just pulled a rabbit out of his hat.

His arguments were certainly compelling, with a deep intuitive appeal, and from a scientific perspective they would move from compelling to overwhelming when I later investigated the scientific support and evidence for his views. But there was one point that seemed like it needed to be addressed.

"You know, I was just thinking," I said, "and I completely agree that cultivating the attitudes or views you mentioned can help us cope with adversity, help us deal with life's problems. As usual, your suggestions are grounded in good common sense as well. But I'm not sure how effective it is to look at the reality of a situation when you are going through a crisis or dealing with adversity, seeing it from a wider perspective. After all, you have mentioned in the past how when we are experiencing strong emotions like anger or anxiety, our perspective seems to narrow—so it seems that at those moments we may not have the *capacity* to see things from this wider perspective, to analyze or to investigate the reality of the situation more holistically, and look at the different angles and so on."

"That's true, Howard," he replied, "so this is why we need to make an effort to think about these things ahead of time, repeatedly, familiarizing yourself with these ways of thinking over a period of time. And we need to reflect on these kinds of views very deeply, reinforcing them, so that they are part of our fundamental outlook. That way, when problems come up, these attitudes and holistic ways of perceiving things will arise naturally."

The Dalai Lama looked at his watch and I realized our time was coming to a close.

"I know we have to end soon, but are there any other thoughts you have regarding ways to help us cope, before we end?"

"Yes," he answered, "it is important to have a variety of approaches we can use to help us cope with our environment, and the problems that come up in daily life. For example, if you are living in an environment where there are bombs constantly exploding around us, analyzing the situation from a wider perspective or looking at different angles of the situation isn't the best approach for 'coping.' " He chuckled briefly. "In that case, the best approach is to run for cover!

"So, one thing . . . although the main approach that we are using here to help us cope involves developing a certain outlook or attitudes, cultivating our inner resources, I think that our external experiences can also play a role in how we cope with adversity."

"Can you explain a bit more about how our external experiences can enhance our ability to cope with adversity, deal with problems, or help us regulate our negative emotions and so on?"

"Yes. But I think we should end here for today. We will continue tomorrow."

A while back, as part of a workshop I was conducting on the Art of Happiness, I asked the participants to complete an exercise in practicing positive reappraisal of adverse circumstances, situations, or events. The exercise involved asking participants to select an experience of adversity or a period of hardship or suffering that they have gone through, an experience that is now in the past. After writing down this experience, they were asked to reframe and reappraise it, looking at the experience from alternate angles, listing any positive outcomes or benefits that ultimately resulted from the experience, either directly or indirectly.

I suggested that they consider questions such as, Was there anything useful that I learned from the experience, about myself, others, or about other aspects of life? Did I meet anyone as a result of the experience, either directly or indirectly, who has played a significant role in my life? Did I ultimately grow in any way from it? Did it lead to any beneficial changes that would not have happened, had I not gone through the experience? Did the experience ultimately open any new doors, provide any new opportunities?

The size of this particular workshop was deliberately kept small so each participant would have an opportunity to share their experiences with the others if they so wished. Thus, in the second stage of this exercise, the participants were invited to share their experience with the group. Sitting in a circle, we began with the first person, Joseph, a well-dressed, intelligent, and articulate professional gentleman in his sixties.

"I just don't know what to say," Joseph began. "It was easy to come up with a period of suffering—my daughter died four years ago from leukemia. But I've been sitting here thinking, and I just can't see anything positive about it. I can't see anything good that came from it in any way, nothing that I learned from it except pain, and no beneficial or positive changes that came about, either directly or indirectly—it was just bad." His tone was not overtly angry or challenging; his eyes and expression conveyed mostly a kind of weariness and a kind of hollow emptiness, except for perhaps a subtle measure of residual sadness and bitterness—and the unmistakable tone of a father who clearly adored his daughter. He went on to explain how he had become a father late in life, in his fifties, and he had always considered that he might not have been around to see his grandchildren, but never considered the possibility of either of his two children dying before him.

Acknowledging the sad truth that sometimes one's suffering is so great and the tragedy so overwhelming that it is impossible for an individual to see an event from any other angle, several group members offered a few words of understanding and sympathy, and we moved on to the next person to share her story. While generally it was suggested that people first practicing this exercise start with more mundane day-to-day problems and build up to the bigger problems, that afternoon a number of the people in the group had also chosen their biggest challenge in life—moving stories of surviving cancer, dealing with the painful deaths of loved ones, facing bankruptcies after a lifetime of hard work, and others—each of them revealing ultimate benefits, the "one door closes, another door opens" principle. After the last person had shared their story, as we were about to move on, Joseph raised his hand and asked to say a few words.

"You know," he said, "I'd like to amend what I said earlier. I've been listening to these stories and thinking, and the more I thought about it, I realized that despite the pain, I could think of two benefits that ultimately resulted. First, I think the experience made me stronger in some way. . . ."

"In what way?" I asked.

"Well, the death of my child is the very worst thing I can imagine. I think that going through the very worst thing that I could ever imagine, and surviving it, has given me a kind of inner strength—knowing that if I could deal with that, I feel I could deal with *anything*. There's nothing left to fear, because no matter how hard things get, I know that I've survived worse.

"And there's another thing—I think her death has really made me appreciate my younger daughter, Chloe, much more. It made me realize what a gift she is, each day, and not to take her for granted, and as a result I think I'm a better father to her. So, I think that's another ultimate change that is positive."

As our exploration continued, the Dalai Lama added another ingredient to his recipe for coping with life's adversities and finding happiness in our troubled world: *Optimism*. As he suggests, there is a close link between optimism and hope—the more optimistic one is, the more likely one will be able to maintain hope during troubled times. Most researchers categorize optimism as one of the positive emotions, in the same family as hope, since both have a "future" orientation, with a general expectation of positive outcomes in the future. Optimism is one of the most well studied positive emotions. Studies have shown that optimism can play a significant role in helping us cope with the full spectrum of life's adversities and troubles, from minor everyday annoyances to trauma, loss, and catastrophes. As with other positive emotions, it has myriad benefits in enhancing our physical, mental, and social well-being—associated with better health, longer life, stronger marriages, and greater success at school or work.

The Dalai Lama's method of cultivating greater optimism involves essentially the same general technique used to cultivate hope—looking at negative circumstances and events from a broader perspective, looking at adverse situations from different angles, and so on. In this conversation, however, he elaborated on this approach by explaining that the technique involves actively looking for some *positive* aspect to the situation or event, some potential benefit or positive outcome. This technique is sometimes known as reframing, *positive reappraisal,* or benefit finding.

In seeking a better understanding of this technique and why it is so effective, it is helpful to return to the Dalai Lama's initial premise: *"how we view the world around us . . . how you interpret your circumstances and the events going on around you can definitely affect how we might respond to our world and its problems. . . . I think this is directly related to our ability to cope with problems and maintain happiness."* Research has confirmed that optimism is largely a matter of how one perceives and interprets one's circumstances and the bad events that occur in life, the problems, failures, and setbacks. It is clear that when something bad happens, people tend to ask, why? Their assessment of the cause, their answer to this question, determines how they respond to the bad event.

Some of the seminal research in this field was conducted by Dr. Martin Seligman, one of the foremost experts on optimism, who developed an interest in the subject early in his career at the University of Pennsylvania. Seligman came up with the theory that the difference between optimists and pessimists is their "explanatory style," the way that they explain the bad things that happen to them. According to research conducted by Seligman and others, there are two crucial dimensions to a person's explanatory style: *permanence* and *pervasiveness*. When explaining a bad situation, pessimists tend to attribute it to causes or negative conditions that will persist for a long time, and will *affect other areas of their life,* undermining everything they do. When confronting failure or misfortune, optimists see things in exactly the opposite manner; they believe that the underlying causes are just temporary and are confined to just this one particular case. Thus, if a pessimist experiences a failure of some kind, such as failing an exam, he might attribute the reason to his innate lack of intelligence or fundamental lack of study skills, and think, "I'll probably fail this class and end up flunking out of school!" An optimist, on the other hand, might attribute the cause to not putting in enough study time for this test, and think, "I've failed this exam. But that does not mean I'll fail others." The optimist would simply see this as a temporary setback and a challenge to do better next time.

Because optimism and pessimism are largely a matter of explanatory style, psychologists today recognize optimism as something that can be learned—we can learn to alter our emotional reaction to a situation or event by changing how we perceive or interpret that situation. The primary technique used to build optimism is a classic *cognitive technique*, a technique with a large body of scientific evidence proving its effectiveness: first identify your pessimistic, negative thoughts; underlying assumptions; and beliefs; then actively challenge and dispute those thoughts, looking for evidence that refutes those thoughts or alternative explanations that are more optimistic.

Here we can see the Dalai Lama's approach to coping with our troubled world converging with the techniques that are widely practiced in Western psychology. What he calls "cultivating a realistic outlook" or "looking from wider perspective," psychologists call "cognitive techniques." Both approaches involve positive reappraisal. The ability to reframe and reappraise one's negative experiences and perceive them from a wider perspective, a more positive angle, is one of the key strategies for building resilience, hope, optimism, and a wide array of positive emotions. This method can be boiled down, distilled to its essence, and encapsulated in a single sentence, by asking ourselves: "How can I see this differently?" This technique has a broad range of applications. There are many ways that we can react to adverse situations and events. For example, we might react with anger, rage, jealousy, hatred, extreme anxiety, or depression. All of these are destructive emotions that can undermine happiness. This method can be applied in situations giving rise to any of these destructive emotions. It can help us deal with the situation more effectively, combat the negative emotion, and increase our overall sense of well-being.

When we speak about looking at adversity and problems from a more positive perspective, however, looking for positive aspects of a negative situation, and so on, there is a common objection that arises: Many people may ask, "Isn't this strategy the same thing as 'positive thinking,' where people tell themselves all sorts of positive things, always 'looking on the bright side,' while ignoring or denying the negative aspects of reality? Isn't this just 'Pollyannaism,' where individuals are deluding themselves?"

Of course, like other psychological traits, there can be considerable variation between people in their customary level of optimism, and when optimism becomes extreme, it can become unrealistic and potentially get us into trouble—underestimating risks, exaggerating our abilities, or constantly blaming others for our problems even when the problem is caused by our own behavior. In addition, past studies provide some evidence that optimists do tend to filter information with a positive bias, essentially allowing positive information to pass through to the conscious mind while filtering out negative information. These studies found that, in fact, people who were mildly depressed or sad tended to perceive reality more accurately.

It is here that the Dalai Lama's insights can become very important. As we've seen, the Dalai Lama's approach is built on a foundation of "realistic thinking." By assuring that one's perception or interpretation of events is always based on reality, the Dalai Lama's "realistic approach" has a built-in safety mechanism that prevents the dangers associated with extreme or unrealistic optimism.

It would seem on the surface that it might be impossible to see certain situations from a positive angle. But like the illustration of Joseph, the father who had lost his child, if one investigates carefully, there are always ways of perceiving problems in an optimistic manner, yet in ways that do not deny reality. After all, because of the relative nature of things, there is never just a single way to look at something, so we can choose to pay a greater share of attention to the positive aspects of our experience and cultivate an outlook grounded in gratitude for the good things in our life, without denying reality. And since none of us can truly predict the future, and we don't really know what will happen, we can choose to take an optimistic outlook, without denying reality. And even when the reality of a situation is extremely negative—we can *still* have an outlook that views problems as challenges, with an orientation toward problem solving, striving for one's goals, and being on the lookout for potential opportunities to bring about beneficial changes.

Interestingly, recent research reveals that most optimists would fit the description of the Dalai Lama's model of a "realistic optimist." Despite the rather common perception of optimists as being more likely than pessimists to live in their own fantasy world, and the past evidence that mildly depressed people see reality more clearly, there has been growing evidence that refutes this view, finding that pessimists are more likely to delude themselves and deny reality than optimists are.

In fact, there is considerable research showing that optimistic people cope better than pessimists under difficult conditions, and experience less distress. Research on the differences in coping styles shows that optimists have a more active problem-solving coping style and continue to exert effort even when dealing with a serious problem, whereas it is the pessimists who are more likely to avoid the situation or pretend that the problem does not exist. Optimists are found to be more flexible in finding solutions, more likely to reassess their situation as they go along, according to the reality of the situation. And when the situation is beyond their control or unsolvable, optimists generally make an effort to accept the reality of the stressful events, but this is not a stoic kind of resignation or fatalistically giving up, but rather an attempt to accept reality and integrate it into their overall outlook or worldview. They then use cognitive techniques to try to see a bad situation in the best possible light, and try to learn something even from adversity.

Optimism, like all the positive emotions, is a multifaceted state of mind, with one's capacity for optimism determined in part by one's basic disposition, upbringing, life experience, and natural ability to regulate one's own emotions. But one thing that is clear is that no matter what one's basic disposition or experiences might be, optimism can be deliberately cultivated through one's own effort and, as the Dalai Lama suggests, reshaping one's basic outlook on life as needed.

Resilience

At seventy-four years old, the Dalai Lama has led a truly remarkable life, a life marked by sudden and wildly shifting fortune. He is no stranger to hardship, disappointment, or failure.

At two years old, he was living with his family in a Tibetan village of twenty families in a remote region far from the capital of Lhasa. His family's poor farm grew a little buckwheat, barley, and potatoes. He slept by the woodstove in the kitchen every night, and by day toddled around the yard with chickens and *dzomos* (a cross between a yak and a cow).

By the age of ten, that two-year-old Lhamo Döndrub had become Jetsun Jamphel Ngawang Lobsang Yeshe Tenzin Gyatso, supreme ruler of the ancient land, loved and worshipped by all. Beyond having the role of an ordinary king, he is seen as the fourteenth incarnation of the Dalai Lama. In a tradition dating back six hundred years, he is the embodiment of Chenrizig, the Deity of Compassion, patron deity of Tibet. He has begun his lifelong study of Buddhism as a monk. Whenever venturing out of the magnificent thousand-chambered Potala, the winter palace of the Dalai Lamas, he was surrounded by a huge retinue; wherever he went he was carried on an ornate yellow palanquin carried by eight elaborately dressed bearers, with a hundred more people in every procession. The entire city would come just to catch a glimpse as he passed, falling silent with awe, tears in their eyes as they lay prostrate on the ground.

By the age of fifteen, he is formally enthroned to assume the mantle of full political power, but he was not wholly ready for what lay ahead for Tibet. He was taking over leadership of a country on the verge of war with the most populous nation on Earth, whose Communist troops were already invading the country, causing suffering to the people that would pale by comparison with what would soon come.

At twenty-four, he was forced to flee his beloved country in disguise, barely escaping, arriving on the Indian border after weeks of tortuous travel crossing the Himalayas. He arrived exhausted on the back of a *dzomo,* soaked from torrential freezing rains, feverish, and with dysentery. Having left most everything behind, he arrived with virtually nothing.

On March 10, 2008, a group of Tibetan monks living inside Tibet staged a peaceful demonstration protesting decades of tyranny and oppression under Chinese rule. It was the forty-ninth anniversary of the failed uprising that led to the Dalai Lama's escape into exile in northern India. From the Tibetan capital, Lhasa, similar protests began to spread across Tibet and even into neighboring Chinese provinces with large Tibetan populations. Many of these protests quickly veered out of control. Within days, the world was to witness the greatest period of unrest, violence, rioting, and repression inside Tibet in at least the past twenty years. The Chinese response was swift and harsh, with a crackdown by Chinese troops that included mass arrests, detentions, many casualties, and essentially placing all of Tibet in lockdown mode. . . . The Dalai Lama immediately issued a plea to both sides to stop the violence, and throughout the worst of the crisis period and afterward maintained his firm call for nonviolence, issuing open letters to both the Tibetans and the Chinese that called for mutual understanding, to refrain from further violence, and for compassion even for one's enemies.

In response to the call by world leaders for the Chinese to engage in dialogue with the Dalai Lama's emissaries to ease tensions and find some resolution to the problem, the Chinese officials did schedule a meeting. Ordinarily they would likely have ignored such requests, but they were concerned about putting on a good face before the upcoming Olympics in China.

I met with the Dalai Lama in November 2008 to discuss the situation with him. Having lost faith in the Chinese leadership as true negotiating partners, at that time he felt that the situation was desperate, but was out of ideas, so that week he had convened a special meeting of Tibetans, asking them to come to Dharamsala from all around the world—for a kind of referendum on his Middle Way approach and a forum to discuss new ideas. Before describing the Dalai Lama's personal reaction to these events, it is important to put the events in context, so a brief review of the history of the Tibet–China issue since 1959 can be helpful.

In 1959, the Dalai Lama fled into exile in northern India, along with around 100,000 other Tibetans, after an unsuccessful uprising by the Tibetan people against the invasion and occupation by Chinese forces. The years have passed, marked by endless suffering for the Tibetans. In earlier decades there were countless people imprisoned, tortured, starved, or killed. There were thousands of Buddhist monasteries leveled to the ground, along with a systematic effort to eradicate the practice and spirit of Buddhism in Tibet. Today, the religion, culture, language, and Tibetan identity are nearing extinction in what has been called a "cultural genocide." And of greatest concern is the government's deliberate resettlement plan—a policy of large-scale population transfer of Han Chinese into Tibet, seeking to render Tibetans powerless by eventually making them a minority in their own country the way the Chinese government did in Inner Mongolia, where the original local inhabitants are now only 20 percent of the total population.

For fifty years, seeking a peaceful resolution to the problem, the Dalai Lama had attempted to enter into serious negotiations. Since 2002 there had been eight rounds of talks between the Dalai Lama's emissaries and Chinese officials. During the years in exile he had developed compromise positions with his Middle Way approach and Five Point Peace Plan, in which he offered to give up the call for independence in exchange for meaningful autonomy, human rights, and greater freedom for his people. None of the talks had made any real progress in the acceptance of these plans or even serious negotiation. The final meeting took place in 2008, after the March riots and crackdown. In that meeting it finally became clear that the Chinese were not negotiating in good faith: Not only was no progress made, but they reverted back to the same positions they had taken twenty years earlier, placing nearly impossible demands on the Dalai Lama, such as requiring him to formally acknowledge that Tibet has always been part of China, before they will agree to proceed with further talks—a fact that is simply untrue and is at the very heart of the dispute.

Thus, after fifty years of ceaseless efforts, it was clear to the Dalai Lama and others that they had made no progress at all with the Chinese government. Of course, there had been plenty of evidence of that before then.

In recent years government officials have ratcheted up their anti-Dalai Lama rhetoric to levels never seen before, labeling him a "separatist," "criminal," "traitor," and spewing out a stream of slurs, blatant lies, and distortions that could start to become quite annoying (at least to those who know the Dalai Lama) if it were not for the comic relief provided by some of the insults hurled at him. My favorite perhaps was: "A wolf in monk's robes, a devil with a human face but the heart of a beast!"—a little gem contributed by the head of the Communist Party of the Tibet Autonomous Region.

In addition, the Chinese have stepped up their attempt to discredit and marginalize the Dalai Lama. With the world in the middle of an extreme financial crisis, China has used her economic clout to try to aggressively bully and intimidate every single world leader, government official, prominent individual, or organization to shun the Dalai Lama. When French president Nicolas Sarkozy met with the Dalai Lama in 2008, for example, in retaliation China suddenly pulled out of a major summit with the European Union that had been scheduled to address critical issues related to the financial crisis. In fact, by March 2009, China's foreign minister Yang Jiechi boldly declared that shunning the Dalai Lama should be considered one of the "basic principles of international relations [with China]."

After the failed talks in 2008, many believed it was clear that all along the Chinese government had just been stalling, waiting for the Dalai Lama to die, so they could install a puppet. Of course, that should not have been a surprise either. There had been some evidence of that as well.

In fact, they seemed to be taking active steps to prepare for this. At times these measures bordered on the absurd, and at other times they clearly crossed over that border, penetrating deep into territory of the bizarre. In 2007, for instance, this staunchly atheistic, antireligious Communist government passed a unique series of laws: the Management Measures on Reincarnation (MMR) issued by the State Administration for Religious Affairs (SARA). These laws gave the government complete control over reincarnation! Yes, that's right. The laws state that only the government can authorize a dead lama to reincarnate! The law gave the government the power to *deny permission* for a Tibetan Buddhist lama to be reincarnated after he died! In fact, the laws stated that the government had sole control over the reincarnation of high Buddhist lamas, and no foreign organization or individual can interfere in the selection of reincarnate lamas. It also required that all Tibetan lamas be reborn within the PRC (People's Republic of China) and not abroad! How convenient! According to Tibetan tradition, each Dalai Lama is the reincarnation of all the Dalai Lamas before him, chosen according to ancient Tibetan Buddhist traditions and rituals, which seek to identify the young reincarnated Dalai Lama when the old one dies—until now, at least.

With this as a background, I met with the Dalai Lama at his home in November 2008. After so many decades of complete failure at finding a peaceful resolution to the situation, the events of 2008 seemed to have taken a toll. As I began to question him about the March riots and subsequent crackdown, the troubled expression on his face and the weariness in his voice conveyed a level of discouragement that I had *never* seen throughout the more than twenty-five years since we first met.

"Since the March crisis happened, I really felt a sense of helplessness," he explained. As if it was difficult to find the right words, he stopped to gather up his thoughts for a moment before proceeding in a softer, quieter tone of voice. "I felt as if it was the same experience I had in 1959, the tenth of March." Again he fell silent for some time and sat in a kind of reverie for a few moments before continuing. "At that time also the Tibetan people trusted me, put a lot of hope in me, and I could not do anything. I felt really very, very sad. Very sad."

As we started to speak, I was really concerned to see how overcome he was. We spoke for more than two hours about his reaction to the recent events in Tibet and his long-standing history of failure in resolving the Tibet issue. As our meeting progressed, however, I witnessed a remarkable process. Although discouraged and concerned, when I inquired if he had lost hope, his answer was clearly no. In response to my question he started to give reason after reason why his objectives—the objectives of the Tibetan people, he made clear, as he was just acting on their behalf—could ultimately be achieved without violence. He explained how the events of 2008 had finally made him lose faith, at least for the time being, in the Chinese government and leadership as true partners in bringing about mutually beneficial change. But he went on to say how his faith and confidence in the Chinese people were stronger than ever—and that is the direction he looked toward to find hope. He noted increased interest in the Tibet issue and growing solidarity among more and more Chinese writers, academics, intellectuals, and others. He mentioned how several distinct changes in the general philosophy of the Chinese leadership over the decades has made it more and more likely that their rule will come to an end. Also, he cited other reasons that are supported by both common sense and scientific research. For example, he mentioned that the government's focus on the creation of wealth and increasingly capitalistic practices will eventually result in growing affluence among a larger and larger segment of the population. He suggested that at a certain point when the people have their basic survival needs met, along with a certain minimum standard of living, then issues like freedom, democracy, and so on start to become increasingly important. As a result, eventually change will inevitably occur.

Every one of his arguments was supported by common sense and based on reality rather than false hopes. And as our meeting progressed, I saw a transformation—in pain and discouraged at first, as I questioned him and he gave his arguments he became more and more animated, confident, optimistic. I could clearly sense his inner strength and resolve, and I could see his spirits lift right in front of me, so that by the end of the meeting, although still very concerned, there was no trace of hopelessness or fear.

By the end of our meeting that day, I had witnessed resilience in action.

Picking up our discussion the following afternoon, I began, "Your Holiness, yesterday we left off with you saying something about how our external experiences can play a role in how we cope with adversity . . ."

"That's right," he replied.

"So, can you explain?"

"Now, in developing an inner strength that can help sustain us during difficult times, what we really need is a kind of resilience, the ability to face our difficulties without losing hope or becoming overwhelmed. Our experiences can be a factor that helps build resilience. I think that those who have experienced hardship in the past may sometimes deal more effectively with problems and adversity that arise in the present. For example, like in the case of Europeans who have seen two world wars fought on their soil, because of this experience, when they encounter major crises, although they appreciate its seriousness, at the same time their response would be something like, 'Yes, we have seen this before; we have gone through it and survived.' Whereas, in societies where they have not experienced that kind of suffering before, people's resilience would be perhaps weaker. Sometimes, they may even see the suffering to be unbearable, beyond their imagination, and might react to it in an exaggerated manner.

"This principle, the capacity of hardship to help build resilience, of course operates on both the individual level as well as the societal level. For example, you see this quite often among some children who come from wealthy families, those raised in pleasant surroundings, never experiencing tragedy, hardship, or adversity. Because everything has been provided for them, often they go through life with the attitude, 'I'm healthy, I'm wealthy, I will get everything I need,' as if they don't expect to encounter problems in life. This is a delusion. Unrealistic. So when they are confronted with a problem or difficulty, they may become totally overwhelmed.

"So if you look among people who have had very hard lives, you generally find they have a greater resilience. This resilience that people have built up as a result of encountering tragedies creates a certain kind of stability, and a different outlook or attitude toward adversity or suffering, so that when they encounter new tragedies or situations that are adverse, there is a greater degree of acceptance so that it doesn't disturb them as much. There is a certain strength, a settled quality of mind, which can be of great benefit in helping people cope."

"You know, Your Holiness, I think you raise a very valid point about the role of hardship in building resilience. But as far as a practical method to help one build resilience, a technique that a person can employ or practice, I'm not sure how helpful this is. Because after all, no matter how helpful hardship might be in building resilience, we are not going to go out and deliberately seek hardships," I replied.

The Dalai Lama shook his head. "A person does not need to deliberately go out and seek hardship; hardship will seek them. Problems are bound to arise; that is the nature of life. And this process is not something that a person needs to intentionally practice; it is a natural process that will occur on its own."

"But when we were talking before about developing a certain outlook or attitudes about suffering and adversity, you often mentioned that this has to involve a more active process of learning, investigating, analysis, increasing one's awareness and—"

"But here we are talking about something else," he pointed out. "In this case hardship can be seen as the various obstacles that will arise in one's life. And in a sense these obstacles act in opposition to our efforts to achieve happiness, to acquire the sources of happiness and satisfaction. It is this opposition that builds our strength. This law of opposition is part of the natural world. For example, if one wants to build a stronger body, resistance is required for the muscles to grow—an opposing force is required. Earlier, we spoke of how opposing forces are necessary for maintaining equilibrium within the body. And how oppositions or challenges to our viewpoints can result in new ideas and growth, and so on. A similar process is operating here in the case of building resilience.

"So, in any case," he concluded, "it is from this perspective that we can view one's obstacles in life from a positive angle, as having some potential benefit—contributing to greater resilience and inner strength."

The Dalai Lama paused briefly before resuming. "This reminds me of a spiritual principle in the Tibetan tradition of practices generally known as *lojong*, 'mind training.' According to this, there is the idea that more advanced spiritual practitioners will not only be able to endure adversities, but, in fact, they will be able to creatively transform adversities into opportunities."

"Can you explain exactly how you go about doing that?"

"Well, the key approach here, once again, is to have a wider perspective. So, for example, if you happen to suffer from some illness, instead of being overwhelmed and discouraged by this experience thinking, 'Why me?' you can use it as a basis for a deeper appreciation of what are the things that are most dear to you in your life. When you are in that situation, the experience could open you to a real possibility of recognizing what is truly important in life, in contrast to so many of the things that used to preoccupy so much of your time and seem so important to you, that you now realize are so trivial. For some, it could also be an opportunity that deepens their compassion for fellow human beings."

Recalling an incident a couple years prior, I said, "Your Holiness, what you were just saying reminded me of when you had a serious illness. That was when you had to cancel a Kalachakra initiation. I heard you had a serious gastrointestinal disorder of some kind, but I don't know the details. When you were suffering from that illness, did you practice any of these techniques? Can you fill me in on some details about what happened then?"

"Yes. At that time I arrived in Bodhgaya and had some days of preparation before the Kalachakra initiation. I took the opportunity to make a pilgrimage to Rajgir and Nalanda. So, on the way back, we drove through Patna, and I started to have pain here"—pointing to his lower abdomen—"The pain became very bad, strong, intense pain. The pain was so strong I was sweating. I could not sleep, could not lie down stretched out, I just remained bent over, like, like . . ."

"Fetal position?"

"Yes, fetal position. So, driving through Patna, this is in Bihar state. Bihar is very poor, almost poorest state in India. There are so many poor people, and especially I noticed the children, boys and girls barefoot, carrying their schoolbags, and picking up cow dung to burn for fuel. And then I noticed one boy. He looked like maybe ten years old, maybe younger. And he had these braces on both legs, from polio I think, and crutches under both arms. He just remained on the street, and it looked like he had no one taking care of him. Then, not far from there I saw an old man lying in a . . . like a stall, an old hut, just lying or sleeping there. From his appearance—his long, messy hair, mustache, beard, his clothes—it was evident that nobody was taking care of this old man. So then I had a very strong feeling, a kind of hopelessness, and helplessness; I felt very strongly, I can't help these people, I can't help them and there are so many. I thought of how they should be the concern of the state government, and there are good people who want to help, but there is also a lot of corruption in Bihar state, so the conditions there remain very poor. It is so very sad.

"So at that time, I was having intense pain, but instead of concentrating my mind on my own pain, I reflected on these poor people and I especially thought of that young boy and that old man, with a constant feeling of concern for these people. I thought of how fortunate I am, with so many people to look after me, to show sympathy, and here were these people who were the same, these people who were human beings the same as me, but no one was taking care of them. . . . Anyway, thinking in this way diverted my mind from my thinking of my own illness and pain. . . . And this experience gave me renewed appreciation of compassion, a new conviction of the benefits of compassion."

The Dalai Lama's voice trailed off into silence for a moment, then he suddenly laughed. "You see, although it was these others who I was concerned about, I was the one who benefited—because I experienced reduced pain.

"So," he concluded, "I had to cancel the Kalachakra and they announced postponement. I went to a hospital in Bombay, and they did testing and found an intestinal infection. After some treatment with antibiotics, and also taking some Tibetan medicine, I recovered completely."

The Dalai Lama stopped talking for a little while, gazing off into the distance in a kind of reverie, caught up in his own private reflections. Thinking about the Dalai Lama's own personal history, so full of obstacles, I couldn't help wondering about the nature of his reflections, and asked, "Well, speaking of life's ups and downs and difficulties, I'm wondering, from your personal perspective, what was your period of greatest obstacles in your own life, on a personal level, your most difficult or unhappiest moment, or even difficulties you might have had as a child?"

My question seemed to shake him from his brief reverie, but he still paused another moment, and surprisingly he then began to laugh. "As far as difficulties during childhood, my teacher, Ling Rinpoche, would sometimes reprimand me, and this was very terrifying. Sometimes when I was scolded by him, I was so devastated that I would run to my mother! And she would give me some breads and comfort me." He laughed again. "Of course you cannot take the experience of childhood very seriously. . . ." Quickly becoming more somber, he continued. "But probably the most difficult moment was the night I left Lhasa, the night I fled Tibet. Everything was so uncertain. On a personal level, even my life was in danger. And the life of the Tibetan nation was hanging in the air. So it was a moment of great uncertainty, doubt, and sadness. . . .

"And then also, maybe another period, when Ling Rinpoche passed away. . . . No, not when he passed away, but when I heard the news that he had suffered a stroke. . . . Another of my teachers had passed away a day earlier. So I received the news of this death and of Ling Rinpoche's stroke at the same time and in the very same message." He paused again, and quietly said in a sad tone, "I was in Switzerland at the time." He added simply, "That was a very sad moment."

"Looking back, to what degree do you think those experiences strengthened your resilience?" I asked.

"Well, Howard, I cannot claim to be one of the most resilient people in the world. But on the other hand, I'm not on the other extreme either, one who is vulnerable to everything that happens. But these experiences do have some effect.

"So in my own case, if I had lived in Tibet and spent my life in Potala and Norbulingka, living a trouble-free life of comfort, perhaps I would be a very different Dalai Lama today. Of course, my spiritual practices made a difference, too. But in addition, I also had to deal with real-life situations where there are a lot of complications. So in a sense, one could say there are two opportunities for meditation practice. One is the meditation practice in terms of contemplation, your daily spiritual practices. The other is the practice of life, your daily life, where you have to undergo the experience of all sorts of adversities and challenges, and then you change and grow from these."

As the Dalai Lama appeared to be concluding his comments on hardship, another thought seemed to surface, and he added, "You know, in talking about hardships, there is a particular image of the Buddha that I personally find deeply inspiring. It is an icon of the Buddha in almost a skeletal form, representing an earlier period in his life when he underwent a time of great aestheticism and hardship. The original statue exists today in the Lahore Museum in Pakistan. I have a photograph of this icon in my home. To me, this image conveys the powerful message that it is through hardship, it's through constant effort, that the Buddha attained full awakening. Whenever I see that image, I feel deeply moved and it gives me a sense of courage."

"You know, Your Holiness, I just thought of something as you spoke of 'adversities and challenges,' speaking of these two things as if they are equivalent. So, part of what you are saying here is that we can view our problems as challenges to be overcome, and as we overcome these challenges we become stronger and more resilient, better able to cope with life's difficulties."

"That's right."

"This actually reminds me of a series of experiments that were done to investigate resilience, and look at factors that could enhance the person's capacity to bounce back from adversity or crisis. . . ."

At this point I described the experiments conducted by Barbara Fredrickson and colleagues, leading to the Undoing Hypothesis, when, as described earlier, they induced a state of anxiety and stress in a group of subjects by telling them they had only minutes to prepare a speech. The subjects were then told the speech was canceled, and investigators were able to determine the subject's level of resilience by measuring how long it took for them to recover from the stress response—in this case measuring how long it took for their heart rate and blood pressure to return to normal. I described the first series of experiments in which positive emotions were shown to enhance resilience, speeding up the recovery process. But now, I went on to identify another factor that could also act to increase the subject's resilience.

"Anyway," I continued, "when conducting these series of experiments, investigators noticed that all of the subjects experienced around the same degree of stress, but not all of the subjects recovered at the same rate. Some subjects had naturally high resilience while others had low resilience. So, in this experiment they divided the subjects into two groups. When the experimenters were giving the instructions about preparing the speech, they gave one group instructions that encouraged them to perceive the exercise in a positive light, *as a challenge to be met and overcome, and to think of themselves as someone capable of meeting that challenge.* The instructions in the second group led the subjects *to see the speech as more of a threat,* telling them that this speech was going to be analyzed by experts and this evaluation was going to be used to predict their future success.

"The researchers found that this change made no difference to the high-resilience subjects—just as before, they bounced back quickly from the stress reaction. But this change did make a difference among the low-resilience group—those who deliberately viewed the speech as a challenge recovered from the stress effects much more quickly, while those who continued to see the speech as threatening still took much longer to recover. I was reminded of this experiment, because I think it is a great illustration of your point about how our outlook or perception alone can have an effect on our ability to cope with problems, and in this case a pretty dramatic effect, a physical effect."

"Yes, that's a good example." The Dalai Lama agreed.

Life is uncertain. The Dalai Lama's personal history is a testament to that—from a poor village boy at two; to the ruler of an ancient nation at fifteen; to a negotiator struggling with Chairman Mao at nineteen; to a refugee in his thirties still loved by his people and known in the Buddhist world perhaps but living in relative obscurity and virtually forgotten by the rest of the world. For many a deposed leader, the story would have ended there, much like the last emperor of China. In the Dalai Lama's case, however, he became a citizen of the world, a great spiritual teacher, a Nobel Peace Prize laureate, and a representative of nonviolence, world peace, human rights, and interfaith harmony. While the Dalai Lama denies any claim to being the world's most resilient person, clearly resilience has played a role in his ability to deal so successfully with the many changes and adversities he has faced.

To our growing collection of tools to help us cope with life's changes and adversities, the Dalai Lama adds another: *resilience.* The concept of resilience is closely related to cultivating hope and optimism, as all three are involved in helping an individual deal with life's difficulties and stresses. Unlike hope or optimism, however, resilience is a broader concept that includes the sum of our inner resources—resilience is our capacity to bounce back from adversity, traumatic experiences, hardship, and loss. In addition to helping us cope effectively with major life problems and move on, it also helps a person deal with life's everyday stresses and adapt to a changing world.

There are many factors that may potentially play a role in a given individual's customary level of resilience. For example, maintaining good relationships, having an optimistic view of the world, keeping things in perspective, setting goals and taking steps to reach them, being self-confident, and being able to regulate one's emotions have all been associated with greater resilience.

Individuals may differ in the specific strategies or traits that they rely on to help them cope. Research on resilience finds that some people try to cope with stresses and adversities by "repressive coping," simply attempting to ignore it. In other cases, it has been found that those high in the trait of "self-enhancement" seem to handle traumatic events better than others. This characteristic is associated with people particularly strong in self-esteem and those who exhibit a tendency to see themselves in the best possible light. While this trait may give individuals greater confidence to deal with traumatic events, the rest of the time other people tend to see them as arrogant or annoying.

In examining the Dalai Lama's approach to building resilience, we can begin with his initial premise that our outlook on life, how we perceive our problems, plays a key role in how we cope. This view is supported by a large body of scientific research. In summarizing the current evidence, University of Notre Dame psychologists Anthony Ong and Cindy S. Bergeman, experts in the field of human resilience, point out "differences in adaptation to stress may follow from one's habitual outlook on life; that is, how individuals react to, appraise, and interpret life experiences." In the experiment I described to the Dalai Lama, we can clearly see how our perception of a problem can profoundly affect how quickly we recover from the effects of stress. In this case, whether the subject perceived the problem as a challenge or as a threat made a big difference in their ability to cope with the situation.

Even more important, this experiment shows that an individual can deliberately *change* how they perceive a threatening situation. In this instance, all it took was asking the low-resilience individuals to look at the stressful assignment as a challenge rather than a threat! Looking at the situation as a challenge instead of as a threat is an example *of positive reappraisal*—the very same technique we have been discussing as being so effective in cultivating hope and optimism. It is one of the methods we can use to look at negative situations and events from a broader perspective, which in turn is the primary strategy recommended by the Dalai Lama for cultivating a realistic outlook.

There is a great deal of evidence confirming the fact that looking at a problem from a broader perspective can increase resilience. This can be done by positive reappraisal—finding some positive meaning, higher purpose, or potential benefit related to the adversity, either in the short term or long term. Positive reappraisal can also include reframing the negative situation in a more positive light by looking for lessons that can be learned, or potential positive outcomes, either as a direct or indirect result of the situation. The cognitive techniques described earlier can also be helpful here.

These methods of positive reappraisal, looking from a broader perspective, are the very same techniques we discussed earlier for increasing hope and optimism. In fact, these techniques are not only useful in cultivating hope or optimism, but they can also be used to help regulate emotions in general, voluntarily reducing negative emotions and increasing positive emotions. In looking at the factors that can help build resilience, both hope and optimism can play an important role—the more hope and optimism one has, the more resilient one will be. But hope and optimism are not the only positive emotions that can enhance resilience. Research has shown that essentially any of the positive emotions or states of mind (serenity, joy, mirth, contentment, happiness in general, etc.) can enhance resilience.

One of the researchers looking at the link between positive emotions and resilience is Barbara Fredrickson. In one study Fredrickson and her colleagues surveyed a group of University of Michigan students several months prior to 9/11, measuring levels of resilience. They tested them again after 9/11. After 9/11, of course nearly everyone felt sad, angry, and somewhat afraid. Both the high- and low-resilience students experienced negative emotions and were deeply moved by the national tragedy. Yet those individuals who had been identified as high resilience before 9/11 showed more positive emotion after 9/11; even though feeling sad and angry, they were not overwhelmed by the experience, and along with their negative emotions they also felt grateful for the good things still in their lives. They felt that they had learned something positive from the crisis, and were more optimistic in general. People high in resilience have the capacity to experience positive emotions even in the midst of stressful events. These positive feelings seemed to buffer the negative effects of the trauma, helping them cope better and, compared with those lower in resilience and positive emotions, reducing their likelihood of suffering from depression. Investigators reported that those high in the trait of resilience "emerged from their anguish more satisfied with life, more optimistic, more tranquil—and likely more resilient—than before."

In view of the many benefits of positive emotions, including the ability to enhance resilience and the ability to cope with the many problems of today's world, it is fortunate that there are effective strategies that can directly increase these positive states of mind. While techniques such as positive reappraisal and looking at problems from a broader perspective are the main methods of cultivating positive emotions that we have been focusing on, there are also other strategies that can be used to increase positive emotions. Formal meditation and relaxation techniques have been shown to increase positive emotions such as serenity, tranquillity, etc. The use of humor and laughter is also effective. It therefore isn't surprising that many studies have shown that humor and laughter help us cope with a wide array of daily problems. I think it is not by accident that the Dalai Lama not only seems to be able to cope with problems so effectively, but he is also well known for his robust sense of humor and the ease with which he breaks into a hearty laugh.

When searching for an approach to maintain happiness in the face of so many problems in the world today, we have identified multiple factors that can play a critical role in helping us cope: hope, optimism, resilience, positive emotions in general, a broader mind-set, positive reappraisal, a found meaning, and so on. Sometimes it seems that there are so many players here that one needs a scorecard to keep track of them!

In a 2004 study by Michele M. Tugade from Boston College and Barbara Fredrickson, citing others' work as well as their own findings, the authors describe the relationship among some of these factors: "Coping benefits are likely to accrue because the broadening effects of positive emotions increase the likelihood that individuals find positive meaning in stressful circumstances. . . . Positive emotions can beget positive-meaning finding, which by consequence, can beget further experiences of positive emotions. In this way, positive-meaning finding represents the broadening of one's mind-set when coping, which subsequently helps to build psychological resources, like resilience. This cycle can continue in an 'upward spiral' toward enhanced emotional well-being."

Huh? In looking at the relationship among these various factors, we find a complex web of interconnectivity that can seem confusing at times. It seems that any of these factors can enhance all of the other factors, in a reciprocal relationship. For example, a broader perspective can help increase hope, and the more hope one has, the easier it is to see a problem from a broader perspective. Pick any two of these factors and you'll find that they can enhance each other. Fortunately, it is easy to simplify the complex interactions among the many factors that can help us cope with our troubled world: Looking at problems and adversity from a broader perspective helps us see the potential positive angles to the situation. The more hope, optimism, and other positive emotions that we have, the easier it is to cope with our external problems while maintaining inner happiness.

Chapter 12

INNER HAPPINESS, OUTER HAPPINESS,
AND TRUST

WE CONTINUED our conversation the next morning with an issue I felt still needed to be addressed.

"Your Holiness, yesterday you were discussing the practice of looking at problems from a wider perspective as a method to develop inner strength to help us cope, to maintain optimism or hope and so on. When you were discussing the various ways that we can see things from this wider perspective, one suggestion you had was to remember that we are part of a greater community, we have this connection to others, we are not isolated and alone and so on."

"Yes."

"Well," I continued, "this just reminded me of our first discussions in Dharamsala on these topics. I remembered that during one discussion you mentioned your feeling that there was a lack of sense of community in many societies, a growing sense of isolation and loneliness, and that this was one of the primary factors that undermined happiness on a societal level. So, it occurred to me that the strategy you mentioned yesterday—the idea that remembering our connection to a community will give us a feeling of comfort and inner strength and confidence— wouldn't really work very well if a person feels isolated and cut off from the community. So, this brings us back to the topic of this lack of a sense of community.

"In our last series of meetings in Dharamsala we moved to a discussion of violence and conflict in society and so on, but it felt like we never really finished our discussion about community. You outlined several steps we can take to build a stronger sense of community, like reflecting on the benefits of having these community bonds, investigating the background or characteristics that you may have in common with others, and then taking action by going out and joining a group or relating to others in some way. But it seems as if we never finished discussing how to form bonds with others on a deeper, more fundamental level."

He considered this point for a moment before responding. "I think that our underlying sense of community can be closely related to the issue of trust."

"Related in what way?" I asked.

"Of course, this lack of sense of community can have many different causes, and there are always many different factors that could contribute to the problem. But I think that this lack of community, this loneliness and alienation, are all due in part to an underlying distrust between people. Of course, at the same time, where there is a lack of feeling of connection to others, a lack of personal contact between members of a community or a society, and an absence of the spirit of community, this creates the conditions that can lead to a feeling of mistrust. So, it can go both ways."

Some time had elapsed between our last series of discussions in India and the continuation of our exploration of human happiness in Tucson. In the interim I had done some further study on happiness on a broader societal level. Upon investigating the Dalai Lama's claim that lacking a sense of community undermined the level of happiness in a society, I had come across data linking the issue of trust with both our sense of community and with happiness. Supplied with ample scientific evidence supporting his views, I had planned on bringing up the subject of trust myself.

Eager to share this information with the Dalai Lama, I continued: "Your Holiness, during the intervening time since our first meetings in Dharamsala, I have done a little research on these topics. I think it is really interesting that you identify both trust and our sense of community as key factors in promoting human happiness on the societal level. One great study I found, the World Values Survey, looked at different countries and assessed the average levels of happiness of their citizens. The researchers then went on to identify six key factors that accounted for most of the variation in levels of happiness between countries. The number of people who are connected with social organizations, and thus have a connection with others, is one of the six factors. Another factor that correlated with the average level of happiness in a society was the proportion of people who say other people can be trusted.*

"There was also a study done by the University of Cambridge in England, which analyzed the results of an extensive survey among tens of thousands of people in many regions throughout Europe, and they found that regions with the highest levels of happiness also reported the highest levels of trust in their governments, laws, and each other. So, the evidence seems unequivocal. No matter what study one looks at, Scandinavia is always among the world's happiest regions. If you look at the characteristics of people in that region, you'll find a strong sense of community and underlying feeling of trust in others. In one study researchers asked children between eleven and fifteen, 'Do you feel, generally speaking, your classmates are kind and helpful?' A high percentage said yes, which I think is a pretty good general measure of

---

* According to the World Values Survey, studying levels of happiness in fifty countries, the six factors referred to are divorce rate, unemployment rate, level of trust, membership in social organizations (nonreligious), quality of government, and percentage of population believing in God. These six factors are thought to explain approximately 80 percent of the variation in levels of happiness among these countries.

'Do you trust them?' So the scientific evidence certainly seems to support your observations. A feeling of trust can really make a difference in one's customary level of happiness."

The Dalai Lama seemed engaged by these findings and leaned forward in his chair with focused attention.

"It is true that trust can contribute to one's happiness on an individual level," he agreed. "A feeling of mistrust can lead to a suspicious, fearful attitude, and more mental unrest, whereas a more trusting attitude can contribute to a calmer, happier state of mind. But trust can also be important on other levels. On a wider level, trust can be a factor not only in building a stronger sense of community, and overcoming the loneliness and alienation we spoke about, but it can also be helpful in dealing with many of the problems in society that we have discussed. For example, in one discussion we spoke about the importance of finding solutions to our conflicts through dialogue rather than through violence. The spirit of dialogue. This is a critical issue. And here, trust plays an important role—for a dialogue to be successful it is important to try to build trust between the parties. So," he repeated, "you can see how trust is important in so many ways."

In the opening chapters of this book, the Dalai Lama mentioned the Tibetan community as an illustration of a population with a strong spirit of community, which is so often absent in contemporary Western society. Thinking back to my very first visit to Dharamsala, India, home to the Dalai Lama and a thriving Tibetan community in exile, there is no question in my mind that his illustration was justified. Evidence of an active community life was ever present, both among the monastic community and the lay community. There was virtually total support for local institutions, including the Tibetan Children's Village, associations to preserve traditional Tibetan culture and art, and a myriad of organizations devoted to the study and practice of Buddhism. Yet the spirit of community was not merely preserved in these many institutions but was reflected in every face, heard in the laughter of children playing in the street, seen in the smiles of neighbors stopping to chat in doorways, the devotion of the elderly spinning prayer wheels, and the sound of monks chanting in the distance. One could sense the spirit of unity almost as if it was carried on the subtle scent of Tibetan incense wafting through the air, a fresh woody fragrance of burning juniper and Himalayan herbs.

I also recalled the first time I joined in a gathering with a large numbers of Tibetans. The occasion was a series of teachings given by the Dalai Lama in the northeastern Indian town of Bodhgaya, the sacred Buddhist site where Prince Siddhartha Gautama sat down under a tree to meditate 2,500 years ago, achieved enlightenment, and became the Buddha. Today it is the site of the Bodhi Tree, said to be a direct descendant of the tree under which the Buddha sat. There is also a central temple complex, with many small chorten (stupas) and shrines, surrounding the Mahabodhi Temple, with its richly sculpted stone balustrades and finely carved pyramidal tower rising majestically in the air.

Tibetans had come in the thousands from all over India and Nepal, even a few from Tibet itself, creating a festival-like atmosphere, accentuated by the many colorful prayer flags strung from the trees, gently flapping in the wind. It was a powerful immersion in the Tibetan spirit of community. Families had spread blankets on the ground to sit on during the teachings, and for the first time I noticed a small detail about the community, one that was not of monumental importance but which for some reason struck me as one of the most moving and endearing signs of community ties and cohesion: the contingent of toddlers clearly enjoying the communal feeling, some just learning to walk, wobbling, unsteady, and falling into the laps of smiling and welcoming strangers. The older children sometimes went off to play by themselves, but they did not seem to have the urgency to ditch their parents that American kids might display in similar circumstances. The parents kept an intermittent watch on their children out of the corner of their eye, but an untroubled eye as the children were mostly allowed to roam free, secure in the sense of safety of the group (as large as it was), with none of the fear that characterizes so many parents in America when their young children are exposed to the wider community of strangers.

For some reason the sight of children in the crowd created a strong feeling of nostalgia for me that day so many years ago and I remember wondering why it evoked such a response, because the experience of these children growing up in a different land and a different culture could not have been more different from my own. But it soon occurred to me that it was the pervasive feeling of safety and security, of trust.

There was a time, of course, when that same sense of trust and safety was widespread in American society as well. When I was a child, every summer my parents loaded up my brothers and sister in an old station wagon and drove to Venice, California, where they rented an apartment by the sea for the summer. In those days, many parts of Venice were a slum, the chief attraction, besides the ocean, being cheap apartments. Dubbed "Appalachia by the Sea" by the local media, Venice was a unique mix of gentle elderly Jewish men and women, mostly Eastern European immigrants, spending their final days on Earth chatting together on benches lining the beach and of members of the youthful counterculture movement, beatniks in the late fifties and early sixties, followed by the hippies in the mid and later sixties. The daily routine for my brothers and me was much the same: After breakfast, we ran outdoors and spent the day at the beach, the pier, or up and down the Venice boardwalk, never returning home until dinnertime. By the age of seven or eight, I was allowed to spend the day unsupervised, or at least supervised only by my brother who is a year and a half older, enjoying what seemed like an infinite variety of activities—fishing off the Santa Monica Pier, feasting on corn dogs, haunting the souvenir shops, longing for their treasures we couldn't afford, even spending an occasional day at Pacific Ocean Park, an amusement park built on a wide pier jutting out over the ocean.

In many communities today, a parent who regularly allowed their eight-year-old child to roam the streets unsupervised would be reported to child protective services, yet in those days this was standard procedure. With the pervasive fear in many of today's Western societies, by seven years old, the child has no doubt already undergone Stranger Danger training, as if preparing for battle. In fact, I hear that now even Stranger Danger training is outmoded, replaced more recently in schools with the ominously named Lock-Down Drills, which are apparently meant to prepare for school shootings. Students find places to hide and are instructed not to speak, move, or make any noise whatsoever. Protection, safety, security, and precaution are the primary concerns and bywords today. No longer are children free to hop on their bikes and roam the community. Now, before hopping on bikes, they are strapped into helmets, knee pads, wrist gloves, and elbow pads. Then the bikes are strapped on tailgates and driven to a supervised bike-riding zone. Prearranged formal "play dates" are set up in advance between parents acting like social secretaries for their budding CEOs.

As children in American society continue to be conditioned not to trust anyone outside their immediate circle, or in-group, it raises very real questions about the possibility of reversing this troubling trend. But I wondered what the Dalai Lama might have to say on the subject.

"Unfortunately," I said to the Dalai Lama as our conversation continued, "it seems that the level of trust between people has been going down and down in many societies in the world today. For example, in Britain and America, they did a study and they asked people, 'Do you feel that people generally can be trusted, or do you feel that you can't be too careful when dealing with people, that you should always be cautious?' So the number of people who trust other people has decreased by 50 percent since the 1950s, which is huge.

"You know, Your Holiness, here we are in Tucson again, many years after our first discussions here. Being here reminds me of when I used to live here, for four years when I went to medical school at the university. I was just remembering how I lived in a small house across the street from the medical school and for the entire four years I lived here I always left the front door to my house unlocked—day and night. In my case, it seems that I trust people less than I used to—at least in the sense that these days I would never even consider leaving my home unlocked as I did in those days."

"Howard, I don't know if this is only a matter of trusting people," he said with a light joking tone. "I hope it was not just the case that you had nothing to steal then!"

"Well, come to think of it," I confessed, "I guess that was probably the case. In fact, it was the case," I added, recalling my Spartan living conditions in those days.

"So," the Dalai Lama continued, "you need to be practical. If your conditions are such that you need to lock your doors now, then that is simply prudence. Not acting in a prudent manner, simply because you recognize the basic good nature of human beings, or because you feel a sense of connection to others in general or you have a sense of trust toward those members of your community, is unrealistic. You can be a kind, gentle person but realistic at the same time.

"This talk of locks and so on reminds me of Spiti Valley in northern India, in these remote villages, in the past there was no custom of putting locks on doors. No locks at all. Travelers would come and they could just help themselves. It was just taken for granted."

For a moment his words conjured up a powerful image: a community without locks, a world of complete trust, the vision of a world where the basic goodness of human beings could be expressed. But that image was quickly replaced with a vision of today's world, with all its troubles.

"Is that still the case in that region these days?" I asked.

"Oh, it's changing, naturally," he replied, "although it's difficult to say to what extent."

"Changing in terms of the overall levels of trust, putting locks on doors, that type of thing?"

"Yes . . ."

"So what do you attribute those types of changes to? Why is there less and less trust?"

"Previously, I think, there were very, very few visitors," he answered. "I think they remained mostly within their own community. And nowadays it's different, of course. There is more tourism, and then you have new people working on the road construction. . . ."

"Still, Your Holiness, I think you bring up an important point that seems to be a common feature of modern society: It is this idea that there are more and more strangers in communities. This relates to what we have discussed in our earlier conversations in Dharamsala, this idea of greater mobility in modern industrialized society, people moving from one place to another. And this idea of a constant influx of new people in a community has the potential to cause some mistrust as well as stress.

"For example, I recently came across an interesting study related to this idea that involved a brand-new community in Britain where they built this new housing or apartment complex. The complex was several stories high. After it was completed and people moved in, someone noticed that the people on the ground floor started to develop increased rates of mental illness.

"Anyway, the people who designed the buildings decided to do an experiment. What they did was build some walls. These walls cut off the paths that went in front of these people's windows on the bottom floor, so that very few strangers were walking by their windows. They redesigned it so when a person looked out their front window, they were more likely to see a neighbor, somebody that they were familiar with. And just by doing that, redesigning the pathways, there was a 24 percent decrease in mental illness.

"But the problem of course is you can't go around with a bunch of bricks and mortar, building walls in society. So I'm wondering, do you have any suggestions about how to counteract that force, the destructive force of distrust?"

Thinking for a moment, he replied, "Here, in this case, there could be many factors one might need to take into consideration. Of course when dealing with mental illness, it will vary according to different personalities and psychological make-ups of the individuals. And then in general, I think that in Western society there is a tendency to look to external means to solve all our problems, and to provide our happiness and satisfaction. So, perhaps this orientation makes people more inclined to be affected by changes in the external environment. I don't know.

"But the main point in our exploration is to identify skills that individuals can use to build their inner resources, so that we don't have to build walls from the outside," the Dalai Lama remarked.

"Exactly!" I said. I was glad that he had brought up the idea of inner skills. "So then how do you avoid an erosion of trust?"

"This can be complicated, because there can be many factors involved, so we need to recognize that there may be a variety of approaches that may be required on different levels. But one thing, for example, personal contact and getting to know the other person, can help to build greater trust. I think that some of the approaches we discussed in the past in regard to building the spirit of dialogue can also apply to building trust."

"But in those cases where there are lots of new people moving into your community, like in Spiti Valley, where people are now putting locks on their doors, and you don't have the opportunity to have personal contact with them all . . ."

"Howard, just because one sees more precautions in these communities does not mean that there has necessarily been any dramatic change in the level of trust, or there is widespread suspicion. For example there might be a community where there are one hundred people, and people may have a feeling of trust for ninety-nine of those people, but if people don't trust that one last person, of course, people are going to take precautions. But that does not mean that you need to be suspicious of everyone.

"So, I think once again it comes down to having a realistic outlook. You can take precautions to protect yourself because you recognize that there may be a small percentage of people with bad intentions, but at the same time if you look at things from a wider perspective, if you look at the reality, you will see that most people are decent people. If you maintain a realistic view and do not exaggerate the degree of the problem, then this will not change your fundamental view of human nature. So, there is no need to develop a suspicious attitude toward all newcomers to the community."

So, things change. Suburban parents no longer allow their children to roam free in the summers. A psychiatrist living in Phoenix and a

Tibetan villager living in the remote Spiti Valley in the Himalayas no longer leave their doors unlocked at night. What can we do? Are we required to ignore the dangers of the world in order to return to a more innocent time, in order to restore our levels of trust in one another and regain our sense of community?

In asking the Dalai Lama the fundamental question here—how can we cultivate greater trust?—his responses initially disappointed me. These were the same old responses and strategies he had already covered. And covered: We need a variety of approaches—evasive! Personal contact—boring! Realistic outlook—God help us! Didn't he have anything *new* to add? In one conversation he mentioned how some of his Tibetan friends found his constant use of the term "realistic approach" to be annoying. Well, I hadn't yet reached the stage of feeling annoyed, but that possibility was on the horizon.

It was not until some time after these discussions that I took a closer look at the Dalai Lama's views and his approach to cultivating hope, optimism, resilience, and trust, all of which he felt could be cultivated using the same approach: his "realistic outlook." Of course, I had some awareness of the correlation between his views and the scientific research at the time of our discussions, but it was not until I spent some additional time reflecting on his words and researching the latest scientific studies on happiness and positive emotions, and correlating the two, that I began to see his approach in a deeper way and realize its profound depth. What had started to appear to me as a tired cliché—his "realistic outlook"—I soon realized was deceptively simple, and actually had tremendous wisdom and insight behind it, layer upon layer. It was more of a code word, and although it was expressed in common secular terminology, it seemed to cloak a variety of very profound Buddhist principles and practices. These simple terms he used, such as "awareness" or "realistic outlook," represented a variety of effective strategies to increase happiness and help us cope with the world—strategies that were based on fundamental Buddhist principles and supported by modern science. For example, as we have seen, his "realistic approach" includes the same techniques that psychologists call positive reappraisal, reframing, benefit-finding, looking for positive meaning, cognitive techniques, cognitive-behavioral techniques, and so on—all of which have a large body of scientific evidence proving their effectiveness.

Admittedly, at one point I was disappointed that the Dalai Lama seemed to offer his realistic outlook as the main technique to cultivate whatever positive emotion we were talking about. It didn't bother me much at first, but by the time we got to the topic of trust and he was *still* using the same method, I was ready for a different technique. However, in looking at the scientific evidence, the Dalai Lama's approach begins to make perfect sense and fall into place. For example, the Dalai Lama began that week with a discussion of his realistic approach ("wider perspective" and so on), then hope and optimism, followed by resilience and trust. This was by no accident—our objective was to explore how to cope with our troubled world and still remain happy. While according to the research all of the positive emotions can act as an antidote to the effects of negative emotions and stress, and all can contribute to greater personal happiness, there are a specific group of positive emotions that are particularly effective in helping us cope with adversity, external obstacles and problems, and so on. And what emotions are classified as being in this group? This group includes: hope, optimism, resilience and, yes—trust! Some investigators add faith and confidence to this group. Clearly, not all researchers classify positive emotions the same way—in fact there can be a wide variability. But at least there is a rationale here. These emotions are grouped together by positive psychologists such as Dr. Martin Seligman because they share a general "future" orientation, involving positive expectation of one kind or another. For example, the object of hope is generally some specific goal or objective in the future, while optimism involves more of a general expectation of positive outcomes. With trust, the object of the positive expectation is generally a person.

As we look from a "wider perspective," it may not seem so surprising that the Dalai Lama would choose to use the same strategy to cultivate hope, optimism, resilience, and trust, since they are seen as being in the same family. We saw earlier how the research indicates that all of the various positive mental states and techniques that we have discussed seem to reinforce one another, so choosing one powerful, proven strategy should be enough to enhance a variety of positive emotions, all of which can help us cope more effectively with our troubled world.

Now recognizing that the Dalai Lama did not suggest his "realistic approach" as a technique to help build trust simply because he ran out of fresh ideas and had to keep recycling the same old technique, we can take a final look at his views on cultivating trust.

The Dalai Lama offers us an approach in which we can maintain a general feeling of trust in people, which creates an openness—an openness that carries with it the possibility of connection, a potential bond. When we reach out to another human being and make that connection, establish that bond, this becomes the basis for our sense of community. Of course, the key question is, how can we maintain that feeling of trust? The Dalai Lama's approach is based on a fearless commitment to discovering reality, and the willingness to accept that reality, to live by that truth. In this case, for instance, his approach begins by developing a deep understanding of human nature, and the recognition that the majority of human beings are good, decent people—people who just want to be happy, just want to be loved, who don't want to suffer. Just like you.

At the same time, there is an equal understanding of the reality that there are some people who have malicious intent, those who will harm other human beings. At the intersection of these two divergent views lies common sense and reason. With this view, you can always trust people—you can trust human beings to be human beings: Some will be mainly good, some mainly bad, and all of us some mix of good and bad. This means that most people you will encounter will be good and not abuse your trust, while a small minority will be bad and abuse your trust. But with the Dalai Lama's approach you can take precautions against being harmed, you can do whatever you need to protect yourself from that small minority, but at the same time you can maintain a general feeling of trust toward others, without letting a small minority distort your perception, outlook, or attitudes.

The Convergence of Personal and Societal Happiness

"You know," I said, "as you were talking about the benefits of trust, a critical point has just occurred to me. This week we have been discussing factors that can help us cope with our troubled world internally and find happiness. In some of our past discussions we have spoken about the various external problems in our society and in the world, exploring ways to overcome these problems. But it seems to me that you've essentially hit on an approach that sort of 'kills two birds with one stone,' simultaneously bringing about inner happiness and societal happiness. You just mentioned how trust can contribute to one's personal happiness, but at the same time trust can be an important factor in helping solve some of the world's problems. Greater trust could help build a stronger sense of community, and trust is important in facilitating a more successful dialogue in the process of conflict resolution."

"Yes, of course," the Dalai Lama said, as if this was the most natural and obvious observation in the world, even though these ideas were just beginning to dawn on me.

"It seems that the other positive mental factors we have been discussing are the same in that way—on one hand, positive mental states or emotions such as hope, optimism, resilience, and so on make a direct contribution to one's own happiness. And at the same time, they are also factors that play a role in giving one strength, that directly help a person to continue to work toward a better world. Like in your case, it is hope and optimism that allows you to continue to fight for human rights and greater autonomy in Tibet, despite fifty years without success."

"That's right," he said again.

I felt a building excitement as the divergent themes and variety of separate topics that we had been discussing for so long now began to coalesce, merging into an elegant, unified system in which inner happiness and societal happiness were connected along the same continuum. The struggle to overcome inner problems and find inner happiness and the struggle to overcome the problems of our world and create

happier societies no longer appeared to be two separate and unconnected pursuits. It wasn't as if some startling new fact was revealed, or
cutting-edge new information, but rather the existing information just
seemed to fit together and fall into place.

"You know, this is where inner and outer happiness seem to converge. And, come to think of it, this principle isn't limited only to particular positive mental states like hope, optimism, or trust, but in fact
it seems that *all* of the positive emotions and happiness in general, all
share this same quality, the potential of promoting both inner and
outer happiness. It reminds me of all the studies showing how happy
individuals are more altruistic, more willing to reach out and help,
more charitable—so here again, inner happiness and working toward a
better world seem to merge."

"And, it works the other way too," he reminded me. "Not only is
it the case that happy people are more willing to help others, but as I
generally mention, helping others is the best way to help yourself, the
best way to promote your own happiness. It is you, yourself, who will
receive the benefit."

"I guess that at this point we can view the cultivation of positive
emotions as something which directly contributes to one's personal
happiness as well as something which helps overcome societal problems (directly or indirectly), thus contributing to a happier world."

Smiling, the Dalai Lama merely nodded in agreement.

Here we added a critical issue, highlighting the point at which our inner world and our outer world intersect, revealing an approach that
can simultaneously build personal happiness and societal happiness. In
trust we have added another dimension, showing how it could have
a positive impact on a wider societal level. As we have seen, studies
show that the level of trust in a society is directly related to the level
of happiness in that society. Trust can also have many specific benefits
in overcoming societal problems—trust between groups reduces sus-

picion and fear, and promotes a more peaceful society. Greater trust reduces prejudice, discrimination, and conflict. If conflict does happen to arise, trust reduces the likelihood of violence.

Some of the most fascinating and revolutionary findings of this research is the studies showing the potential of positive emotions to transform our exterior world as well as our interior world. In fact, there now appears to be a substantial body of empirical evidence that these positive states of mind can directly contribute not only to *coping* with the world's problems but also in beginning to actively *change* them.

Positive Emotions as an Antidote to Societal Problems

Finally we can begin to see a wider approach to finding happiness in our troubled world, with a strategy that can work toward increasing personal happiness and societal happiness at the same time. Since positive emotions directly contribute to greater personal happiness, it is likewise worthwhile looking at how positive emotions may potentially help reduce societal problems.

When we began to address human happiness in the context of societal trouble, one of the first problems the Dalai Lama identified was the growing lack of social connectedness in many societies. So far when discussing the link between happiness and social connectedness, we have focused on the capacity of these social bonds to increase our level of happiness. Not only does our close connection to others lead to greater happiness, but our happiness or positive emotions lead to better social interactions. New studies have provided experimental evidence showing that happiness and positive states of mind directly cause people to be more sociable and have more successful social relationships. Inducing a happy mood in a subject will increase the likelihood of that individual striking up a conversation with a stranger—and when they do connect with strangers or friends, they tend to disclose more personal information, and there is a tendency to form deeper bonds with others. These kinds of changes would clearly make it easier for someone to follow the Dalai Lama's advice, and increase their success in bonding with a social organization or group of people.

Positive Emotions in Dialogue and Conflict Resolution

In our discussion the Dalai Lama mentioned his firm belief that war and violence was outmoded as a way of dealing with conflict and he envisioned the next stage in the world's cultural evolution, when dialogue is used to resolve our disputes instead of violence. He did, however, point to a number of challenges that must be overcome in order to engage in successful dialogue: He mentioned we need to find a way to be able to let go of past resentments and find a way to let go of the same old rigid ways of looking at the situation. We need to find a way to look at the disputed issues in new and creative ways, with a fresh perspective. We need to be able to expand our perspective and use our imagination, so we can also see the other side's views. We need to have a broadened, integrative way of thinking that will allow us to be able to see areas of mutual benefit, where both sides get their most important needs met.

Well, let's see . . . we need to apply a way of thinking that is less rigid, that is more flexible and creative, that is less self-focused, that can integrate differing viewpoints and find common themes, that can look at situations in new ways, from different angles, open to new information . . . hmmm. . . .

Yes, that is a good description of *precisely* the kinds of thinking that have been found to be associated with positive emotions, in experiment after experiment. In fact, positive emotions create a way of thinking that is ideal for engaging in successful dialogue to settle a dispute.

In the same way that negative emotions are associated with certain specific narrowed kinds of thinking, positive emotions are also associated with their own characteristic broadened kinds of thinking, using the higher reasoning areas of the brain—and it almost seems as if this kind of thinking was designed to be used in conflict situations where two or more sides are attempting to resolve a dispute: Positive emotion enhances integrative thinking, where the individual will look at a wide range of facts related to a situation, and be more effective in integrating diverse facts to come up with a new solution. A positive state of mind also results in more flexible thinking, a more supple mind that can look at a problem from different angles. Finally, positive emotions make one's mind receptive to new information, new ways of looking at things—a kind of thinking that would definitely facilitate greater openness to other viewpoints, an important ingredient in successful dialogue in attempting to resolve a conflict.

Earlier we described several experiments demonstrating how positive emotions create changes in thinking that result in a greater ability to see the "big picture," to think more creatively, and to find new ways to achieve one's goals—all types of thinking that would be helpful in negotiating a successful resolution of a conflict or dispute. There have been many more experiments documenting the effects of positive mood. Alice Isen, along with her colleagues at Cornell University, have conducted many of the key studies on the effects of happiness on thinking, and twenty years of experiments have confirmed that when people feel good, their thinking becomes more creative, integrative, flexible, and open to information.

In one experiment the researchers gathered together a group of physicians as test subjects. After inducing a positive mood in some of these subjects, she presented them each with a case history of a patient and relevant diagnostic studies. The doctors were then asked to "think out loud," while analyzing the case step-by-step to come up with a diagnosis (which was liver disease). In later analyzing the content of these assessments, the researchers found that those doctors who were feeling happy exhibited better critical thinking, reasoning, and clinical skills. They were faster to integrate case information and less likely to become anchored on initial thoughts or come to premature closure in their diagnosis. This ability to be less rigid in one's thinking, less likely to come to a quick judgment and simply hold on to your view, greater openness, etc., is the same type of thinking that would be more likely to have a successful outcome in conflict resolution. In another experiment, Isen and colleagues showed that negotiators induced to feel good in a complex bargaining task were more likely to discover integrative solutions, resulting in a successful outcome.

The deliberate cultivation of positive emotions can lead to new ways of thinking: facilitating dialogue and creating a greater potential for conflict resolution. The Dalai Lama's vision of a better future, a nonviolent future, may someday come to pass—not a Utopia where human beings never fight, or are never violent, but a future where peaceful dialogue is not the exception but the norm for the vast majority of humanity, the standard approach, and one in which there is always a good likelihood of success.

Chapter 13

POSITIVE EMOTIONS AND BUILDING
A NEW WORLD

How We Relate to One Another

It felt as if we were making great strides, connecting our inner world with the larger problems of society. The Dalai Lama also seemed fully engaged, but hearing the bustle of activity outside the hotel suite, I knew our time was short.

"Your Holiness, you've discussed in some detail the issue of trust, which you linked with our sense of community, so it seems that we've come full circle back to the issues that we began to discuss in Dharamsala when you pointed out a general lack of trust within a community decreases community bonds, but the growing social isolation and decline in sense of community lead to lack of trust as well.

"Now in trying to understand the causes of this lack of trust and deterioration of community, I had identified our increasingly mobile society as one of the causes. But you felt that our increased mobility did not necessarily have to lead to an erosion of trust or lack of sense of community. As you have mentioned, there can be many factors that cause these kinds of widespread problems. Can you identify some underlying cause that is common to both the erosion of trust in our society as well as the decline in our sense of community, or a common factor that links these together?"

He thought before answering. "This actually brings us back to what we discussed when we first took a look at these subjects. That is, both of these pertain to the question of how we relate to each other, what is the basis. Do we relate to each other on the basis of what differentiates us or on the basis of what unites us?"

"Your Holiness," I said warily, hoping he would not classify the question under our category of Silly Questions, "just for clarity, since you indicate that the basis of a relationship is a critical factor, could you briefly elaborate on what you feel are the customary distinctions that people in our society normally base their relationships on."

Apparently not inclined to take issue with my question this time, he answered, "Of course, there can be many ways that people relate to each other. They can relate to each other based on what is their family background, what is their financial situation, what is their level of education, ethnicity, language, and so on.

"This tendency to relate to each other on the basis of what differentiates us is so prevalent in today's society. It's given great importance and seems to be a reflection of our societal values, with our emphasis on acquisition of material wealth. People seem to be so preoccupied with how much they earn, how much they are worth, and what kind of social status they happen to have. In fact, I was told, that, if asked, people are generally reluctant to tell you how much money they make because it's seen as an indication of their worth and who they are as a person. But one fundamental problem with this kind of approach is that you can end up relating to the person's money, their status or power, rather than the person himself or herself. You are relating more on the basis of your own hopes or expectations, the things that you hope to get from them, and so on. And then if there is a change of that person's financial status or position, your relationship goes along with it.

"So when you take these as very important factors, the family background, the financial situations, the social status, the kind of work you do and so on, and then if you treat the basic humanity as less important, then it focuses on our differences and creates a feeling of distance between people. Then," he concluded, "of course this opens us up to all these problems, including lack of trust."

"You know, Your Holiness, thinking back to our original discussion of the spirit of community and so on, we also discussed how it also leaves the door open for the kinds of Us Against Them divisions that—"

Anticipating the direction where I was heading and the question I was about to raise, the Dalai Lama cut in and said, "Yes, but there is another very important factor to remember. It's critical. Now, as we mentioned there are different levels of 'community' that can be formed on the basis of living in the same neighborhood, or a common religion, culture, shared interests, and so on. But in a sense I think this level can be seen as focusing more on *external* characteristics that we share. But there is also a deeper level, in which we can relate on a more fundamental level, relating to others based on our *inner qualities*. These are our common characteristics that we all share as human beings, our basic human qualities.

"So, here we are adding this deeper level as well, connecting to others based on these common human characteristics. *No matter what other factors serve as the basis for our sense of community, no matter what other ways that we may relate to others, if we can maintain a feeling of connection to others based on our common humanity, it will prevent all these problems from arising.*"

"So, Your Holiness, here it seems that we are no longer talking just about cultivating a sense of community, strengthening community bonds, or a feeling of trust. From what you are saying, it seems that finding a solution to all of the problems we have discussed—violence, racism, and so on—seems to converge on this fundamental issue of how human beings relate to each other. It seems to ultimately come down to how we connect with each other."

"That's right, that's right!" the Dalai Lama affirmed, nodding his head vigorously.

"Actually, Your Holiness, that brings up a question that I have been wondering about ever since those first series of discussions about shifting our outlook from Me to We. In those discussions, I think you also briefly brought up the importance of relating to others on this fundamental human level. But how does one exactly go about doing that? Are there specific techniques or methods, or meditations that can help reinforce this capacity to relate to others on this fundamental level you are talking about?"

As I asked this question, I checked my watch, realized we had only five minutes left until the end of our scheduled meeting, and braced myself for the response I was quite sure to follow.

The Dalai Lama, too, checked his watch and, laughing, replied, "Howard, this is a huge question to cover in five minutes! Perhaps it's better to wait when we have more time."

In our discussion that morning, the Dalai Lama raised a critically important issue, tracing the common roots of both the erosion of trust and the decline in our sense of community in modern society: relating to others more on the basis of our differences than our similarities. How can we achieve a state of mind where we still have a good sense of our own identity, a sense of our own integrity, and yet also have a capacity to merge with another, almost as if we are a part of each other? On the group level, how can we expand our scope of our identity, incorporating other groups into those who we see as Us?

Here we have raised the question of the potential role of positive emotions in solutions to our societal problems. Continued research in the fields of positive psychology and neuroscience has revealed that positive emotions serve to promote a way of relating to others based on what unites us more than what differentiates us! These emotions cause changes in our thinking that result in a tendency to perceive ourselves and others as being more similar. The positive emotions tend to expand the boundaries of our identity, making those boundaries more like a permeable membrane rather than an impenetrable wall.

Experimental evidence has now shown that positive emotions cause a direct shift in our outlook—from Me to We! This takes place on both an interpersonal level and intergroup level. On the interpersonal level, for example, in one study researchers got subjects talking about their personal relationships. After taking a break, during which they induced a happy mood in some of the subjects, they had them continue talking about their relationships. The investigators found that those subjects who felt happier increased their use of the words "we" and "us," and reduced references to "me" and "I" in discussing their relationships!

Similar effects have been found on a group level. The beneficial effects of positive emotions in this case are again due to some of the characteristic changes in thinking associated with positive emotions. One of these changes involves seeing things in a "more inclusive" way, a tendency to see how separate categories can be grouped together and included in a larger all-encompassing category. This also manifests in general as a diminished tendency to divide things into categories. In one experiment, for instance, subjects were given a set of fourteen colored chips and were asked to sort them into groups by color—those in a good mood arranged them into fewer categories than those in a neutral or negative mood.

Those experiencing positive emotions also tend to have a greater sense of interconnectedness, they see relatedness easier, and tend to extend or expand the normal boundaries of categories. In one experiment involving word association, subjects experiencing positive emotions were more likely to see the connection between "elevator" and "camel"—recognizing they are both examples of the category "vehicle" (as they both convey people from one place to another).

While categorizing colored chips and connecting word pairs may not seem very relevant to the social problems in today's world, in fact this turns out to potentially have profound significance—because the different way of thinking associated with a happy state of mind seems to be applied to how we perceive *social categories* as well. Experimental evidence has shown that a person in a happy mood will tend to be more inclusive when perceiving different social categories, will see the interconnectedness among people and groups more easily, and will tend to focus less on the differences among social groups—perceiving less difference between one's own in-group and other groups as well as perceiving less difference between the other out-groups. In other words, not only does this kind of thinking make other groups appear to be more similar to our own group, but it also makes other social groups appear to be more similar to one another.

On a practical level, experiments have shown that inducing positive affect makes it easier to see common bonds with members of other social groups, fosters a common in-group identity, and reduces intergroup bias and conflict. If there are several groups represented in some joint activity, for example, those with a positive mood are more willing to see "them" as part of a more-inclusive, wider "us," and more likely to find a common in-group identity, more likely to view each of the groups as part of one larger, all-encompassing group. This will increase the variety of individuals with whom one can work, and foster a greater degree of cooperation between groups.

Positive Emotions and Prejudice

The changes in thinking caused by positive emotions are also the type of thinking that would encourage seeing members of other groups as all part of the category "human being," rather than as separate, rigidly defined racial, national, or social categories. This could serve to reduce prejudice and the potential negative sequelae of prejudice, such as discrimination, racism, hatred, conflict, and violence. *In fact, there is experimental evidence showing that those in a happier frame of mind perceive members of other groups with less prejudice and hatred.*

In one experiment, for example, Barbara Fredrickson and colleagues demonstrated the effect of inducing a happy mood on the phenomenon of Own Race Bias (ORB). ORB is a well-known and well-documented psychological phenomenon that has been studied for decades. ORB means that people are generally much better able to recognize and distinguish between faces of members of their own race than other races—in common parlance, the "they all look alike to me" syndrome. This is thought to be due to the natural bias against other races that we spoke of earlier, which leads people to process information differently when they look at the face of a member of their own race versus looking at the face of another race.

To understand the origin of ORB, it is helpful to take a brief look at what happens inside the brain when we look at faces. The area in the brain that is responsible for recognizing faces is called the fusiform face area, or FFA. This is the area of the brain that is activated whenever we look at the faces of members of our own race. Brain imaging studies have shown that when we look at faces of members of another race, however, the activation of the FAA is generally dramatically diminished. Why? Earlier we discussed how our instinctual bias against out-groups, such as other races, is associated with the activation of the area of the brain called the amygdala. As it turns out, when the amygdala is activated, it sends signals to the FAA, lowering the activation of the FAA, and thus lowering the ability to distinguish unique facial features.

In Fredrickson's experiment, the researchers showed photos of both black and white faces to a group of white subjects. These subjects exhibited ORB, and when tested later, they were better able to recognize the white faces that they had seen before than the black faces (in this experiment they studied white subjects, but ORB is found among all races). This of course is an automatic process, not under conscious control, and subjects generally do not even notice that they are exhibiting ORB. *After inducing a positive mood in the subjects, however, they retested the subjects and discovered that the positive mood eliminated the own-race bias!* Their ability to recall white faces remained the same, but their difficulty recognizing black faces disappeared—in other words, *the positive mood resulted in the white subjects perceiving black faces in exactly the same way they perceived faces of their own race, essentially, seeing "them" as one of "us,"* as far as the limits of this test were concerned.

One interesting feature of this experiment is that under normal circumstances, if there is no ORB, the brain tends to recognize faces in a "holistic" manner—as a collective whole instead of as a collection of parts. As we discussed earlier, one of the effects of positive emotions in general is to enhance a person's ability to see things more holistically, to see "the big picture." It is likely that this ability to see things more holistically plays a role in the tendency of positive emotions to reduce ORB. It has been proposed that when ORB occurs, faces of other races are not processed holistically, but rather they are processed more like inanimate objects than faces. Under these conditions, the image of the face stored in memory is usually distorted by a person's racial stereotypes of the other race—a black face, for example, may be remembered as darker in color than it is in reality, and the facial features are remembered in a way that more closely resembles stereotypes. Under the influence of positive emotions, however, as the ORB disappears, a member of another race is more likely to be seen as an individual, a complex human being, and less likely to be seen as a one-dimensional stereotype, based on their race.

Positive Emotions as a Strategy for Social Change

We have been making a case for the idea of positive emotions as a solution to some of the societal problems we have presented. As the Dalai Lama says frequently, we need to have many methods and solutions at our disposal. There is no single panacea, no one cure for society's ills. *But there is considerable evidence that the cultivation of positive emotions is one strategy that can contribute directly to personal happiness while at the same time create ways of thinking and acting that would tend to reduce many of the problems in today's world.*

Needless to say, the challenge in using this strategy to overcome societal problems is to figure out how to induce positive emotions on a wide scale. In experiments researchers have induced positive emotions on a temporary basis by methods such as having subjects watch uplifting or amusing film clips, giving subjects a small bag of candy, or arranging for them to unexpectedly find money in a phone booth. But to increase the average level of happiness in a nation is an entirely different matter. Fortunately, research has shown that there are ways to produce more sustained increases in happiness. For example, the Dalai Lama's approach, involving changes to one's fundamental outlook, is effective. His method of increasing hope and optimism, by looking at situations from a wider perspective, positive reappraisal and so on, has a much wider application and can be used to reduce negative emotions and cultivate more positive emotions in general. There are also other scientifically proven methods to increase positive emotions, including meditation, practicing gratitude, physical exercise, and others. The problem is that you can't force people to change their way of thinking or their behavior, even if it will result in greater happiness for themselves and their families, and contribute to a happier society, one in which there is less prejudice, hatred, conflict, violence, and so on.

But the cultivation of positive emotion holds great promise as at least one approach among many that we can use to help overcome some of our societal or global problems, if there is a concerted effort, as the Dalai Lama always recommends, to educate people, through the media and so on, about the benefits of positive emotions and the practical strategies to achieve a happier state of mind. This approach to overcoming our societal problems could potentially be much faster and more effective than instituting other kinds of education and awareness programs designed to reduce prejudice, racism, or violence. One reason, for example, is because it would seem to be much easier to convince members of society to adopt practices that will lead to their own happiness and welfare than to convince them to adopt programs to reduce various social problems.

Second, the cultivation of happiness and positive emotions produces a particular "side effect" that makes it ideally suited to bringing about social change and building a better world. Studies have shown that increasing happiness and positive emotions cause an individual to be more altruistic, more charitable, more willing to reach out and help others. As with other features of positive emotions, this would tend to bring about social change more rapidly than if we were attempting to tackle one social problem at a time, relying on methods for changing the behavior of only one member of that society at a time.

Another advantage lies in that the cultivation of positive emotions automatically leads to changes in thinking and behavior, and therein to greater happiness. Unlike with other kinds of education or awareness programs, these changes produced by the nurturing positive feelings should gather momentum, snowballing to even greater effect.

Additionally—*positive emotions are contagious*. Though some may need to make a concerted effort to change their basic outlook and increase their positive emotions or everyday happiness, others' level of happiness can be increased to some degree merely by contact with happy people.

In one of our conversations the Dalai Lama said, "The creation of a more peaceful and happier society has to begin from the level of the individual, and from there it can expand to one's family, to one's neighborhood, to one's community, and so on."

These words take on even greater meaning in the light of some startling new studies on the contagious nature of emotions, showing how a person's happiness can *literally* "expand to one's family, to one's neighborhood, to one's community and so on."

This contagious nature of emotions has been known for some time, and is based on research that shows that when we witness others expressing certain emotions, we tend to experience it ourselves. In investigating the brain mechanisms responsible for this phenomenon, some neuroscientists have come to believe that "mirror neurons" may be involved. A mirror neuron is a brain cell that fires both when performing an action and when observing the same action performed by another. It is thought that they may help attune us or help us resonate with the emotional state of others, and that they may play a role in empathy.

In a stunning study published in the *British Medical Journal* (January 2009), researchers from the University of California–San Diego and Harvard University found that the infectious nature of happiness is much more profound, extensive, and long-lasting than we could have imagined, spreading in social networks just like a virus. They discovered that having happy people in a person's social network can dramatically increase that person's chance of being happy.

If you become happy, you increase your next-door neighbor's odds of being happy by 34 percent, and increase your friend's odds of being happy by 25 percent, if that friend lives within a mile of you! They found that the degree of the contagious effect depends on the type of relationship and also on your geographical distance from the other person. On average, however, the authors report that every happy person in your social network increases your own chance of being happy by 9 percent. It works both ways: Having happy family or friends in your social network increases your odds of being happy too. Remarkably, the researchers found that happiness spreads in a person's social network up to "three degrees of separation." Your happiness can affect not only your friend, but also a friend of your friend, and even a friend of a friend of your friend—someone you may never even meet or hear of. In addition to the longer reach of this transmittable effect, the durability of the effect is far stronger than had been estimated previously. In fact, the researchers say the effects of catching happiness from someone else *can last up to one year*! As the happiness and positive emotions spread throughout social networks, communities, and societies, the social benefits will spread and take root in a society right along with the personal benefits.

The role of happiness and positive emotions in promoting social change and building a better world goes beyond the issues we discussed here. For example, Ronald Inglehart, a professor at the Center for Political Studies at the University of Michigan, has done studies pointing out that increasing the average level of happiness among the population of a nation will result in an increase in freedom and democracy in that country. So, it seems almost as if the benefits of happiness and positive emotions are unrivaled. Instead of perceiving the pursuit of greater personal happiness as a self-absorbed, self-indulgent luxury, it could be argued that if you are truly concerned about others' welfare and building a better world, it is your *duty* to be happy, or do what you can to become happier.

Positive Emotions, the Brain, and Hope for the Future

Ultimately, when investigating the serious problems facing the world today, we can trace the source of all these social problems to the human heart and mind. And in seeking to determine our potential for overcoming all these problems, at least from a scientific perspective, it is important to consider the biological substrate of our human emotions and ways of thinking: the brain. This is the organ that leads us to perceive all of these supposed distinctions and differences between people and is the organ responsible for creating the hostile, fearful, or aggressive emotions that lead us to violent, cruel, and stupid behavior in which we seek to harm one another.

Earlier we discussed how the human brain evolved mostly during the Pleistocene age, evolving to its current anatomical structure around 100,000 years ago. It was adapted for the common problems encountered by our remote ancestors. The Dalai Lama pointed out, however, that the modern world is vastly different from the world inhabited by our remote ancestors, so responding in ways that were once adaptive and helpful could potentially cause our own destruction today. While these impulses may have protected early humans from truly life-threatening dangers, we often react in the same way to threats based on imagination or mental projection.

One might wonder, if modern humans are simply walking around with caveman brains encased in our twenty-first-century skulls, brains stamped with a date that expired 100,000 years ago, aren't we doomed? After all, with the technological capacity to completely destroy all life on earth, do we really have the luxury of sitting around playing checkers for the next hundred thousand or million years until evolutionary forces can catch up and adapt our brains to modern conditions?

Fortunately, we are *not* doomed. Our brains may have circuitry that was adapted to the problems of our seemingly endless period of hunter-gatherer societies, but our brains have vast resources as well, resources that can be used to modify and reshape our customary ways of thinking and responding to the world around us. In fact, we have almost limitless untapped resources at our disposal. Even though we have the brain circuitry to act on earlier programming, and even brain circuits hardwired during a more primitive time *urging* us to act in certain ways, we are not compelled to do that. Yes, we have the capacity for anger, hatred, prejudice, and exaggerated fears, but we also have the capacity for kindness, compassion, tolerance, and altruism. Yes, we have the more primitive emotions of the limbic system, but we also have the more advanced neocortex, with its capacity for reasoning, critical thinking, creativity, and higher brain functions. And we have the choice of which responses to cultivate and strengthen.

Every moment of our lives, for instance, new connections—*synapses*—are being formed between our nerve cells in response to new learning, to new experience. In fact, *one million* new connections are being formed for *every second* of our lives! We have the capacity to develop new circuits, establish new connections between nerve fibers in the brain, and forge new neural pathways that can reshape the very structure and function of the brain. This amazing capacity of the brain is called neural plasticity and increases in our understanding of brain plasticity have helped us realize that the brain is not an irrevocably fixed organ—so we can establish new programming that determines how we might respond to situations, even to train our minds to perceive things in new ways.

It is these features of the brain that will allow us to find new nonviolent ways to resolve disputes, new ways of interacting with our fellow human beings, and it is the capacity responsible for the fundamental premise of the Art of Happiness series: the fact that we can train our minds to be happy, genuinely happy, to be kinder and more compassionate.

Now all we need is the will, and a bit of practice. From the perspective of the neural equipment we're all issued at birth, the path to a more peaceful, nonviolent world—one in which individuals enjoy inner personal happiness and outer societal happiness—is inside us. So, there is cause for optimism, even celebration. The Dalai Lama's vision of a world dominated by kindness instead of cruelty, where our human conflicts are predominantly solved by dialogue instead of violence, is a very real possibility.

Chapter 14

FINDING OUR COMMON HUMANITY

"YOUR HOLINESS, I know that you are leaving Tucson tomorrow to go on to the next city on your tour. But I am jumping off here and won't be joining you to the next city. So this will be our last meeting for a little while. But this question about a more specific method to establish a deep feeling of connection with others has been something that I have been wanting to ask you for quite a while. Of course, yesterday, we didn't have time to go into it. So that's why I want to be sure and start off today's meeting with that question."

"Okay. Let's start," said the Dalai Lama.

"So, to review," I began, "yesterday we concluded that most of our societal problems in one way or another seem to be related to this inability to connect to others on a deep level, a basic human level that perceives others to be just a human being like oneself. So, this issue is so important, I'm hoping that today we can examine this issue thoroughly and come up with a practical approach to cultivating that kind of connection with people, even with people who appear to have nothing in common with you."

"In that case," he said, "perhaps, we could use a popular method of the Buddhist approach to addressing problems. Here, I mean using the analogy of curing an illness. First, we understand what the problem is; second, we examine its causes and conditions; third, we inquire whether or not there is a possible cure; and then, finally, if we know there is a cure, we seek to apply the necessary remedy."

"Yes, Your Holiness, I like that model," I responded enthusiastically. "So, using this model, Your Holiness, the problems we have been discussing in our last few series of discussions could be considered some of the major ills of society—these illnesses would include, for example, lack of sense of community, increasing alienation and isolation, lack of trust, as well as the more acute ailments involving acts of prejudice, conflict, violence, and things like that. Am I right?" I asked.

"Yes, that's right," replied the Dalai Lama.

Since this was our final meeting for this series of discussions, I asked, "To review, the causes of these illnesses would be things like our destructive emotions, distorted ways of thinking, plus the conditioning we receive from our environment, and on a more fundamental level our tendency to divide ourselves into groups, 'us' and 'them.' And then some of these 'illnesses' arise as groups develop prejudices against one another, and the more active forms of discrimination. True?" I asked.

"Yes," he confirmed again, then added, "Perhaps, extreme individualism where one feels so self-sufficient that they don't need others, and false sense of superiority should also be included in this category. But of course, when dealing with these problems you will find many different causes, many factors involved."

"Now to follow through with the medical analogy, Your Holiness, what would you include in the category of remedies?" I asked.

"As I usually point out," replied the Dalai Lama, "when dealing with human problems we need a variety of approaches on many different levels. For example, we have spoken about the critical importance of *realistic thinking*—examining any given situation or a problem with a clear understanding of the reality. And I think *personal contact is another key factor* with these kinds of problems, in dealing, for example, with human violence—personal contact and dialogue are critical for resolving conflicts without violence. And personal contact also creates a basis for a greater sense of community. These are always helpful. So, many of the specific remedies related to specific problems, we have already discussed."

"That's true," I affirmed. "So, to get back to the main question, I guess now we are looking for more of an all-purpose remedy for global or societal problems. So, sticking with your medical model, let's say that you determine that there is a cure for these problems. Let's say that we determine that the ability to connect with others on a deep level, cultivating a feeling of affinity on a basic human level, where we feel that all human beings are our brothers and sisters, can act as a powerful general remedy to prevent or overcome all of these problems. So then how do we 'apply the remedy'? I mean are there practical methods or strategies that can help create such a connection?" I asked.

"Yes, creating such a sense of connection to others may require a fundamental transformation both in our outlook and the way we relate to others," he replied.

"Well, I guess I'm wondering more specifically, if we really want to change our perspective, and develop that genuine sense of connectedness to others, to all human beings, where do we start?"

"Once again it all comes down to awareness."

I laughed. "So, once again, we're back to awareness—it seems as if we keep circling around back to awareness! I think in those first discussions in Dharamsala you also mentioned how we need to cultivate greater awareness of our common humanity. But given the importance of these ideas, and their implications related to empathy and compassion, which I want to bring up with you, I'm wondering if you can describe more precisely what we should become aware of. I mean like identifying some concrete facts or ideas that we could 'be aware of' or think about, that might help transform our underlying outlook in this way, helping us to cultivate a deeper feeling of connection to all human beings."

Half expecting his standard response, about how it depends on the circumstances, context, individual, and so on, I was surprised by the definitive nature of his reply. "Yes. I think here three things." He replied decisively, "Number one, *reflecting on our social nature*; number two, *reflecting on our interdependence*; and finally, *reflecting on our common humanity*."

Contemplating Our Social Nature

"Your Holiness," I responded, "that sounds good. So, let's say that in order to cure our societal and individual ills, we need to develop a deep awareness of these three things. Now, I am wondering if you could elaborate or detail specifically what sorts of points one might contemplate in regards to these three essential facts."

"As I mentioned, I think the very first thing is to recognize that we human beings are basically social animals. We need to cultivate a deep appreciation of *our social nature*. It is part of our basic nature to come together, to form community bonds, to work together with a spirit of cooperation. Now look at these bees—their survival depends on cooperation. If one bee goes here, one bee goes there, they die. Everyone! So, without religion, without laws, without a constitution, these small animals cooperate—they know they need to work together to survive. So, basically that's our nature, too.

"Now if we appreciate our social nature and the need to work cooperatively with each other, naturally we will pay attention to others' welfare. This will create a society that is stable, happier, more peaceful—and the result is that everybody enjoys the benefit. There's no doubt about this. Otherwise, if the recognition of the social nature of human beings is not appreciated, and people completely disregard the welfare of others, then ultimately everyone suffers, including yourself. Isn't it?"

"So, given the importance of cultivating awareness of our social nature, before we go on, can you think of any additional ways to increase awareness of this?"

"In fact, this can simply be a matter of keeping on the lookout for evidence or examples of this social nature," he replied.

"Can you think of any examples right now?" I asked.

He took a moment to consider. "Yes. Now look at what happens when a community faces some crisis. This is often when you will see our cooperative nature coming out, when people pull together to deal with the crisis, with the well-being of the community foremost in their minds. This is a very basic human response, the reliance upon each other for support, for protection, and suggests the expression of our social nature.

"For example, look at what happened in New York following the tragedy of September 11. In the face of this crisis, the people of that city pulled together like never before, solidifying their sense of community, working together cooperatively, and the barriers between people suddenly began to disintegrate, people connecting like they never did before. I heard that people looked at each other in the eye, acknowledged each other on the streets, and related to each other as fellow New Yorkers, no matter what social status one had or how another was dressed and so on. And I think that this had even a more long-lasting impact. When there was a blackout in New York City, I heard that the spirit of cooperation was remarkable, people were open to one another, more helpful, had more of an attitude of a shared experience."

I added, "Of course, the question is why we don't always act in that manner, why it takes a crisis to pull us together."

For a moment the Dalai Lama remained silent. Sometimes he would unexpectedly stop to reflect on some point. Usually such reflections were brief. His reflective expression suggested that he was carefully turning over some question in his mind, perhaps seeking a deeper understanding of some fundamental issue. Sitting cross-legged, he would sway back and forth slightly as he thought. Like so many other times over the years, I marveled at the way he would explore issues with a real spirit of discovery. Even if we were discussing a topic that he had discussed countless times, there was still a freshness in his approach and a willingness to revise his views at any time.

Apparently having completed his brief inner contemplation, he resumed our discussion as unexpectedly as he had stopped. "So, Howard, I think this is in line with the medical analogy we are using, when we are really in physical pain, we seek medication. But otherwise, if it is not obvious to the person that he or she is sick, then he wouldn't want to seek medication. You might see causes of a problem already developing but you don't care if there is no pain. Because there is no immediate threat or pain there. Usually it takes a strong sensation of pain before you react."

"Well," I pointed out, "here we are talking about ways to increase our sense of connection to others. And we can say that one thing that brings people together, with a spirit of cooperation and sense of connection, is a crisis or shared suffering. But somehow," I said somewhat jokingly, "I'm not sure if the deliberate creation of crises and suffering we can share is the most effective approach to building a sense of bonding and community among people!"

The Dalai Lama chuckled briefly. "Then, continuing with this medical analogy, in the case of sick person, a prudent person would not wait until it comes to the crisis point of unbearable pain before he takes care of his illness. It is much better if you can educate yourself, recognize the symptoms of the illness and become more aware of the causes of the problem, before the pain develops. You may want to check what is going on. This way you can take better care of yourself. Similarly, even without a crisis, if individuals in a given society reflect a bit more deeply, they would see their deeply social nature and the interconnectedness of the well-being of all the members of the society. So the prudent thing would be to try to recognize this before crisis strikes.

"Therefore, if people do spend a little bit of time to reflect upon this, they will come to know that the well-being of one individual within a society is contingent upon the well-being of the society, that the interests are intertwined. Now, I mentioned how we can increase our awareness of these things by looking for examples, for evidence of our social nature. And, fortunately, if we look for it, the evidence will be there—because the fact of the matter is that normally people *can* come together. It's an expression of our basic nature."

In pondering the great mysteries, the broad eternal questions, and the origins of the distinguishing characteristics of human existence, such as our deeply ingrained social nature, there is one place where we might start: with the one feature that sets us apart from all other animals, our human brain. Or, alternatively, perhaps we might start with the one thing that is solely responsible for all the great achievements of human beings, responsible for all the magnificent works of human civilization that resulted from our big brain: *a piece of unripe fruit.*

No, here I'm not talking about Eve's apple, growing on the forbidden tree of knowledge of good and evil. I'm talking about an ordinary piece of unripe fruit, hanging on an ordinary tree, growing in an African forest around fifteen or twenty million years ago. One morning around that time, there was a little monkey who missed breakfast, so she was pretty hungry. She had missed breakfast because she slept in, and all the ripe fruit that had fallen from the trees had already been gobbled up by her friends. Her stomach was growling, and she was so hungry she decided to take a bite out of a piece that was unripe, knowing of course that it wouldn't do her much good, since monkeys can't digest unripe fruit. Lo and behold, she discovered that she was able to tolerate the unripe fruit—in fact, she found that it satisfied her hunger and she could digest it! Well, that was her lucky day, because from then on this genetic mutation allowed her to have her fill of fruit every day—everyone else had to wait until the ripe fruit fell, but she could grab herself a snack anytime she wanted. Not having to spend all her time scavenging for ripe fruit left her plenty of time to mate, and she had lots of kids who could eat unripe fruit, too. Well, within a few generations there was an entire band of monkeys living in the forest who could digest unripe fruit, and they were just living it up.

Now, at that time, there was a whole clan of cousins of the unripe-fruit-eaters who were also living in the forest and who still were able only to digest ripe fruit; they were frankly getting annoyed. All of a sudden there was an awful lot of fruit going missing from the trees, even before it had a chance to ripen, and the fruit-eaters were getting hungry. It wasn't fair! Finally, it got so bad that a few of the cousins decided they were fed up, and they decided to move out of the forest, or at least to the edge of the forest, bordering the savannas. Sure enough, they found more food there—with less competition from those damn unripe-fruit-eaters! But, sure enough, now there was another problem: There were some strange fearsome creatures living there, big cats and dogs, who turned out to enjoy eating little monkeys as much as the monkeys enjoyed eating ripe fruit.

Well, none of them wanted to go back into the forest where it was safe but where they went hungry most of the time. In the forest, they had gotten used to being pretty independent, as each monkey was fully capable of picking up the ripe fruit that fell on the ground, so they didn't really have to work together very much. But now, the monkeys realized that if they worked together as a team, warning each other about the predators, trying to fend them off as a group, then all of them would stand a much better chance of survival. So, they gave it a try and it worked! Still, things were not exactly perfect—in the forest, each monkey could do pretty much what she or he wanted to do. Now that they had to work in groups, they still wanted to do whatever they felt like doing but they had to balance their own needs in a way that wouldn't interfere with the functioning of the group, and things started to become more complicated. As the size of the group grew, alliances formed and there was a more nuanced and complex dance to life, just to stay safe, get some food, and get laid once in a while.

These savanna dwellers were the remote ancestors of chimps, gorillas, and humans, and this was the origin of our big brains, at least according to a number of top primatologists who have been studying primates for decades. There is a kind of popular notion in our culture that the evolution of our large brains vaguely had something to do with our opposable thumbs, and we evolved our large brains to make tools and outwit our neighbors of other species. But this theory, called the Machiavellian Intelligence (or the "social brain") theory, *attributes the evolution of our large brains to our social nature.* The main idea is that we rose from a lineage in which both individual and group success depended on balancing the need to work with others with the need to hold our own, to thrive both as an individual and as a group, to compete and cooperate at the same time. Once we started to live together in groups, this placed a whole new load on our brain: The members had to develop the intelligence to balance their individual needs with those of the group, learning how to cooperate and exercise some individual restraint when necessary. It also required understanding the behavior of other group members, forming alliances that were dynamic and might change, and so on. And as social structures became more complex, our ability to reason and plan and develop complex strategies was helpful if one wanted to stay safe, get enough to eat, and continue to mate, without being isolated from the group, which put one in peril of death.

Primatologists find this theory very appealing, as it fits the information on hand, such as the fact that among primate species the relative size of the neocortex (the most recent, "thinking" center of the brain, you know) in relation to the rest of the brain is directly related to the size of the social groups formed by the species. In fact, primatologists can look at the size of a primate's neocortex upon autopsy and accurately predict the group size of that species. This unripe-fruit theory is also consistent with the growth in body size of later primates (which conferred a greater chance of defending themselves against the predators), and it explains a wide range of primate behavior, such as grooming, which is thought to have evolved to solidify alliances within the group and form closer bonds.

If this theory is correct, then the human brain, the distinguishing characteristic of our species, was designed specifically for us to work together cooperatively, and our social nature, as the Dalai Lama suggests, is the very core of what it means to be human.

This discovery of the relationship between social group and brain size in primates has led some to calculate the maximum size of natural social groups for humans as well—and researchers have come up with a figure of around 150 to 200 people. That is the size group that our brains were designed to live among, keeping in mind the human brain was adapted for hunter-gatherer societies. "Natural group size" is the size of group that we can live in and develop the most efficient, smoothly running social organization, where we can keep track of the various personal characteristics of group members, thus being able to predict behaviors of other group members—it is the size of group that we can maintain with optimal interpersonal relationships, interacting smoothly on a personal basis with everyone. At this level, peer pressure serves to keep behavior in proper bounds and group members can work out problems directly among themselves without having to defer to all sorts of rules and authorities, etc. One recollection that fascinated me after learning of this figure was of the Dalai Lama saying that they had chosen to organize their refugee population into "camps" of 160 people when they set up their refugee communities in India.

What is the implication for our twenty-first century when we live in "groups" of hundreds of millions of individuals organized into "nation-states"? Well, it's not great. This means that we have the capacity, at least based on brain anatomy, to connect on a "personal" level with roughly 150 people at a given time—beyond that, people just become abstract members of some group, with stereotyped characteristics. In a sense, this figure of 150 represents that maximum number of people whom the brain can simultaneously keep track of as real human beings, each with personal human characteristics, those with whom one feels a personal sense of connection. Beyond that, we have evolved many other strategies to deal with the human beings we live among: We share a language, with which we can communicate information about people without having to live in small groups where we must learn information about others firsthand. We have developed social hierarchies and governments with authorities who represent large numbers of people. We liberally use stereotyping, perceiving members of large groups to have certain attributes, as a means of "knowing" something about a large number of individuals without being able to meet everyone.

But from a biological perspective, at least some argue, the more the group expands in size, the more other people seem on a gut level like nameless, faceless objects, an "it" or a "thing" rather than a "he" or a "she." We can be surrounded by thousands of other people every day, even come into personal contact with them, but we block out their personhood—someone delivers our mail every day, but unless we know them personally, on a gut (or brain) level, they are simply "the thing that brings the mail"; or someone thankfully hauls away our trash once a week, and they have a huge impact on the quality of our lives (imagine if nobody hauled away your and your neighbor's trash—ever), yet normally we conceptualize them simply as "the thing that makes the garbage go away."

This explains a lot. The closer another person is to one's "group," the more the other person seems "real" and the more likely we are to experience compassion and caring for them. That's why we may feel more emotion for the death of a next-door neighbor than for a dozen youngsters in a bus accident on the other side of town whom we hear about on the news, and why we feel more for the death of a dozen young residents of our own town than fifty thousand people dying in an earthquake on the other side of the world. Perhaps this is why, on that morning of my first meeting with the Dalai Lama as I sat listening to the news, recounted in the opening of this book, the stories of genuine human suffering, the suffering of human beings just like me, had little impact on a deep emotional level.

Needless to say, this is just one among many factors contributing to the problems of the modern world. But fortunately, there are ways to turn "the thing that makes the garbage go away" into a real person, ways to "personalize" a stereotyped individual, to see others as real human beings, worthy of human dignity and respect, as people for whom we can feel empathy and compassion. We have already covered some of these methods—such as Susan Fiske's "vegetable" technique or the strategy of personal face-to-face contact. And here, the Dalai Lama adds a final method: developing a deep awareness of our social nature, our interdependence, and our common humanity, so that everyone we meet is seen through this lens.

No matter what one's opinion of the true nature of human beings, there is one thing that is for certain—from an evolutionary and biological perspective the Dalai Lama is absolutely correct that we evolved to work together in groups, and human beings cannot survive without working cooperatively with one another. Of course, this characteristic is not limited to human beings—most other primates, like their human cousins, live in groups and show clear signs of sadness when separated from the group. In experiments in which they isolate an individual monkey from the group, the monkey will pull a lever over and over again, with no other reward than just getting a glimpse of another monkey. In fact, whether seen from the perspective of sociobiologists or evolutionary psychologists, most scientists agree that this is a genetically hardwired feature of human behavior, and there is a vast amount of scientific evidence supporting the Dalai Lama's view of the social nature of human beings.

But as the Dalai Lama reminds us, recognizing and understanding our social nature is not something that is merely of scientific interest. It is not merely a matter of philosophy, religion, or academic theory, but rather something that is essential to our existence. In an age when, for one reason or another, more and more people lead relatively insulated lives, going about their daily business under the illusion that they are independent and self-sufficient, it seems that many have developed the notion that we have no real need for connection to the wider community or humanity, that this is something optional. Somehow in the past century or two we have lost sight of the basic human need for social connection, somehow forgotten that this is a matter of our survival. As our conversation continued, he reminded us of this fundamental truth with utter clarity.

Contemplating Our Interdependence

"We are caught in an inescapable web of mutuality, tied in a single garment of destiny. Whatever affects one directly, affects all indirectly. That is the way the world is made."
—DR. MARTIN LUTHER KING

The Dalai Lama spoke convincingly about our social nature as human beings, and how a deep recognition and understanding of this can perhaps alter our perception of ourselves, and reshape our attitudes toward others. So, we went on to the second essential fact.

I asked, "Your Holiness, you have discussed the first factor that we can contemplate, that can be used to cultivate a sense of commonality with all human beings. That is our social nature. Can you now speak about the second one you mentioned?"

"Yes," he immediately replied. "I think the next factor that ties us together is our *interdependence*. As human beings we depend on one another for our very survival. And I think that in modern society, we are becoming even more interdependent and interconnected. Now, in the past, more people lived separately, as farmers and as nomads. They were not so dependent on each other. So maybe in the old days it was more realistic to have a feeling of independence—as the individual farmers worked hard, tilled the land, and created their own sustenance. But things have changed. More and more people live in cities, and the whole basis of creating metropolitan communities involves human beings coming together and working together. Of course we can see from early tribal groups to today, it seems that human beings like to live together; we naturally tend to group together. But as society has become more complex, and we have developed these modern megacities, it seems that more than ever we need a sense of cooperation, a sense of community.

"So, I often mention how the world is becoming smaller," the Dalai Lama continued. "This means that through modern technology and communications we have opportunities to come into contact with others throughout the world at an ever-increasing rate, and through things like the modern economic structure our lives are becoming increasingly intertwined. And our welfare and others' welfare are closely linked to one another. For example, anytime there is a resurgence of violence in the Middle East, it immediately affects oil prices; there is a kind of a domino effect through a chain reaction the consequence of which is ultimately felt acutely even by an ordinary family living on the other side of the globe.

"Today, our lives are directly affected by what happens in the societies surrounding us, and even globally. For example, excessive pollution created in your area by local industries or certain lifestyles may have far-reaching effects that extend beyond your own community or even country—it could even have a global impact on the ozone layer and so on. But often, as we have discussed, people don't think about the effect of their actions on others, and we tend to have a feeling of independence from others, no feeling of connection to the wider community or society."

"I was just thinking," I went on, "it seems almost paradoxical that despite the heavily interdependent and interconnected nature of today's world, we seem to have an even greater sense of isolation and independence. . . .

"For example, people may work in some industry, or work for some company, and it may take many people to run their company or produce the product they sell. Yet when they get their own individual paycheck every two weeks, there is a kind of feeling of, 'Well, I did my job, I worked hard in my own office and I got paid for my work, and I'm supporting myself, so it does not make any difference what others at the company do; that's their business.' This kind of thing . . ."

He nodded, with a thoughtful expression. "You know, it seems that when we are very young, from a very early age, we have this innate sense of connection with our mothers, we have a feeling that we can depend on our mother's care and concern—but somehow later on, as we grow up, we feel that we can get by completely on our own, as if we can exist independently from others. I think that's a mistake.

"For instance, in your example of someone working for a big company," he said, perking up as he became more engrossed in the conversation, "it all comes down to one's attitude and outlook. There is a kind of community in a large company. For instance in the car-making industry, although individuals may be working on an assembly line where there is only one part that is being produced, collectively they will produce a car, so people will say, 'We produce a car,' not 'I produce a car.' Therefore there is an understanding that each is a part of the bigger network collectively making this product.

"So, it becomes a matter of perspective," the Dalai Lama continued, "a question of attitude that makes the difference. People have a choice. They can choose to acknowledge their interdependence, like a worker who feels a sense of connection with all the others who are working on the car they are producing. Or, they can maintain the attitude, 'Yes, I am free and independent, I earn my own money and I buy my own things.' Of course, that kind of outlook will lead to a sense of lack of dependence upon others, and the result will be a lack of feeling of connection with others."

If one gives it some thought, it isn't difficult to come up with countless ways that our world is interdependent, how we are becoming more closely connected with each passing year. Modern history has been characterized by an exponentially growing interconnection and interdependency on every level—in the advances in communications, the Internet, transportation, the intertwining of economies, the advent of weaponry of such nightmarish proportions that concepts such as Mutually Assured Destruction have been conceived; the idea of deterring nuclear war based on the knowledge that such an act would assure total annihilation of both sides. The advances in modern technology have proceeded at such a blinding pace. Consider that during the Oldowan period the technology of the day—stone tools—stayed the same, with a few minor refinements, for *two million years*. The next big breakthrough came around 300,000 years ago when some genius figured out that you could put a handle on your stone ax and have a tool with more than a single component. Although advances initially developed at a glacial pace, we have seen human civilization developing technologically (among other ways) at an increasingly rapid rate, down through the ages, until the speed of technological change has almost defied imagination. In just the past couple centuries we have witnessed the world-shaking transformation of the Industrial Revolution and have seen the changes continue to accelerate throughout the last century as well, when the primary basis of interdependence was either economic—for example, events such as the 1929 Wall Street crash, which had repercussions around the world—or military, with two world wars casting a net that swept up nations all over the globe with horrible consequences for civilians as well as combatants who were caught up in devastating "collateral damage."

Finally, we come to the present day, when it seems that our lives are turned upside-down almost daily by some new invention. Even the interdependency of just the last century pales in comparison to the ways the world is "shrinking" today, as the Dalai Lama points out. A multifaceted interdependence of increasing complexity is joining people across the globe in all facets of life—some of it good, some of it bad. The traditional economic or military interconnection continues to escalate—to the point, for example, where the interpenetration of investment capital and "market" links is creating an economic interdependence that directly links the socioeconomic destiny of virtually the entire planet. Even cultures are interacting and impacting one another, as our cultural icons, fashions, and popular ideas cross borders as well, linking individuals in all parts of the globe. In fact, the Dalai Lama himself is a good illustration of that—his name, face, and his message of kindness, universal responsibility, human rights, and so on, is known around the world.

There's no question the world is becoming more interdependent, making cooperation between communities and nations a critical issue. The Dalai Lama extends the principle of interdependence to all levels of human existence, personal as well as global, understanding that one's own welfare is inextricably linked to the welfare of others. In fact, if one searches carefully, one can find examples of interconnecting agents on every scale imaginable, from the planetary scale to the microbial level. On the planetary scale, for example, no issue is of greater importance than environmental interdependence, as the Dalai Lama points out. The sudden massive changes in patterns of consumption, the growth of technology, manufacturing, and mass transportation of the twentieth century have placed ecological interdependence center stage as the threat of nuclear disasters such as Chernobyl, the destruction of our rain forests, industrial pollution, and the use of substances like CFC gases have created environmental damage that affects us all, insidiously spreading across national boundaries unimpeded. And even on the microbial level, of course, viruses and bacteria could be seen from that perspective, as having no respect for national borders—carried by living beings to connect people across the world with deadly results, from the time of the Spanish conquistadors who carried pathogens from Spain to the Native Americans in the New World, decimating eighty million people in the sixteenth century, to the tragic AIDS epidemic of our times.

It is easy to see the principle of interdependence operating on every level—even on an individual level; one popular and powerful method of contemplating our interdependence has been the notion of Six Degrees of Separation. These days the concept is most well known for the game Six Degrees of Kevin Bacon, a game seeking to connect any actor to actor Kevin Bacon, by no more than six links. The concept originated with a Hungarian writer, Frigyes Karinthy, who wrote a volume of short stories in 1929, one of which was titled "Chain-Links," in which a character claimed that the modern world was shrinking due to the ever-increasing connectedness of human beings, as a result of technological advances in communications and travel. His characters created a game based on the idea that you could choose any stranger living on the face of the earth and using no more than *five* individuals, one of whom is a personal acquaintance of yours, you could contact the selected individual using nothing except the network of personal acquaintances (i.e., you knew someone, who knew someone else, who knew someone else, etc. . . . who knew the person named). But the main issue here, as the Dalai Lama makes clear, is not so much the particular facts one chooses to illustrate or reinforce our sense of interdependence, but the willingness to consider the critical importance of interdependence, and its relevance to our lives in a personal and intimate way—by recognizing that our happiness, to a large degree, is dependent on others, and therefore our welfare and others' welfare are inextricably linked. Unless one is a completely self-sufficient hermit living in a cave or stranded on a deserted island, like the Tom Hanks character in the film *Cast Away*, one's very survival depends on others.

In reminding ourselves of our fundamental social nature and our interdependence, how we are born to live and work with others, and how human survival is dependent on others, there is a simple thought experiment that can act as a powerful exercise to help reinforce this idea: To try this exercise, you can choose any product that you rely upon or use regularly, or something that is important to you or that you enjoy (inanimate goods of some kind). Next, spend at least five minutes imagining as many people as you can who were personally involved in the manufacture, preparation, or transport of that object, including all the components and raw materials for that object. Use your imagination and among the thousands who may have contributed, try to visualize at least some of them as real human beings, maybe trying to picture what they might look like, what they might be wearing, and whether they have a family, and so on.

It can be a powerful practice to try this daily for a week, or even longer. You can experiment and modify the exercise according to what seems to have the most impact for you, but it is helpful to choose a different object or product every day. Frequently people choose a meal as a subject—for example, a poached egg and some toast—and imagine the person who brought the food home if not the diner himself, then the check-out person at the supermarket, the stocker, the trucker who delivered it to the market, the farmer who collected and those who packaged the egg that is now on the plate, the individuals who grew and harvested and delivered the chicken feed to the farmer . . . It can go on and on, as detailed as you like, and go in any direction. You could imagine all those who assembled the tractor used in cultivating the wheat for the toast, the miners in foreign lands who mined the ore to make the metal for the tractor, and so on. With a little practice, this exercise will help us appreciate how we are connected with so many people, dependent on so many people throughout the world just to meet our basic needs, and as that awareness grows, it is joined by a growing sense of gratitude.

A friend recently tried this exercise while she was eating a piece of ordinary prepackaged frozen chocolate cake she had defrosted. She described the various people she visualized, including the workers cutting the sugarcane in a humid field on a tropical island, those who grew the wheat, manufactured the flour, and gathered the cocoa beans, and a worker wearing a white apron in a large factory, surrounded by the aroma of a thousand chocolate cakes freshly baked. She said that when she was done with the exercise, imagining the thousands who worked hard to supply all the ingredients, put them together, ship it, and so on, she felt like some exotic ancient supreme potentate who had commanded a thousand people, working in every corner of the world, just to bring her a piece of chocolate cake—and she said that for a moment it tasted like the most rare and special thing she had ever eaten.

Contemplating Our Common Humanity

Having reflected on our social nature and our interdependence, we now move on to the third truth that the Dalai Lama suggests we contemplate: "our common humanity." He recommends that we reflect on these three truths as a means of achieving a deep sense of connection with all human beings, a way of relating to others based more on what unites us than on what separates us. On the surface, it might seem that contemplating our common humanity alone should be enough to evoke a deep sense of our connection to others. In fact, by comparison, the contemplation of our social nature and our interdependence may seem a bit dry and academic to some. Why bother to contemplate our social nature and interdependence first?

Upon further reflection, we can perceive the Dalai Lama's great wisdom in including the contemplation of our social nature and our interdependence. First, understanding that we are social animals, that our social nature goes to the heart of who we are, underscores the importance of these issues, helping us see how they are critical to our survival as a species. Furthermore, contemplating our interdependence helps us understand how our own welfare is inextricably linked with the welfare of others. After contemplating our social nature and our growing interdependence, we can approach these issues more as a matter of survival, and as a matter where our own personal happiness and welfare are at stake—thus strongly reinforcing the importance and practical value of cultivating a greater awareness of our common humanity, rather than thinking of "our common humanity" as a purely religious, moral, or academic issue.

"So, Your Holiness, we have come to the third of your contemplations. So, before we proceed, just to be clear, can you explain briefly what exactly do you mean by your phrase 'common humanity'?" I asked.

"This is in a way a simple idea. In order to contemplate our common humanity, we begin by investigating what are the most basic traits that all human beings share. So if you reflect carefully, you will realize that we all have the basic aspiration to seek happiness and to overcome suffering. For me this is the most fundamental truth of our nature. But of course, our shared characteristics also include a need for a deep appreciation of others' affection, our capacity for empathy. We humans also have this marvelous intelligence as well as rich imaginative faculty.

"I think that cultivating an awareness of the fundamental equality of all human beings is perhaps the most important thing here," the Dalai Lama continued. "We all have the same human body, the same human emotions, and the same human mind. If you get stabbed, you bleed; if I get stabbed, I bleed. If you lose someone you love, you feel sad; and if I lose someone I deeply care about, I feel sad. If you reflect on an important truth, you gain new insight; and if I reflect on an important truth, I gain a new knowledge.

"To me, all these features which differentiate us, like wealth, position, status, and so on, are secondary. I truly believe we can learn to relate to one another on a deeper level, based on our shared humanity. And the main point here is that if individuals relate to each other on the fundamental level of humanity, so long as they possess the human qualities, then there will be immediately a basis for trust."

Finally the Dalai Lama distilled the essence of this profound practice by saying, "So, in my own personal dealings with people, for instance, whether the other person is a president or a big business person, or an ordinary householder, or even a beggar, or someone suffering from AIDS, the immediate connection with the individual is our fundamental humanity, our common humanity." He concluded by saying, "This is the level on which I try to relate to the other person. That's what enables me to feel deeply connected with the other person. This is the key."

The Dalai Lama uttered these last words in a simple, direct way, sharing his personal experiences in his typical open, honest, and unaffected manner. There was nothing particularly remarkable about how he said those words, but having witnessed him relating and connecting with others for more than two decades, in exactly the way he claimed, I could not help but feel moved. I had seen him connect with so many people from all around the world, people from all strata of society. I had witnessed the way he treats all with equal respect and regard, affording them a certain kind of human dignity. I had watched so many people, meeting him for the first time, spontaneously break into tears, weeping with joy—a reaction that was not limited only to Tibetans, for whom meeting the Dalai Lama was the fulfillment of a lifelong dream.

One can never tell what is in the hearts of others, or why so many people from diverse backgrounds would spontaneously react to meeting the Dalai Lama with tears of gladness and joy. But I wonder if part of that reaction may be due to the unusual experience of being treated as a worthy fellow human being and being respected, loved, and respected on that basis—unlike their customary interactions in which others related to them based on whatever role they were playing at the moment (that of a friend, employee, boss, student, or whatever). And finally, I had seen people leave after those meetings with him invariably smiling, relaxed, as if they were suddenly nourished after a long fast.

So, now we move to the final contemplation—our common humanity. In the opening chapters of this book the Dalai Lama prescribed an approach to building greater trust and a sense of community by joining some kind of wider group with others who share a similar background or interests. In a way, this could be seen as a prescription that treats the symptoms of the societal illness, and one that offers temporary relief. But here he offers another prescription, one that heals on a more basic level, an approach to treating societal ills that could be seen as strengthening the underlying emotional immune system of society. He suggests going beyond our common interests—as bowlers, or Elks, or Methodists, softball players, chess players, bicycling enthusiasts, truffle-eaters, or cat fanciers—to discover our underlying common characteristics as human beings, the qualities and traits that we share with every single human being whom we will encounter in the course of our daily life: our common humanity. A fundamental transformation of our basic outlook, in which we have a deep sense of our commonalities as human beings as well as our differences as individuals, is the ultimate solution to creating a happier society, in which the members of that society have a sense of connection and trust, an underlying bond with every other member of that society.

Of course, even though this solution may sound simple, that does not mean it will necessarily be easy. It requires more than simply acknowledging our commonalities with other human beings, more than a simple recognition of our social nature, interdependence, or common traits. It requires a deliberate and conscious reflection on this, over and over again, deep reflection, repeated reflection, until this view becomes internalized, and becomes part of our fundamental outlook, our automatic perception or attitude that arises spontaneously as we encounter any given human being, friend or enemy.

Although this may not be easy, fortunately it is possible to undergo this internal transformation, to reshape our outlook, to approach other human beings on the basis of our shared humanity, on our commonalities instead of our differences—and the Dalai Lama, among others, is living proof that it is possible.

Thinking about how the Dalai Lama relates to every person he meets on the basis of our common humanity, treating all with the same respect and human dignity, I find that a flood of images from the last twenty-five years flashes through my mind, bearing witness to this simple truth. Searching for an illustration, however, I find that the scenes are racing by in memory so fast that it is difficult to stop and select any one in particular. But for some reason, at this moment I recall a brief interlude that took place at a Businessperson's Lunch in Minneapolis some years ago, during one of his U.S. tours on which I had tagged along. It was a very exclusive and restricted event, organized for the local movers and shakers, the rich and powerful, to meet the Dalai

Lama. We arrived at the building from the back, and in order to get to the ballroom, the DSS security team had planned a route through a maze of back corridors, passageways, and the kitchen. The kitchen staff and busboys and dishwashers had assembled to see the Dalai Lama go by, lining the corridors as he passed by, smiling and greeting them warmly. The Dalai Lama was scheduled to give an address before lunch, and the timing was such that we had to stand backstage for a few minutes while the speaker on the stage introduced him. A young busboy had happened to be standing near the spot where we stopped, so while we were waiting, the Dalai Lama and he exchanged a few words of small talk. When the introduction was finished, we emerged onto the low platform acting as a stage and the Dalai Lama gave his address. There was nothing very extraordinary about the Dalai Lama's brief exchange with the busboy backstage. It was just a spontaneous and natural response to the moment, with no pretense, no ulterior motives, no fanfare. Well, nothing extraordinary other than the busboy's surprise, I suppose. But what struck me so forcibly later on was how the Dalai Lama interacted exactly the same with the rich and powerful people at that luncheon as he did with the busboy—exhibiting the same level of interest in both, giving them his full attention, the same warmth, and, when speaking with them, acting as if they were the most important person in the world at that moment, as if they were the *only* person.

There was one other small detail of that lunch that I remember, another ordinary detail of no consequence but which struck me as a metaphor of the truth that we are all human beings, with no great differences among us on that fundamental human level. When we came out in front, I noticed the backdrop that separated the stage from the work area and kitchen—it was just a very thin wall of plywood, covered with a very thin dark wood veneer. All that separated these rich businesspeople eating their roast duck at their tables of white linen and crystal and silver from the workers who invisibly prepared all this food and the elegant trappings, all that separated these two completely different environments and kinds of people was just that quarter of an inch!

For some reason that struck me as a powerful metaphor for how we think we have this vast gulf between ourselves and others, how we think that there are such huge differences between people, particularly between the rich and the poor, the powerful and the humble, and so on. We think there is so much that differentiates us, but in reality that is often an illusion; in reality there is very little that separates us—and it seems as if the Dalai Lama instinctively acts based on this reality, realizing that we are all the same, at least on that fundamental level, and treats people accordingly.

While it is quite clear that the Dalai Lama has a great capacity to connect with others on this fundamental human level, the question is, how can the rest of us develop the same capacity? Knowing that his attitude was largely the result of years of spiritual practice, I asked, "Your Holiness, I'm just wondering if there are any formal meditations, techniques, or exercises that people could practice regularly to generate this deep sense of trust and a feeling of connection with others—perhaps some kind of Buddhist meditation that was designed to generate this state of mind but that could be practiced by non-Buddhists as well."

"There are many meditations and different kinds of practices. But there will be individual differences in which practice a particular person might find to be most effective. However, even without a formal sitting meditation," he explained, "one can use the ideas we have been discussing as a kind of 'analytic meditation.'"

Ah, now we're getting somewhere, I thought. I suppose I was hoping he would have some kind of special Buddhist method of generating this state of mind. Or, perhaps I had been expecting he might somehow encapsulate our discussions on these topics in some fresh and uniquely Buddhist way, according to some secret formula that could be used as a daily meditation practice. I'm not sure. But in eager anticipation of the Dalai Lama revealing a more structured meditation technique designed to cultivate this sense of our common humanity, I said, "To be more specific about this analytic meditation, then."

"Well, to be more specific," he responded, "we could deliberately reflect on, *one*, we are social animals. This idea could be reinforced by thinking about the other social animals, and how they depend on one another for survival. Then, *two*, in the modern world in particular, all our interests and our welfare are so intertwined. The world is getting smaller and smaller each day—we are becoming more and more interdependent, and our own welfare is closely connected with the welfare of those around us. And *three*, we could reflect on our fundamental equality as human beings, such as the idea that each of us wants happiness and wants to avoid suffering."

"But these are the same three things that you were just talking about!" I complained.

"Exactly!" he said, smiling broadly, as if I finally got it.

Chapter 15

EMPATHY, COMPASSION, AND FINDING
HAPPINESS IN OUR TROUBLED WORLD

"YOUR HOLINESS, since this is our last meeting here, I want to see if we can tie together several subjects that we have discussed and see if there is a kind of unifying principle related to finding happiness in a world with so many problems."

"Good," said the Dalai Lama cheerfully, as if ready to tackle any topic.

In mentioning that this was our last meeting in Tucson, I briefly thought back to our first series of meetings in Tucson so many years before. One of the very first questions I had asked at that time was "Your Holiness, are *you* happy?" I recalled his response: "Yes, definitely."

Now a new question arose, a question more in the context of our current discussions. I asked, "Your Holiness, over the years I have noticed that you seem to be a genuinely happy person, despite the fact that your life has not always been an easy one. In fact, I remember asking you once if you were happy, and you told me yes. So, I'm wondering if maybe your happiness has something to do, in part at least, with the way that you relate to others on the basis of our common humanity?"

"Yes, I think so," he said simply.

"So then, first, I was wondering if you could briefly elaborate on some of the benefits or the effects of relating to others in this way."

"About the effects . . ." the Dalai Lama began slowly, "yes, I think when you relate to others on this fundamental human level, there is a sense of freedom. It opens a kind of inner door, from where you can reach out to others more easily. There will be a sense of basic trust and lack of insecurity."

"So, on a practical level," I interrupted, "I assume that you feel that this basic trust will help overcome problems like prejudice, or the lack of sense of community that we have spoken about."

"That's right," he confirmed, then continued. "So, when you relate on that level, when you meet other people, there will be actually no need for introduction. You will feel as if you already know the person, even though you might be meeting the other person for the first time. In this sense, there will be no real strangers for you.

"When you can learn to do this, you will then allow your natural capacity for empathy to express itself more spontaneously. I think this kind of empathy is one of the most wonderful human qualities. Because when you are deeply aware of the fundamental truth of our human existence—that just as I do, others too wish to achieve happiness and wish to overcome suffering, and have the equal right to obtain happiness—you automatically feel empathy and closeness for them. You will then be able to easily relate to others' welfare out of a genuine sense of caring. This is compassion."

"I'm glad that you brought up empathy and compassion," I said, "because that is actually what I wanted to bring up with you, in order to clarify a few things. First, about empathy—by definition, empathy involves our ability to connect with others, our ability to relate to them, understand their feelings, to share their experience and so on. So, it seems that connecting or relating to others based on our common humanity, our shared characteristics as human beings, is essentially a method of creating empathy. But with this kind of empathy you can relate to all human beings, and it does not depend on being able to relate to their individual characteristics or personal experiences."

"That's right," he said.

"And then, empathy and compassion are closely linked too," I continued. "Compassion involves opening oneself to another's suffering, sharing their experience of suffering and wishing them to be free of their suffering. So, empathy is an absolute requirement for compassion, because you need to be able to relate to that person, to share that person's experience, feel what they are going through in order to feel genuine compassion.

"So, to summarize these things, and how they fit together, we can say that cultivating a sense of our common humanity is a way of creating empathy, and the deeper one's empathy is, the stronger one's compassion will be."

"That's right," the Dalai Lama said again.

"So, at this point, I'm wondering if you have anything to add about compassion, specifically in the context of finding happiness—both inner happiness and a happier society, one in which we begin to overcome some of the problems in today's world."

The Dalai Lama took a moment to organize his thoughts, then said, "Yes. First, as I always point out, when you experience compassion for others, the first person to benefit is actually you. Compassion is a true source of happiness. Cultivating a close, warm-hearted feeling for others automatically puts the mind at ease, helps remove fears and insecurities and gives us the strength to cope with any obstacles we encounter. It is the ultimate source of success in life. I believe that at every level of society—family, community, national, and global—the key to a happier and more successful world is the growth of compassion. So, you see, compassion is something really worthwhile. It is not just a religious or spiritual subject, not a matter of ideology. It is not a luxury, it is a necessity."

"Your Holiness, I know your views about all the practical benefits and rewards that can come from cultivating greater compassion, and how ultimately even our survival as a species can depend on it. But I think that one reason why more people don't take the cultivation of compassion more seriously is that despite your saying how compassion has practical value and is not merely a religious subject, many people still have an underlying perception of compassion as a spiritual or religious subject. For example, I've heard you mention how compassion enhances our physical and mental health, but most people still think of compassion as a moral issue instead of a health issue.

"In my own case, for instance, when you used to speak of compassion years ago, I could not deny that it was a wonderful thing, but it still struck me as something a little too 'warm and fuzzy' for my taste, something too sweet and sentimental or something, and more of a spiritual topic It took many years for me to start thinking of compassion in terms of its tremendous practical benefits, many years before I could accept your claim that it leads to one's own personal happiness, or has these other practical benefits for society and so on. And one of the main things that changed my mind was the scientific proof of what you were saying, a lot of which didn't come out until the past few years.

"Anyway, Your Holiness, I guess all I'm saying is that I agree that if people adopted some of your views on a widespread scale and took compassion more seriously, for example, that it would have a profound impact on our society. However, since it is unlikely that most people in the West will 'convert' to Buddhism as their primary spiritual path, if these principles are to be widely adopted in Western society they need to be presented in a secular context, which generally means investigating and presenting them from a scientific perspective."

"Yes, that's true," said the Dalai Lama.

"Fortunately," I continued, "there is now a wide body of scientific evidence of all these benefits of compassion, which I know you are very familiar with, as a result of all your meetings with scientists. Not only that, but there is also scientific evidence showing how people can train their minds to become more compassionate and happier, and how training the mind to be more compassionate can actually change the very structure and function of the brain. I think that's very important too because a lot of people may have the misconception that compassion and kindness is a matter of one's genetic temperament or innate disposition—the idea that you're either born as a naturally compassionate person or you're not, but if you are not a naturally warm or compassionate person, there's nothing you can do about it, in the same way that you can't change how tall you are. But of course that's not true.

"So," I concluded, "my point is that there is now a lot of science that supports your views, which are based on Buddhist principles, but in order for that research to have an effect on society, the information needs to move beyond the universities, laboratories, scientific journals, and conferences so that average people begin to change their attitudes about compassion."

"Yes, I agree with what you are saying," said the Dalai Lama, "which is why I generally try to point out to people how we need to promote these ideas in society, how we need to educate people. This can take place through the media, through the education system, and so on. And Howard, you also should do some research, some investigation, and share this kind of evidence in our book. We should try to promote these ideas in whatever way we can. And of course, here we must not only learn to recognize the importance of empathy, compassion, and so on, and not only talk about these things, but we must reinforce these ideas so that they become translated into our actions, into how we interact with other people and with the world around us."

Having added the final topics to our discussion—empathy and compassion—it felt as if all the pieces, the diverse topics we had addressed in our many conversations, now fit together nicely.

As the Dalai Lama made his final remarks, summarizing our discussion, there was an unmistakable note of confidence and hope in his voice, generated by his firm belief in the possibility of a better future, a better world that can come about through our own actions.

"So," the Dalai Lama concluded, "if each of us can learn to relate to each other more out of compassion, with a sense of connection to each other and a deep recognition of our common humanity, and more important, teach this to our children, I believe that this can go a long way in reducing many of the conflicts and problems that we see today in the world. So, in this way, I believe that we can help create happier individuals and happier society, as well as a more peaceful world."

Here we begin the final step toward our goal of finding happiness in our troubled world, an approach that involves cultivating inner happiness while taking steps toward overcoming the many problems facing the world today. In this final conversation, the Dalai Lama added the last elements to complete his coherent, reasoned method of achieving our goal. To summarize:

> *The method begins by cultivating a deep sense of our common humanity, a profound awareness of the common characteristics we share with every other human being. This becomes the basis for generating a sense of empathy for every human being. This empathy becomes the basis for generating compassion. Generating a feeling of compassion will lead directly to greater personal happiness. Acting on the basis of that compassion will result in taking steps to overcome the problems of today's world, and will eventually lead to "a happier society, as well as a more peaceful world."*

To some, this approach may seem simplistic or naive. It is neither. In fact, this is a tremendously powerful and effective approach. It only requires the willingness to try it. Following the Dalai Lama's suggestion, here I have supplemented our conversation with some of the empiric evidence and scientific research that support the validity and effectiveness of his approach. Augmented by this information, the immense depth, wisdom, and power of his approach come into clearer focus and are plainly revealed. Before I go on to present some of that evidence, however, it is worthwhile to do a brief review, to place this method in the proper context.

Brief Review: Dealing with the Problems of Today's World

Throughout the course of our conversations the Dalai Lama identified a variety of problems facing us in today's world—lack of community, social alienation, prejudice, hatred, racism, conflicts, and violence, among others. These problems can undermine human happiness on multiple levels—individual, community, society, and global. In addressing these problems, the Dalai Lama began by reminding us that there can be many causes and conditions leading to these societal problems, and these causes can be on many levels—on both the "internal" level, which includes factors such as negative emotions or false or distorted beliefs and stereotypes, and on the "external" level, for example, adverse social conditions or situational factors. Because of this, the Dalai Lama also reminds us that we need many strategies and approaches to overcome these problems. In earlier chapters, we discussed some of the more specific causes of these problems and some specific strategies we can use to deal with them. Using the "medical model" that the Dalai Lama is fond of, we can say that the specific strategies for dealing with some of the more specific causes of our societal problems, could be seen as symptomatic treatments, specific remedies to treat various symptoms of our troubled world.

At this point, however, we are revisiting the underlying cause of these troubles on a deeper, more fundamental level. *Here, the Dalai Lama has identified a more systemic cause for our social ills: tracing the origin of all these societal "diseases" back to how we relate to other people, whether we relate to others based on how we are different or how we are similar, based on what unites us or on what separates us.* In fact, this is the fundamental cause of many of our troubles on *every* level—whether the problems are global, societal, community, or even interpersonal.

At this deeper level, the antidote is to relate to others in ways that unify, overcoming the rigid impenetrable boundaries between "me" and "we," or between "us" and "them." Transforming how we relate to others in this way, on both an interpersonal level and an intergroup level, can be seen as more of a systemic, all-purpose general remedy, perhaps a cure.

We have already examined one antidote, or "treatment," that works at this more fundamental level to change our perception and customary ways of thinking: *the cultivation of positive emotions.* We have seen how positive emotions can change how we relate to others by "broadening" our thinking and perception, expanding the boundaries of our identity from "me" and "we," breaking down barriers between "us" and "them." Incidentally, in our discussion of the beneficial effects of positive emotions, we have defined "positive emotions" very loosely— to include many different positive states of mind. Within this general category of positive emotions we include not only states of mind that are generally considered to be genuine emotions, such as a feeling of joy or happiness, but also positive states of mind that have a cognitive component, positive states of mind that may involve a positive kind of outlook, perception, or attitude.

We have seen how the "broadening" effects, as well as the multitude of other scientifically proven benefits of positive emotions, can be seen to some degree with virtually any positive emotion. We have also identified the cultivation of positive emotions as a practice that can be seen as at the intersection of personal and societal happiness. It is potentially a very powerful strategy for finding happiness in our troubled world, by increasing inner happiness as well as causing changes in behavior that would result in reducing some of the problems of our world today. In addition to the general effects of positive emotions, we have discussed how there may be some variation in the more specific effects of the positive emotions. For example, we saw how the "hope" family (hope, optimism, trust, resilience, etc.) has the same general effects as all the other positive emotions but is particularly useful in helping people get through times of adversity and hardship, helping them persist at working toward their goals even when obstacles arise, and helping them cope with a wide variety of disappointments, setbacks, and problems of everyday life. So, having now identified the fact that there may be some differences or variations among the effects of the positive emotions, we can now go on to discuss a particular positive emotion that the Dalai Lama mentioned in our discussion, which has some unique properties—and add the final pieces to complete our discussion.

As our meeting was coming to a close that day, the Dalai Lama finally identified a specific *positive emotion that can be considered the supreme positive emotion for the cultivation of inner happiness and well-being as well as for the transformative effect it has on how we relate to others: compassion.*

Empathy: Definition and Basic Functions

Before addressing compassion more specifically, it is important to first focus on another positive state of mind, the key factor that gives compassion its power to overcome the societal problems we have spoken about: *Empathy.*

There can be many definitions of empathy. But regardless of the differences between definitions, they all seem to include certain basic features: first, there is some kind of emotional connection with another person. Second, there is also some kind of cognitive component, such as judgments or ideas about the other. And of course there is some kind of mechanism responsible for maintaining boundaries between self and other, something that helps the person keep track of which attributes or emotions are his or her own and which belong to the other.

On a popular level, it seems that empathy is most often thought of as the capacity to "put yourself in another's shoes," the capacity to imagine or sense what another person is experiencing. And in fact, when researchers seek to investigate empathy, the common technique they use to generate empathy is called "perspective-taking," where they ask their subjects to either imagine themselves in the other person's situation or to imagine that they *are* the other person.

As the Dalai Lama points out, our human capacity for empathy is one of our most wonderful attributes, particularly when it is used in the service of love, compassion, and kindness—but even in the absence of these sublime states of mind, empathy plays a critical role in our ordinary day-to-day lives. As the Dalai Lama has pointed out, human beings are social animals. In order to function effectively in groups, we need a way of "reading" other people, of anticipating the behavior and reactions of others—and by facilitating our ability to do this, empathy has played an essential role in human evolution.

Empathy is just as important—or more important—today as it was for the survival of our remote ancestors. The various functions of empathy serve to keep us connected to others and prevent social exclusion. These are critically important functions, as social exclusion can be devastating for a human being and has been shown to have a wide range of detrimental effects on virtually every aspect of functioning—causing poor health, depression, even decreased ability to exhibit logical reasoning. Specifically, empathy helps facilitate smooth social interactions, coordinates social behavior, and adapts or synchronizes our behavior with others in a social group. In general, empathy helps strengthen social bonds—and strong social bonds are a hallmark of psychological wellbeing.

As we have become more interdependent and our social systems more complex, empathy has become even more indispensable in today's world. Empathy helps coordinate and adapt one's behavior to others in a social group, leads to smoother interpersonal relationships, and facilitates social interaction in many ways. In fact, the ability to entertain the perspective of another has long been recognized as a critical ingredient in proper social functioning. As modern society becomes more multicultural and we come into contact with diverse populations and a wider array of people, our capacity for empathy becomes increasingly critical.

EFFECTS OF EMPATHY: SEEING OTHERS AS THE SAME AS YOU

The Dalai Lama has said that the key to overcoming many societal problems is to relate to others based more on your similarities than on what differentiates you. There is an impressive body of research gathered over at least two decades, consistently showing that practicing empathy will produce that specific effect, reducing the gap between self and other.

In one experiment, investigators began by conducting tests to determine the subject's self-concept: identifying the customary ways that the subjects perceived themselves, what characteristics, traits, and attributes they identified with, and so on. Later, in an "unrelated" experiment, the subjects viewed videos of students talking about their experiences at college. One group of subjects was instructed to view the videos while imagining what that person was thinking and feeling, or what it would be like for them if they were in the student's situation. The other group was instructed to watch the video without perspective taking, in a neutral and objective frame of mind, just noting a student's behavior. Both groups were then asked to fill out questionnaires, assessing what they thought of the students in the video, what they might be like in real life, and so on. Those who watched the videos with empathy were much more likely to rate the students as much more like themselves, attributing qualities and traits to the students that they themselves had.

One important detail regarding this change in how we perceive others when we practice empathy, seeing them as more like ourselves, is that generally when we attribute our own traits to another as a result of practicing empathy, we assign our *positive* traits to them, but not our negative traits.

In addition, not only did the empathizing subjects tend to attribute their own traits to the target, but the subjects attributed a higher number of traits to the target in general, demonstrating an increase in the total number of attributes they ascribed to the target. What is the significance of these findings? It means, for one thing, that we perceive the other person in a much more realistic way when we empathize, seeing them as a complex human being with many different characteristics and traits, like ourselves.

Next, surprisingly, when practicing empathy, we tend to perceive others in the same way as we think of ourselves regarding how we explain the causes of their behavior or interpret their actions. Now, normally there are differences between the way we explain our own behavior and the way we explain another's.

Under ordinary conditions we tend to explain the causes of our own behavior as having more to do with situations—i.e., if we come home to our messy apartment, we tend to explain it based on circumstances ("I was working late last night and didn't have time to straighten up the apartment this morning" or "I was running late to work"). On the other hand, when it comes to explaining another's behavior, we tend to attribute the cause to dispositional explanations—i.e., that is "the way they are," it is part of their intrinsic character or disposition. So, if we walk into a neighbor's messy apartment, we might think, she is a messy person—that's just the way she is. This fundamental difference between how we normally explain our own versus another's behavior is called the FAE—the fundamental attribution error.

Studies have shown that when we empathize, the FAE disappears, and we interpret their behavior in the same way as we explain our own—attributing the causes of their behavior to conditions or circumstances, rather than their basic disposition or "the way they are"—once again, *seeing them more like you see yourself.*

Benefits of Empathy: An Antidote to Societal Problems

As we have seen, according to the Dalai Lama, the cause of many societal problems involves how we relate to others—and although there may be many mental factors involved in how we relate to others, it is clear that empathy is the key factor. It has a powerful and almost magical effect in shifting our perspective to view others based on our similarities rather than our differences. This is the factor that helps us to connect to others, to understand what the other is experiencing. There has been a large body of scientific evidence accumulating in recent years showing that empathy has specific effects on our thinking, perception, judgment and behavior—acting in ways as if it was custom designed as a direct antidote for distrust, prejudice, hatred, racism, conflict, and a host of other societal ills.

We recognize that others may have many similar traits and characteristics, their views or behavior may depend on the circumstances the way ours do, they are capable of a range of responses depending on the situation, and so on. While it is true there may be some distortion in projecting your own traits onto them, this is outweighed by the fact that when we practice empathy, *we* see others in much more realistic terms overall, with a richer and more diverse inner life. The result of these changes in thinking and perception caused by empathy is that you begin to gain a better understanding of that person as a real, live, complex human being.

Throughout our discussions, no matter what problem we may have been discussing, the Dalai Lama's approach to dealing with the problem would inevitably include cultivating a "realistic outlook." The scientific studies here support the Dalai Lama's approach. They show that empathizing with another helps us see that person more realistically, and this effect has tremendous significance in overcoming many societal problems. In earlier chapters we saw how *personalizing* a member of a stereotyped out-group, through methods such as the vegetable technique, tends to automatically eradicate our negative bias and stereotyping. The same process occurs when we empathize, as we see the person more as a unique individual—thus, we can view *empathy as an antidote to stereotyping!*

There have been many studies showing how *empathy serves as a direct antidote to prejudice.* One effect that has been well documented with numerous experiments is that not only do we tend to see others as more similar to us when we practice empathy, but we also tend to like them more. *It is a well-known psychological principle that people tend to like those similar to themselves.* In fact, that is one of the dynamics behind in-group favoritism. Once we identify with a group, and it becomes our in-group, we tend to project our own personal attributes onto our own group as well. It is the in-group's association with the self that leads to the in-group favoritism. *One of the important findings in empathy research is that when we practice empathy toward a member of a stereotyped out-group, the change in the way we perceive that individual extends to his/her group as a whole—thus seeing that group as more similar to one's own group, and increasing affection for that group.*

The positive effects and benefits of empathy can be far reaching—

for example, *empathy has been linked with forgiveness, lower intergroup conflict, and facilitating dialogue* as a means of conflict resolution. The practice of empathy also reduces social aggression and improves attitudes and evaluations of out-groups.

The Psychological Mechanisms Underlying Empathy

Many of the investigators who have conducted studies on empathy have proposed that the underlying psychological mechanism is a kind of merging of one's self-concept (our sense of who we are—the sum total of all our characteristics) with one's image of the other person (our view of who the other person is, the sum total of all their characteristics). This involves an underlying sense of incorporating another person into one's self-concept, what they call a "self-other overlap." When this self-other overlap occurs, there is almost a literal kind of psychological merging of oneself with another person, where the boundaries between self and other partially dissolve. The traits we consider as belonging to us and the traits we consider as belonging to others become intertwined, and the sense of self and other merge—we experience a sense of "oneness." *This self-other overlap is considered to be the basic, undifferentiated core of all these beneficial effects, as it is difficult to be biased, prejudiced, violent, etc. if you see the other as being the same person as you are—in a partial, psychological way at least.*

Of course, the practice of empathy takes place on many levels—we are consciously aware of some parts or aspects of the process, while other parts are subconscious and automatic. For example, when we practice empathy we may consciously experience certain aspects of the sense of "oneness" that results from the self-other overlap—for example, we may feel emotional closeness with the person, perceive him or her to be similar to ourselves, feel concern for his or her wellbeing, or simply have a greater feeling of satisfaction with the relationship.

On the other hand, there may be aspects of these underlying psychological processes that we are not consciously aware of at all, which can sometimes have some strange effects. For example, according to

some investigators, this self-other overlap takes place in two directions: In one direction, you project your own traits onto the other, seeing that person as possessing some of your own characteristics, as we
have explained. But it is the inverse direction that can become a bit
bizarre: You also see yourself as possessing some of the same traits as
the other person, assimilating the other into the self. If the target of
your empathy is a member of a stereotyped out-group, there is also a
tendency to take on the stereotyped attributes of that person.

There have been some fascinating experiments demonstrating this
effect. Adam Galinsky, a social psychologist at Northwestern University, has done a series of experiments using images of several stereotyped
groups, showing how individuals can take on the characteristics of a
stereotyped out-group after practicing empathy toward a member of
that group. Researchers showed subjects a photo of an attractive female
cheerleader at a football game, pompoms and all, inducing perspective
taking by asking them to write an essay describing a typical day in the
life of the cheerleader, writing the essay as if they were the cheerleader,
imagining what her life was like, etc. Later, subjects were asked to fill out
a Personality Questionnaire as part of an ostensibly separate and unrelated study. They were asked to describe themselves in detail, including rating how attractive, gorgeous, and sexy they were. Those who had
participated in the perspective-taking exercise, both men and women,
rated themselves as much more attractive and sexier (typical stereotyped
traits of cheerleaders) afterward than a control group who had not "put
themselves in the other's shoes."

Similar experiments were performed "priming" the subjects by
having them take the perspective of various stereotyped groups, sometimes using the "day in the life" essays, or by watching videos of group
members describing their lives, while subjects were instructed to listen with empathy (the control group was instructed to listen objectively, without thinking of the individual's perspective). Members of
groups included a black middle-aged man, a white political science
professor, and an elderly man. Individuals rated themselves as higher
in both positive and negative stereotyped traits for these groups. But
what was even stranger was that individuals were observed to exhibit

behaviors consistent with the stereotypes, such as white male subjects exhibited more loud, aggressive behaviors and hostile gestures after taking the perspective of the black male—and they did more poorly on intellectual testing afterward, consistent with stereotyped views. Those who were primed with elderly stereotypes did worse on memory tasks afterward—and were observed to walk down the hall more slowly afterward, without being consciously aware of this change. Finally, those who watched videos of professors while perspective taking were found to do significantly better afterward on intellectual tasks and formal tests of academic and reasoning abilities.

One strange finding of these experiments was that individuals demonstrated decreased stereotyping and prejudice after practicing empathy, yet showed these stereotyped behaviors—demonstrating a disassociation between behavior and perception and judgment—resulting from separate pathways in the brain responsible for each of these activities.

The Brain Mechanisms Underlying Empathy

While some researchers have investigated explanations for the benefits of empathy from the psychological perspective, such as the self-other overlap, at the same time there has been a tremendous amount of interest in looking for the neural or brain mechanisms underlying empathy—with some amazing discoveries in recent years.

All human beings are born with the capacity for empathy; it comes hardwired in the human brain. It seems clear, however, that like many other innate human characteristics, there are no doubt individual differences in the degree of natural empathy that any particular person might possess—ranging from a small number of individuals whose brain mechanisms for producing empathy may be disordered in some way to those who seem to be born with a tremendous capacity for empathy and compassion.

Much of our understanding of how empathy is produced in the brain, like the other positive emotions, has been discovered within the last two decades—and there have been some astounding findings. One of the most fascinating findings was discovered by accident in the early 1990s. Researchers Giacomo Rizzolatti and Vittorio Gallese at the University of Parma in Italy were studying specific neurons in the brains of macaque monkeys that were responsible for sending instructions to the monkey's arm and hand to reach out and grasp an object, in this case a peanut. (It is well known, of course, that for every function that the body performs, there are specific regions in the brain, consisting of groups of nerve cells, called neurons, that are responsible for that function. Neurons send messages via both chemical and electrical signals, conducted along a series of long nerve fibers, to the target organs, giving instructions on what to do. For example, there is an area that controls the motor movements of the hands, and another area that receives sensory information from the hand, etc.)

One day, one of the researchers reached out for a peanut to give to the monkey. They then saw the same neurons in the monkey's brain starting to fire—exactly as if the monkey was reaching for it himself! This was a strange and completely unexpected finding, and investigating further, the researchers discovered that there were special cells in certain regions of the brain that fired both when the animal performed an action and when the animal observed another performing the same action. The researchers named these cells mirror neurons, since they mirrored another's behavior—acting as though the animal itself was physically enacting a behavior that in reality it was merely witnessing. Later, these same kinds of cells were found in the brains of human beings. So, in a sense this could be seen as a neural correlate of the self-other overlap— since as far as these cells were concerned, they could not distinguish between themselves performing an action and another performing the action. In fact, although these cells were found only in certain regions, such as those related to hand and mouth movements, some researchers feel that these mirror neurons might be located in other areas of the brain, and may be involved in producing empathy.

Further research over the past decade has demonstrated fascinating neural mechanisms linking the "self" with the "other." There is a considerable body of authoritative research and experimental evidence supporting a theory known as the perception-action model, which is thought to play a role in empathy—again perhaps representing the neural (brain) correlate of the self-other overlap. This theory posits that when a person perceives another person experiencing an emotion, the brain automatically activates areas that are responsible for the generation of the same emotions in the observer. Such a system is thought to be responsible for the observer essentially re-creating within the state of the person they are perceiving, helping them "resonate" with the other individual. The brain of the observer activates areas associated with forming an intention to act in some way—as if the observer is getting ready to activate the same motor movements and physiological processes it is observing in the other individual—i.e., as if the observer is the same person as the observed individual.

Studies monitoring what is going on in the brain of subjects, using fMRI machines, as they watch a video of someone receiving a painful stimulus, show that simply watching someone else experience pain would activate in the brain of the observers a number of the areas associated with the firsthand experience of pain; i.e., the same neural circuits showed increased activity when a person experienced pain as when a person observed another experiencing pain. This represents a kind of direct "sharing of experience" on a neural level, a kind of "oneness" of self and other—a neural self-other overlap.

Fortunately, when a subject observes others in pain, this "overlap" does not include stimulation of the areas of the brain that are involved in coding for the sensory aspects of pain, i.e., the part of the brain that tells an individual that the experience physically hurts. The areas of common activation involve the "motivational" and "affective" aspects of pain. This means that the areas of the brain that are involved with preparing the person to move away from the source of the pain (e.g. pulling one's hand away from a fire), and the areas of the brain involved in producing the unpleasant emotional feeling are activated in both the observer and experiencer. No matter what experience one is watching, the "overlap" is only partial; if *all* of the same areas of the brain were activated, it would create a kind of hallucination that re-created the reality of the experience you were witnessing.

Of course, it makes perfect sense why there are differences between one's first-hand experience and an observation experience—or why there is only partial overlap of the neural systems producing pain rather than complete overlap. If *all* the neural systems responsible for producing an experience were activated when observing another's behavior, then the person would think that they were actually experiencing that behavior; it would create a kind of hallucination that re-creates the reality of any given experience.

CULTIVATING GREATER EMPATHY

So, we have seen how there are immense benefits of practicing empathy—both as a specific solution to overcoming societal problems and as an antidote on an ordinary day-to-day level, facilitating everyday social functioning. While each human being may be born with a certain natural level of empathy, there are ample scientific studies showing that a person's capacity for empathy (as with many other skills) can be increased through training and deliberate effort.

The most common way of practicing and strengthening empathy, as we have seen, is through the deliberate practice of perspective taking, imagining oneself in another's position. The cultivation of empathy through perspective taking is effective but has several natural limitations. The Dalai Lama offers an alternative method of generating empathy, a more powerful method that does not depend on one's ability to imagine or relate to the specific circumstances or life conditions of the target of your empathy. The Dalai Lama's radically different approach involves deep contemplation of our common humanity.

CONVENTIONAL EMPATHY: BASED ON PERSPECTIVE TAKING

The conventional method used when one is trying deliberately and consciously to increase empathy involves trying to imagine either yourself in that person's particular set of circumstances or more directly imagine what it might be like to be that person. We have already spoken of the bidirectional nature of the self-other overlap. The first direction involves "projecting into another," seeing the other person as possessing traits that you yourself have. The second direction involves taking on the characteristics of another, perceiving yourself to have the same traits as the target. The first kind requires no knowledge about the other person. One can project one's own characteristics onto anyone—or even a pet, for that matter. The second kind requires some degree of knowledge about the other person, or at least thinking you have knowledge about them. There is some experimental evidence to suggest that one does not need to know any details of the other's personal history in order to feel empathy. However it also seems that empathy is facilitated if one can relate to another's experience as a result of one's own prior experience; i.e., it is easier to experience empathy for a mother if one has been a mother, easier to experience empathy for a firefighter if one has been a firefighter. While knowing something about another, and seeing him or her as similar to you in some way is *not necessary* to experience empathy, *it does help.*

This is one of the limitations of the customary practice of perspective taking as a means of establishing empathy. After all, the specific life circumstances that we might have in common with others is limited. There are other limitations as well: Some researchers have expressed concern, for example, about a situation where one is attempting to establish empathy with a neo-Nazi skinhead. If a person is going to unconsciously take on the stereotyped traits of a group, as described in the experiments above, the skinheads, for example, might not be the best choice of a group to unconsciously mirror—or for that matter, that group might not be the best choice for forming a self-other overlap situation where the person feels the two have similar values or attributes. Fortunately, this is unlikely to happen, since other studies have shown that the "merging" of traits that occurs with empathy and the underlying self-other overlap usually involves positive traits, but what is more likely is public censure and repercussions if one begins to announce that one can see things from the Nazi skinheads' perspective, even if one doesn't agree with that perspective.

ULTIMATE EMPATHY: BASED ON OUR COMMON HUMANITY
This is where the Dalai Lama's method has tremendous advantage: the *connection to others is based on our common humanity!* With perspec-

tive taking we have to rely on our imagination, imagining what it might be like to be in that individual's position and unique situation—marital status, job, children, or background. With the Dalai Lama's "Realistic Approach" you can base your "common ground" on reality—on the undeniable fact that you and the other are both human beings. This takes no guesswork. There is no need to try to imagine the particular circumstances of that person's life, nor to project your own traits onto the other person whether they truly possess those traits or not. With his approach, based on contemplating common humanity, the self-other overlap is built on common characteristics that are shared by every human being—e.g., all want to be happy, all don't want to suffer, all feel pain, all want to be loved, and so on. This makes the empathy more powerful, because one has the power and strength of reality behind you. In addition, with the Dalai Lama's approach one can feel empathy for every human being, even those with whom you may have little in common on the surface.

While we have seen how conventional perspective taking acts to overcome stereotyping and prejudice, how cultivating empathy for a member of a stereotyped out-group expands beyond that single group member to the entire group, so that one is no longer prejudiced against the group, the elimination of stereotyping and prejudice does not extend to *other* stereotyped groups. So, you may overcome your prejudice against African Americans, for instance, through the practice of empathy, but this will have no effect on your feelings about other racial groups. By basing your empathy on your common characteristics as human beings, you are essentially extending your scope of empathy to include all stereotyped groups!

The Power of Empathy

We have already presented the many benefits that can result from the deliberate cultivation of empathy both for individual happiness and in overcoming societal problems. But the true power of empathy extends even beyond what we have discussed thus far. Studies of rescuers of Jews during World War II, for example, have shown that empathy played a major role in their helping behavior. In many cases empathy was the primary factor that motivated the person, enabling them to transcend the evil and tremendous social pressures around them to save Jews from certain death, often at great risk to themselves. This required the very highest levels of inner strength, courage, and moral integrity—and it was often the power of empathy (and of course compassion, which we will address shortly) that helped them mobilize these heroic qualities.

Now, research shows that individuals are more likely to experience empathy for those whom they perceive as similar to them in some way. On a practical level, this means that if rescuers perceived victims as being like themselves, similar in ethnicity, attitudes, personality, or cultural background, then they would more easily identify with the victim, experience more empathy, and be more likely to help. Here we are talking about the conventional kind of empathy, based on perspective-taking. Some Holocaust researchers have proposed the idea that the reason why there were so few rescuers during World War II was because Jews were so seldom found to be similar in these characteristics to other people around them.

However, researchers have also proposed the idea that for the very few Jews who were rescued in Nazi-occupied Europe, there were two types of rescuers. The first type were those rescuers who identified with the victim and saw the victim as similar to themselves based on areas including political, theological, and socioeconomic grounds. These rescuers helped the Jews based on the conventional kind of empathy.

But the other type of rescuers were different. The Holocaust research team of Drs. Sam and Pearl Oliner have identified a particular trait that characterized the second type. They have noted that the other type of rescuers were extremely high in what they call extensivity. This special trait of extensivity was defined as *"a connection to others through a perception of common humanity."* These individuals generated empathy based on their common humanity with the victims, not on any other perceived similarities in specific social, financial, political, or religious attributes.

What was the difference between conventional empathy and empathy based on our common humanity? In Denmark, there was strong identification with the Jew by the non-Jew before the war—and a greater prewar practice of relating to Jews based on common humanity rather than narrow similarities in specific traits. In places like Poland and Lithuania, prewar political and theological differences were pronounced, and individuals were more likely to experience conventional empathy, directed only toward others of the same political, religious, or social group. In Denmark, 96 percent of the Jewish population was rescued! In Poland and Lithuania, 95.5 percent were killed!

A deep understanding of our common humanity, empathy, and compassion, an awareness of the true practical value of these things, and the courage to implement them in daily life can not only determine or influence levels of personal and societal happiness, but also at times can even be a matter of life, death, and survival. Ultimately, they have the potential to shape the future of humanity.

Definition of Compassion

Finally we come to the pinnacle of human emotions: *compassion*. Compassion is commonly defined as a kind of sympathy for or openness to the suffering of another, associated with the wish that they be freed from their suffering. Some people's definitions include the wish to help the suffering person.

For our purposes here, however, at times it may be helpful to think of compassion in terms of a group of related emotions or positive mental states rather than as a single emotion, similar to how we conceptualized the "hope family" earlier. Using this model, we can think of the "compassion family" as including a number of related positive mental and emotional states—empathy, compassion, kindness, and so on. Over the years the Dalai Lama has used many terms to describe the positive states of mind in this family—a "good heart," "affection," and "a warm heart" are three he has often used. When he speaks of friendship, his tone of voice generally conveys the same sense. In more recent years, when he speaks about compassion he seems to be using the word "caring" more frequently.

Benefits of Compassion

Compassion can be considered the state of mind that exists at the crossroads between interior and exterior happiness, where individual happiness and societal happiness converge at a single intersecting point, an all-purpose elixir that can act as an antidote to both personal misery and societal problems. At least according to the Dalai Lama, scientific evidence, and common sense.

How? We have explored many problems in today's world. The Dalai Lama readily acknowledges that we need many approaches and need to act on many levels in order to address the complex and varied problems of today's society. But he also explained how most of the problems of our society are caused on the most fundamental level by certain distortions of perception and thinking, by negative emotions, and by the ways that we customarily relate to one another—which all potentially lead in the direction of destroying each other in one way or another.

Now, besides the more specific "treatments" or remedies for societal problems that we have spoken about in previous chapters, we have also shown how the generation of positive emotions in general can act as antidotes to the underlying or fundamental causes of societal problems. Compassion brings with it all the benefits of both empathy and the positive emotions. As one of the most powerful positive emotions, compassion can yield all the potential benefits of the positive emotions in general—as we have seen, in the studies showing the beneficial effects of positive emotions, researchers found that essentially any of the positive emotions could produce these effects, and it made no difference whether the specific positive emotion that was experimentally induced was amusement, joy, serenity, or more general feelings of "happiness" or "positive affect," etc. So, as one of the most powerful positive emotions, compassion carries all of the same potential benefits as the rest of the positive emotions in general.

Next we saw how the "positive emotion" of empathy carried the same general benefits as the other positive emotions, plus it also had unique properties in that it can transform how we relate to others, thus facilitating social bonds and causing changes in thinking that could help overcome many of the problems in society today. Just like with the benefits of the positive emotions in general, compassion also carries all of the benefits of empathy. This is because empathy is an important component of compassion. Wherever there is compassion you will always find some degree of empathy. Since compassion involves the ability to sense another's suffering, one must have at least some degree of empathy for the other person. Therefore, since compassion requires some degree of empathy, essentially by definition, it is virtually certain that generating a state of compassion will bring all the potential benefits of empathy that have been discussed.

As the Dalai Lama pointed out, there is an intimate connection between empathy and compassion. From the scientific perspective, ample studies point out the link between perspective taking, compassion, and altruism, showing how empathy tends to naturally lead to compassion and the tendency to help others, the objects of your compassion and empathy. Batson, for example, has extensively investigated the relationship between empathy and compassion, and has found that perspective taking increases "empathic concern," a state of mind that leads to helping others, motivated simply by the desire to improve the other's well-being. Of course, there are always variables and many different factors that might contribute to a given individual's capacity for empathy, compassion, and his or her response to another's circumstances. In some cases, seeing things from another's point of view may not always automatically lead to greater compassion for the other person.

In other cases, compassion may not always lead to helping behavior. For example, sometimes a person's empathy and compassion is so great, and the person experiences the other's suffering so acutely, that they are overcome with a feeling of personal distress and are unable to act. In such cases, one may need to use strategies to reduce anxiety and fear, such as we discussed in chapter 9. There are always individual differences. I once asked the Dalai Lama how to deal with such cases. His feeling was that the person may need to work on strengthening compassion more, and eventually it would become strong enough to overcome the feeling of personal distress.

COMPASSION AND SOCIAL CHANGE

In speaking of the potential of compassion to bring about positive changes in society—in eliminating prejudice, discrimination, racism, conflict, violence, and other social problems—it is obvious that compassion alone cannot change society. After all, compassion is a state of mind. In order to bring about societal change, *action is required—we must change the behaviors associated with the destructive states of mind.* Of course, as we have seen, compassion has the potential to overcome destructive states of mind, such as prejudice and hatred, and can transform the way we perceive others, such as seeing others more realistically and less stereotypically. That alone should have the effect of changing the way we relate to those with whom we come into contact, and have a small effect on those within our immediate environment. And *considering the contagious effect of positive emotions and the interdependent nature of our world today, any positive impact we have on our immediate environment will eventually have broader effects, like the ripples spreading out on the surface of a pond.*

Fortunately, the effect of compassion on one's behavior goes beyond simply passively neutralizing any personal tendencies toward prejudice, racism, conflict, or violence. Compassion tends to create the motivation to take more active steps to help others, to reduce others' suffering, and take action to promote the welfare of others. Of course, people differ in their resources, abilities, talents, and capabilities to help others and promote social change. *People must decide for themselves the best and most effective way that they can make a contribution to building a better world. But cultivating a state of mind that motivates a person to make a contribution to a better world is clearly the first step.*

COMPASSION AND PERSONAL HAPPINESS

We have made the case that compassion is the intersecting point between personal and societal happiness, contributing to both. So far we have addressed how compassion can help overcome societal problems, or at least cause changes in thinking most likely to solve societal problems, or at least cause changes in thinking most likely to solve societal problems. So what remains is showing *the link between personal happiness and compassion*. This concept is gradually starting to gain some momentum in the West, although there is still quite a large gap between the Dalai Lama's notion of compassion, which is inextricably linked with one's own personal happiness, and the prevalent Western view.

In our discussion that afternoon in Tucson, the Dalai Lama did not go into great depth in discussing compassion in general. It was a topic that we had spoken of many times in the past, so rather than cover old ground, he distilled his thoughts to capture the essence of compassion, the key message, and directed his comments to our current context. Besides, after going into such depth on cultivating a sense of our common humanity and so on, topics that I had never previously heard him explain in quite the same way, there was not a lot to add. But still, in order to understand his view of the relationship between compassion and personal happiness, it will be helpful to add a few comments here.

Over the years I have explored with the Dalai Lama some of the differences between his view—the Tibetan Buddhist view—of compassion and the Western view. From his perspective, compassion involves the deep awareness of an individual's suffering and a heartfelt caring, a sincere wish that the individual be freed from their suffering, and a desire to do something to relieve their suffering. The Western notion of compassion is tied up with the idea of altruism, which comes prepackaged with a sense of self-sacrifice—where the benefit of one's compassion or altruism is directed 100 percent toward the other guy, and one's own personal happiness does not come into the equation. In fact, there is the sense that if one has any thought for one's own welfare when showing another kindness, it "doesn't count" as an act of altruism or pure compassion. The Dalai Lama, commenting on this omission of oneself as a legitimate object of compassion, felt that the Westerners were really missing the boat. He felt there was nothing wrong in feeling compassion for oneself as well as others, nor was there anything wrong with reaping some personal rewards as a result of feeling compassion for others—i.e., finding personal happiness as a result of generating compassion for others.

Western culture may still not automatically link the concept of compassion with personal happiness, but the findings of science are starting to change that. As soon as these findings begin to make their way out of laboratories and university classrooms, and into the mainstream of modern popular culture, perhaps we will see some dramatic changes in our society as more and more people seek to actively cultivate compassion for others as a means of gaining personal happiness and life-satisfaction.

At the time of the writing of the first volume of the Art of Happiness series, there were relatively few studies on happiness, and it seems even fewer when it came to the scientific study of compassion, particularly the biological aspects. In that volume we mentioned a study or two by a few of the pioneers in happiness research, mavericks at the time. Since that time, however, there has been a worldwide Happiness Revolution, with a virtual explosion of research on positive emotions, leading to a rapidly growing body of evidence establishing the link between personal happiness and compassion. Some of the most exciting research in this field has been conducted by Richard Davidson, director of the Laboratory of Affective Neuroscience at the University of Wisconsin–Madison. This groundbreaking work has partly been inspired by Davidson's contact with the Dalai Lama as part of the ongoing meetings of the Mind and Life Institute. As a result of his studies monitoring brain activity using fMRI brain imaging machines, Davidson located an area of the brain associated with happiness. Specifically, he identified an area of the brain in the left prefrontal cortex that is associated with positive, happy states of mind—such as zeal, enthusiasm, joy, vigor, and mental buoyancy. In one series of experiments Davidson sought to take a look at what was going on in the brain when a person is experiencing compassion.

In one of my favorite experiments on the link between personal happiness and compassion, Dr. Davidson and his colleagues brought a French-Tibetan Buddhist monk into his lab to study the effects of compassion. This monk was a highly trained adept, who had spent many years in the Himalayan region, meditating on compassion. Hooking him up to his EEG and fMRI machines, Davidson began by monitoring the monk's brain function in a resting state to measure baseline brain activity, then he asked him to perform an intensive Buddhist meditation on compassion. The results showed that during his meditation on compassion, there was a dramatic leftward shift in his prefrontal function, lighting up the "happiness region" of the brain, leading Davidson to conclude: "The very act of concern for others' well-being creates a greater sense of well-being within oneself." What could be more conclusive evidence of the link between personal happiness and compassion?

There have also been a number of studies linking personal happiness and kindness. In one experiment, for example, Dr. Sonja Lyubomirsky and colleagues at the University of California at Riverside asked a group of subjects to choose one day each week in which to perform five "random acts of kindness." These did not necessarily need to be heroic acts of self-sacrifice; they could be as simple as opening the door for someone with a warm smile or anonymously dropping a coin in someone's almost-expired parking meter. After six weeks, the subjects in the study experienced a significant increase in their overall levels of happiness and life satisfaction.

Experiments such as these have firmly established the truth of the Dalai Lama's fundamental belief: "If you want others to be happy, practice compassion. If you want to be happy, practice compassion."

In providing evidence of the beneficial effects of compassion, I will add one additional study conducted by Davidson and colleagues. There is now substantial evidence that we can learn to train the mind to overcome negative emotions, as well as to become more compassionate, happier, and so on. So, in this study the experimenters were investigating individuals' ability to train their minds—specifically looking at their ability to regulate their negative emotions. In the first step, subjects were shown some disturbing photos while their brains were being monitored using fMRI brain scanners. The photos used to evoke extreme negative emotional responses were generally photos of people who were diseased or perhaps mutilated, such as a picture of a baby with a large tumor growing out of his eye. Such photos tended to evoke emotions such as disgust, fear, and a general negative emotional state. This was confirmed on the fMRI brain scans by showing activation of structures such as the amygdala, which, as you now know, is involved with emotions such as anxiety and fear, as well as the stress response.

In the next stage of the experiment, the subjects then practiced a technique to decrease their negative emotional response. The technique involved *generating a feeling of compassion*. The subjects were instructed to look at the same picture again, but this time with a sincere aspiration that the suffering of the individual depicted in the picture be relieved and that the outcome be positive. Looking at the photo in this new way acted as an antidote to the negative emotion—the activation of the amygdala was counteracted! Thus there is evidence that a practice of compassion can regulate or decrease negative emotions and stress as well as induce positive emotions and happiness. Incidentally, in a wider sense, this technique can also be seen as an exercise in positive reappraisal of the disturbing photo, or a method of broadening one's point of view, looking at it from a different angle, from a more positive perspective, and so on—the very same technique recommended by the Dalai Lama in earlier chapters as a method to help one cope with adversity and daily problems. Here again, we can see this is a very effective technique for overcoming the negative emotions and acting as an antidote to the stress response.

Thus we have now seen how the practice of compassion not only transforms one's ways of thinking and of relating to others in ways that build trust; reinstills a spirit of community; overcomes stereotyping, prejudice, and racism; and acts as a preventive measure against conflict and violence but we have also seen how compassion can act as an unlimited source of human happiness and well-being on a personal level. From this perspective, it may not be an exaggeration to see compassion as the supreme human emotion or positive state of mind, the intersecting point between individual and societal happiness. And, as the Dalai Lama has shown us, cultivating a very deep understanding and awareness of our common humanity is the most direct and powerful means of establishing a deep feeling of connection to others that can act as the foundation of our compassion.

Changing the Public's Perception of Compassion

Sadly, of course, we do not see compassion and kindness practiced widely enough in today's world. Perhaps one of the primary drawbacks is that the general public still does not perceive compassion as a legitimate source of personal happiness, nor do we widely recognize the vast array of practical benefits to be found from practicing compassion. We still perceive compassion as something that we give the other guy, something disassociated from our own happiness in life. We still perceive compassion as a religious, spiritual, or moral teaching rather than a state of mind with many practical uses, based on an outlook on life that can be deliberately cultivated through proven methods. We still see compassion as something discretionary, as a luxury instead of a necessity.

The challenge seems to be in changing the public's perception about the practice of compassion, to perceive compassion as a state of mind with real practical value, resulting from an outlook that can be deliberately cultivated through one's own effort. Perhaps there may be one glimmer of hope for a speedy popular acceptance of the importance of compassion, holding in mind the possibility of large segments of the American population adopting practices to cultivate greater compassion. This glimmer of hope is to be found in the study just mentioned, conducted by Davidson and colleagues on the regulation of negative emotions. To explain, in that study the researchers were interested in looking at the effects of these techniques not only on the subject's brain function inside the lab, but also in the subject's daily life, outside the lab.

As we mentioned earlier, cortisol is one of the hormones that is released during the stress response. Under normal circumstances, when a person is not under stress, this hormone is released into the bloodstream at high levels in the morning, then it gradually diminishes throughout the day. When plotted on a graph, it shows a steep downward slope or angle from morning to night. When under stress, this hormone is released steadily all day long, resulting in a flat line on a graph. In order to monitor the subject's level of stress during the day, the subjects had their saliva measured at six different times throughout the day. Plotting the levels on a graph, the investigators saw that those who practiced the compassion or "reappraisal" technique showed a steeper slope, indicating less stress.

But, finally, we come to the main point. The flattened cortisol levels, representing the continuous secretion of cortisol due to stress, is associated with a number of effects that damage the body. *One of these effects is a larger waist circumference, a fat belly. The steeper slope results in a reduced waist circumference, a slimmer belly.* Perhaps this could be the key to a dramatic overnight transformation of American society, producing a society that is more compassionate—maybe we've finally found the magic solution to transforming the world and ending violence and hatred. Perhaps all it might take is a few headlines in the supermarket tabloids: NEW!!! AMAZING NEW DISCOVERY!!! BEATS "THE SECRET" ALL TO HELL!!! **THE COMPASSION DIET!!!** YES, THAT'S RIGHT! BE KIND AND COMPASSIONATE AND LOSE 3 INCHES OFF YOUR WAIST VIRTUALLY OVERNIGHT!!!

Joking aside, it is certainly possible that the public's perception of compassion may soon begin to change, and the practice of compassion may become more widely adopted on a popular level as the Dalai Lama and others show us the true value of this state of mind, bringing tremendous benefit for our own happiness and for the world at large. And science may play a significant role here as well, in changing the ways we perceive the practice of empathy, compassion, and the other positive emotions. It may take time, but there are positive signs that these ideas are gaining more widespread acceptance every day. There now appears to be real hope for a genuine path that can lead both to our own personal happiness as well as to a better world.

This last session in Tucson was the culmination of several series of on-going discussions over a period of a few years. Since it could be some time before we resumed another series of discussions, I had brought with me a *kata,* a white silk scarf, which is exchanged both at the times of first greeting and farewell as part of Tibetan custom. The *kata* I had with me was a particularly nice one, approximately ten feet long and two feet wide, woven with patterns of traditional auspicious symbols as well as verses wishing good fortune and happiness.

Our session had come to an end. The Dalai Lama's secretary had already walked into the room to indicate that whoever was scheduled to see him next had already arrived. Acknowledging his secretary with a nod, the Dalai Lama turned to me and said, "So, Howard, it's time to close. And I would like to thank you. I have enjoyed our discussions, and let us hope that when you share our long explorations with others that it may be of benefit to some."

Realizing that there were people waiting, I quickly began to collect my recording equipments and notebooks, feeling slightly flustered as I reached for my *kata* to present to him. I said, "Thank you, Your Holiness, for being so generous with your time. You know, over the years we have touched upon some other topics related to societal issues, such as the gap between rich and poor, the question of personal lifestyle, consumerism, and the issue of greed and so on, but these still remain to be more fully explored. So I hope we can continue our discussions at some later date."

"Okay, very good," he replied.

Although *katas* are generally rolled in such a way that they easily unfold, this one was wrapped so tightly that it took a few moments to unroll it to its full length. As I struggled to unravel it, the Dalai Lama commented, "You know, Howard, this custom of exchanging *katas* has a nice symbolism. The inspiration for the custom came from India, where to mark special occasions people offer flower garlands or silk shawls to each other. The actual material of the *kata* is traditionally woven in China, and it's the Tibetans who use it as part of their custom. So, in this custom, you can see the harmony between the people of three neighbors, India, China, and Tibet. Wonderful!" For one final moment he broke into that wonderful, unaffected, mirthful laughter that never failed to uplift me and give me hope for the possibility of finding true happiness.

And with that the Dalai Lama spontaneously offered his hand to shake while at the same time reaching with the other arm to pull me closer for a friendly bear-hug.

ABOUT THE AUTHORS

His Holiness the Dalai Lama was born on July 6, 1935, to a poor farming family in northeastern Tibet. At the age of two he was recognized as the Dalai Lama, the spiritual and temporal leader of Tibet, the fourteenth in a succession dating back 600 years. At the age of six he began his lifelong training as a Buddhist monk. Since 1959 the Dalai Lama has lived in exile in Dharamsala, India, after escaping Tibet following an unsuccessful uprising by the Tibetan people against the occupation of Tibet by Chinese forces. His tireless efforts on behalf of human rights, world peace, and basic human values have brought him international recognition. He is the recipient of numerous honors and awards, including the 1989 Nobel Prize for Peace, and the U.S. Congressional Gold Medal.

When asked about his role in life, the Dalai Lama will often refer to himself as "a simple Buddhist monk." Many others consider him to be one of the foremost spiritual leaders of our time and one of the world's leading Buddhist scholars and teachers. During the course of his extensive travels he also speaks as a passionate advocate for his three main commitments in life: First, he is committed to the promotion of basic human values, or what he often refers to as "secular ethics." Second, he is committed to the promotion of harmony and understanding among the world's major religious traditions. And third, he is committed to the "Tibet issue," dedicated to the welfare of the Tibetan people, acting as a spokesperson in their struggle for greater human rights, autonomy, and freedom. Wherever he goes, the Dalai Lama makes a sincere appeal to his audience for greater kindness, compassion, tolerance, and universal responsibility.

For more information about the Dalai Lama, including his schedule of teachings, please visit: **www.dalailama.com**

Howard C. Cutler, MD, is a psychiatrist, bestselling author, and speaker. He is co-author with His Holiness the Dalai Lama of the acclaimed Art of Happiness series of books, which have been translated into fifty languages and have appeared on bestseller lists throughout the world. The groundbreaking first volume, *The Art of Happiness: A Handbook for Living,* appeared on *The New York Times* Bestsellers list for ninety-seven weeks. As a leading expert on the science of human happiness and a pioneer in the field of positive psychology, Dr. Cutler gives keynote presentations, workshops, and courses on happiness to individuals and organizations in cities throughout the United States and worldwide.

Dr. Cutler's background includes a BA in art, a BS in zoology, and an MD degree from the University of Arizona College of Medicine, followed by a four-year postgraduate training program in psychiatry. He is a diplomate of the American Board of Psychiatry and Neurology and is on the editorial board of *The American Journal of Psychotherapy.* Dr. Cutler has dedicated his life to helping others find greater happiness, fulfillment, and success. He currently resides in Phoenix, Arizona.

For more information about *The Art of Happiness,* including books, workshops, and courses, or to contact Dr. Cutler, please visit: **www.theartofhappiness.com**

The Art of Happiness book project is a series of books on the theme of human happiness, written by His Holiness the Dalai Lama and Howard C. Cutler, MD. The books examine different facets of human happiness from both the Eastern and Western perspectives, with the Dalai Lama representing the Buddhist perspective and Dr. Cutler, an American psychiatrist, representing the Western scientific perspective. Since the original publication of *The Art of Happiness: A Handbook for Living* in 1998, there has been a rapidly growing interest in the subject of happiness worldwide, including a new field of psychology devoted to the scientific study of human happiness and flourishing. During these years, the Dalai Lama and Dr. Cutler have continued their collaboration. Additional volumes of the Art of Happiness series are currently planned.

books to help you live a good life

Join the conversation and tell
us how you live a #goodlife

🐦 @yellowkitebooks
📘 YellowKiteBooks
📌 Yellow Kite Books
📷 YellowKiteBooks